CONSULTATION

Strategy for Improving Education

CONSULTATION

Strategy for Improving Education

DUANE BROWN
University of North Carolina

MARVIN D. WYNE
University of North Carolina

JACK E. BLACKBURN
Auburn University

W. CONRAD POWELL
University of South Carolina

ALLYN AND BACON, INC.   Boston   London   Sydney

Library of Congress Cataloging in Publication Data

Main entry under title:

Consultation, strategy for improving education.

Includes bibliographies and index.
1. Education–Aims and objectives. 2. Personnel
service in education. I. Brown, Duane.
LB41.C767   370.11   79-10
ISBN 0-205-06554-4

Printed in the United States of America

10 9 8 7 6 5 4 3 2   85 84 83 82 81 80

Production Editor: Sandy Stanewick
Manufacturing Buyer: Linda Card

To Sandra

Contents

Preface

Consultation as a strategy for improving education is not new. Teachers have met informally to improve their own teaching and good administrators have consulted with members of their staff to improve various aspects of the educational enterprise. Books about consultation are new, however. This book systematizes and presents in coherent fashion what has been occurring for decades.

There are certain assumptions underlying this volume that will become immediately obvious to the reader. First, it is assumed that any process will be more successful when the person or persons involved have a rationale for that process. More simply, good practice is based on theory. This is not to suggest that this volume is highly theoretical, for it is not. Second, learning is enhanced when specific suggestions for action are made. In this regard every attempt has been made to provide the "how to's" as well as the "why do's." Third, it is assumed that acquisition of skills can be enhanced by providing examples of the procedures. Case material has been used throughout to illustrate concepts and techniques to help the reader develop consultation skills.

Not only was there concern for theory and practice in the development of this book, but every effort was made to include many points of view about consultation. As a result, humanistic and behavioral consultation approaches are considered along with opposing ideas about organizational consultation. It is too soon to write a definitive statement about consultation. However, it is not too early to detail the application of various principles to the consultation process.

One last consideration is reflected in the book. It is that consultation strategies are applicable with a wide range of persons who either participate directly in or impinge indirectly upon educational practice. Further, it is assumed that consultation procedures can be used to increase the effectiveness of education by involving teachers, parents, students, administrators, governmental officials, and staff members of community agencies. Education is not a process that occurs only between 8:00 A.M. and 3:00 P.M. Consultation offers a method for involving forces that can not only enhance the school day but extend the educational process beyond the boundaries of the school.

Acknowledgements

A number of people have been instrumental in the development of this volume. To my friend Manford Sonstegard, who first demonstrated to me that consultation is a viable approach to pupil development, I owe a special debt of gratitude.

My wife, Sandra, also deserves much credit for the finished product. Not only has she typed and edited much of the material, she has served as critic as well. A practicing educational consultant, she has acted to curtail my tendency to be too idealistic.

A colleague, John Brantley, coordinator of the School Psychology Program at the University of North Carolina, was extremely helpful in conceptualizing some of the early chapters. His advice was invaluable.

The faceless consultants employed by Allyn & Bacon to read and criticize the manuscript deserve much credit. It is ironic that these persons cannot be named, for much of their thinking has been included in the book.

Finally, Mary Allen, overloaded and overworked secretary in the School of Education, helped to make final corrections and get it all together. She and the others mentioned have my eternal gratitude.

DUANE BROWN
Chapel Hill, NC
December, 1978

CONSULTATION

Strategy for Improving Education

CHAPTER ONE Society and Education

Our society faces unprecedented difficulties. The concrete facts concerning divorce rates ranging upward of 35 percent, the presence of forty million individuals in families with substandard incomes, continued discrimination against women and minority group members, spiraling crime rates, increasing drug abuse, high jobless rates, particularly among youth, and an increase in the number of persons requiring mental health services are sufficient evidence of this fact.

The result has been that educational institutions are increasingly confronted with students who have not developed those psychological characteristics that would enable them to benefit fully from their educational experience. This lack has in turn had a disconcerting influence upon many educators who realize that schools are inadequately prepared to design and deliver educational experiences for many students.

Other developments have accelerated the concerns of these same educators. Among these are recent court cases and laws that mandate that all children are entitled to educational opportunities. Perhaps more important, these legal declarations have placed the onus on the schools to identify individuals who have not received adequate educational services and to devise means by which services can be provided. The result has been that students who were formerly excluded from schools – for example, those with visual impairment, the multiple handicapped, and the severely retarded – are now being included. These trends plus the placement of educable mentally retarded students in the regular classroom have added to the difficulties of schools prepared primarily to serve the middle-class student.

Expanding educational knowledge and technology have also contributed to our educational dilemma. The phrase *education should consider individual differences* has taken on new significance with our increased understanding of learning styles, the realization that students respond differentially to various environmental stimuli, and our ability to diagnose learning disabilities, to name but a few developments. Our concerns for individual differences have brought the realization that we need to reconsider instructional styles, reorganize classroom patterns, renovate curriculum, and build multifaceted, multipronged educational programs that will truly serve all students.

Finally, the educational institution must be considered as a part of its own problem. Like most bureaucratic institutions, schools have developed mechanisms that perpetuate institutional inertia. Even though our educational technology is expanding rapidly, our institutions are organized in a fashion that prevents the adoption of new approaches. Educational administrators, teachers, and educational specialists have speculated about this problem and in many places and in many ways have made suggestions aimed at spurring innovation. However, the resistance to change remains and the inertia continues.

In summary, educational institutions are faced with unparalleled problems stemming from a troubled society, a need to design individualized programs to serve the needs of a diverse student population, and the institution's inability to modernize themselves. It is into this situation that educators, generalists and specialists alike, must come and, it is hoped, cope.

EDUCATIONAL SPECIALISTS

At the turn of the century most schools and school systems were small and were staffed primarily by instructional personnel, one of whom was often released part-time to perform administrative tasks. As schools grew and large districts were formed, administrative bureaucracies grew accordingly. However, the personnel employed were assigned administrative duties that must be characterized as routine. In some few instances professional personnel were hired to assist or supervise teachers in the development of instructional procedures or, more likely, in updating their curricular offering. It was not until the fifties and sixties that large numbers of specialists were hired by school districts to assist with the particular needs of students. In the last twenty years the number of school psychologists, school counselors, resource teachers, school social workers, and teachers of those with learning disabilities has increased dramatically. It is to our discredit, however, that in many instances school systems hired specialists instead of making basic changes in the structure and fabric of the educational programs. For example, when the problem of educating the mentally retarded first came to the fore, educational institutions, with some urging from special education groups, opted in some instances for special classrooms or special schools. Some twenty-five years later, we are beginning to realize that isolated classrooms were the wrong approach. We are now attempting to make the needed educational changes so that mentally retarded students can be accommodated within our educational system without being labeled and ostracized.

It is still doubtful that educational institutions are ready for widespread change, which would enable them to serve students more adequately. What is not in doubt is that the educational specialists employed by school districts are increasingly prepared to provide leadership so that planned, orderly change can occur, which will result in more effective educational programs.

School psychologists were perhaps the first educationally based group to recognize that their traditional role as psychodiagnosticians did not allow the latitude required to meet the needs of the students they were hired to serve. A psychodiagnostician is involved in assessing the exact nature of a problem and suggesting specific remedial strategies. Most psychologists realized that there were two rather glaring inadequacies in this role. First, it is more important to develop programs and initiate within the educational institution change that will prevent problems from occurring rather than to remedy them once they occur. Second, given that some problems will arise, a psychologist must possess the ability to enter into a collaborative relationship with teachers, parents, and administrators to help insure that not only are recommendations carried out but also skills will be developed to help the individual deal more effectively with future problems. Therefore, school psychologists began to broaden their role to include consultation (Gallessich, 1974; Pryzwansky, 1974).

School counselors have given lip service for nearly fifteen years to the concept of providing proactive services. The words *preventive, developmental,* and *promotional* abound in the counseling literature and in the role statements published by the American Personnel and Guidance Association (1964; 1974). In fact, however, most school counselors, particularly those at the high school level, continued to function to a very great extent in a crisis-oriented, remedial fashion. Recently, many counselors, realizing that their mode of functioning has many shortcomings, have begun to look for alternative methods. In 1973, C. Gilbert Wrenn listed the use of consultation as a contemporary development in the counseling field. Since then many counselor education programs have instituted courses and practicums aimed at helping counselors develop consultation skills. Perhaps more important, state departments of education and local school districts have developed programs to help in-service counselors utilize consultation procedures in their daily work.

The motivation for school psychologists and counselors to adopt consultation as a part of their roles has been supplied in part, at least, by their desire to influence positively individuals, groups, and systems that have had a debilitative influence on students. Further, counselors and psychologists have wanted to develop alternatives to direct remedial intervention, counseling or therapy. While these same forces have been somewhat influential in getting special educators to incorporate consultation as a part of their role, the hard realities of mainstreaming have probably provided the greatest impetus for this change. Former special education teachers are now learning resource teachers, with not only the function of providing some direct instruction, but also those of influencing the instructional techniques of the regular classroom teacher, involving parents in the educational process, and assisting administrators to design learning environments that will maximize the educational experiences of the special student. Special educators are searching for techniques and methods that will enable them to fulfill these functions successfully. Consultation is being incorporated into the role definition of many educators as one means of insuring this success.

As is perhaps already apparent, this book is aimed at assisting school psychologists, school counselors, and special educators to acquire consultation skills. It may also be obvious that consultation skills are needed by a large number of other educationally based personnel. It is certain that teachers could function more effectively if they understood how best to utilize consultants and if they themselves possessed basic consultation skills. Principals have discovered that the militant new breed of teachers responds less to authoritarian approaches and more to collaborative efforts based upon open communication and mutually established goals, the characteristics of a good consulting relationship. Similarly, supervisors are faced with the problem of involving themselves in productive ways with teachers, principals, counselors, and others in what are essentially consultation situations. Thus, most all educational personnel could benefit from the development of consultation skills.

CONSULTATION DEFINED

One way of defining consultation is by stating what it is not. First, it is not counseling or therapy. Both counseling and therapy in a school setting involve *direct* services to the student or students who have the problem, while consultation involves *indirect* service to these students by assisting others, such as teachers, to provide the needed intervention. Although there are other distinctions between the two approaches, the matter of direct versus indirect service stands as the major one.

Second, consultation is not education, although there is an educational component inherent in consultation. Education, in the sense in which it is used here, is a direct service, not necessarily dependent upon a human relationship and is usually leader- (teacher-) directed and controlled. Further, the goals of education are usually set, at least in part, by external sources such as supervisors, curriculum committees, or departments of education. Consultation is predicated upon a human relationship; it is, as was stated earlier, an indirect service, and it follows agenda set by the consultant and consultee, not by an external person or agency. Let us turn now to look at some more specific definitions of consultation.

A number of such definitions have emerged. Dinkmeyer (1968) and Keat (1974) have developed two that depict consultation as a process in which the consultant and consultee collaborate to develop means of assisting students. Keat points specifically to the need for consultants to use their knowledge to complement that of consultees in assessing pupil needs, developing positive classroom climates, and individualizing instruction.

While the definitions advanced by Dinkmeyer and Keat help us to see what consultation is to accomplish, an earlier definition by Bindman (1964) may help us more fully to understand the consultation process. He stated:

> ... Consultation is an interaction process of interpersonal relationship that takes place between two professional workers, the consultant and the consultee, in which one worker, the consultant, assists the other worker, the consultee, solve a mental health problem of a client or clients, *within the framework of the consultee's usual professional functioning.* The process of consultation depends upon the communication of knowledge, skills and attitudes through this relationship and, therefore, is dependent upon the degree of emotional and intellectual involvement of the two workers. A secondary goal of the process is one of education, so the consultee can learn to handle similar cases in the future in a more effective fashion, and thus enhance his professional skills [p. 367].

In Bindman's definition a number of concepts appear that are worthy of more careful examination. First, he clearly views the consultation process as one predicated upon a human relationship characterized by mutual emotional and intellectual involvement. Second, the consulting relationship is one entered into primarily for the benefit of a third party. Third, the consultant is the more knowledgeable of the dyad, since it is he or she who is there to assist the consultee. Fourth, and perhaps obviously, the consulting relationship is one that occurs in the consultee's professional setting, not the consultant's. Fifth, and finally, consultation has as a secondary goal the education of the consultee in order to enable him or her to function independently in the future.

Caplan (1970) is undoubtedly the leading theorist in the field of mental health consultation. He has distinguished among types of consultation by looking at the focus of the consultation and the consultant-consultee relationship. He indicates that there are two major foci of consultation, individuals and organizations (actually a third, the community, has emerged), and there are essentially two types of consultant-consultee relationships, expert service and collaboration. While these foci are fairly apparent, the nature of the relationships may need some clarification. According to Caplan, in the expert service model, the goal is to assist the consultee to deal more effectively with either specific clients or community problems that retard the development of programs and to help the consultee deal more effectively with similar problems in the future (please note the similarity to Bindman's definition). Clearly the consultant's role is to provide expertise. In the collaborative relationship the consultant and the consultee work together as equals to improve skills either in dealing with clients or in program development.

Pryzwansky (1974) indicates that consultation is usually viewed as it is depicted in Bindman's definition: that is, as a process in which an expert is involved to solve an existing problem. He argues forcefully that support personnel such as counselors, school psychologists, and resource teachers will encounter little success using this traditional approach and advocates a consultation relationship based upon a collaborative model. In fact, Pryzwansky advocates, as do Dinkmeyer and Carlson (1973), that the consultation process be termed collaboration.

The expert service model has several limitations that may limit its utility for a school-based consultant, but that do not eliminate it altogether as an approach. Let us look at some of these limitations. First, the internal consultant may not have the same aura of expertise possessed by those who have traditionally practiced the expert service model: external consultants. The old saying that an expert is anyone fifty miles from home with a briefcase probably is truer than we would like to admit. There is some doubt as to whether internal consultants will be viewed as true experts by those with whom they work, and this suspicion may in turn limit the degree to which solutions developed by the consultant will be implemented.

Second, the expert service model is primarily diagnostic-prescriptive in nature. By this statement is meant that the consultant diagnoses the consultee's problem and then prescribes a course of action. The consultant is typically not involved in the implementation of the prescribed strategies and thus is not able to make adjustments as implementation progresses. One can readily see that the expert service model depends on the collection of comprehensive data about a given situation so that adequate solutions can be devised. The short periods of time most school-based consultants are able to spend with consultees precludes extensive data collection in many instances and may therefore result in the development of inadequate programs, a situation that must obviously be avoided.

Third, external consultants are accountable in only a very limited degree to school districts for the results of their interventions, while internal consultants must directly account for the success or failure of their activities. Perhaps the worst fate that can befall an external consultant is not to be asked to return to a school district for additional consultation. However, internal consultants run the risk of losing their credibility and thus their effectiveness if programs are not implemented properly and outcomes do not take the expected direction. In a very real sense the internal consultant has more to lose than anyone except the student if mutually arrived at solutions to problems are not carefully nurtured when implemented.

Fourth, as has been obvious from the definitions presented, a secondary goal of consultation is to enable the consultee to generalize to similar situations in the future knowledge and skills acquired during the course of consulation. Anyone who has sat with a teacher, principal, or other school personnel in a consulting relationship knows that the design of a strategy or program either on paper or verbally does not signify that the consultee totally understands the rationale for the program or implementation. Without a collaborative effort in the implementation and evaluation phases of consultation, it is likely that the consultee's ability to generalize his or her knowledge and skills will be curtailed. In turn, the consultee may become dependent on the consultant, a situation that should be avoided.

Fifth, the goal of all consultation is change, whether it be in individuals, groups, organizations, or a community. The expert service model assumes that after a series of "talk and tell" sessions, change will occur. Again, those who have consulted with educational personnel know that certain individuals will not implement ideas unless they are carefully demonstrated and unless there is shared responsibility for the outcome.

Sixth, it is sheer folly for either an internal or an external consultant to assume that his or her expertise can unilaterally provide the best possible solutions to problems experienced by a variety of potential consultees. The expert service relationship to a large extent precludes the development of what can be a highly creative and productive relationship in which both the consultee and the consultant bring their personal resources to bear on a particular difficulty. This is the most serious limitation of the expert service approach.

Perhaps enough of a case has been made at this point for a collaborative approach to consultation. But to make the nature of this approach clear, let us state unequivocally that we agree with Pryzwansky (1974) when he states:

> There should be mutual consent on the part of the *two* professionals involved, mutual commitment to the objectives and a means of resolving an agreed upon problem, as well as joint development of an intervention plan and mutual responsibility for implementation and evaluation of that plan.

Having gone on record as strongly favoring the collaborative relationship approach to consultation, we would like now to file a mild disclaimer and simply state that the expert service model has a definite but limited place in the approaches used by school-based consultants. We are particularly mindful of the types of crisis situation that can arise in which immediate and expert attention is demanded. A teacher who is reintegrating an emotionally disturbed child into the regular classroom may need this type of help when the child injures another student. So may the parent who is suddenly faced with a rebellious child who threatens to run away from home if conditions in the home do not improve. In these and other situations, action must be swift and decisive and this fact in itself dictates that the consultant act as an expert, particularly in the design of the intervention. The fact that the consultant plans an intervention to be used to cope with a student does not preclude the consultant from becoming involved in the remainder of the stages of consultation, however, and meeting in this way some of the specifications of the collaborative relationship model.

Finally, our definition of consultation is as follows: consultation is usually a process based upon an equal relationship characterized by mutual trust and open communication, joint approaches to problem identification, the pooling of personal resources to identify and select strategies that will have some probability of solving the problem that has been identified, and shared responsibility in the implementation and evaluation of the program or strategy that has been initiated. A secondary outcome of consultation should be that both the consultant's and the consultee's repertoire of knowledge and skills will be enhanced to the end that both persons will function more effectively in similar situations in the future. Deviations from this approach are made only under those circumstances that demand immediate action and require the consultant to use specialized knowledge to design specific interventions.

The school-based consultant will be involved in a variety of types of consultation aimed at initiating change in different target groups and will use a variety of techniques in his or her attempts to bring about this change. In these efforts the consultant will also use a spectrum of models or approaches to consultation. A conceptual model for this functioning is presented in Figure 1.1. This model has two "ancestors." Perhaps the most obvious one is Caplan's (1970) typology of mental health consultation. The major change in the consultation models presented is that none of the consulting relationships are based upon the expert service model. To Caplan's foci of consultation, which were listed as individual or organizational, we have added group and community. We have also enumerated strategies to be used in the consultation process. The cube itself was designed by Kurpius (1975), although the model that he developed was considerably different.

Targets of Consultation

The school-based consultant will attempt to influence numerous individuals and groups within the educational institutions. The most obvious of these are students, teachers, administrators, and parents. Also, consultants will have organiza-

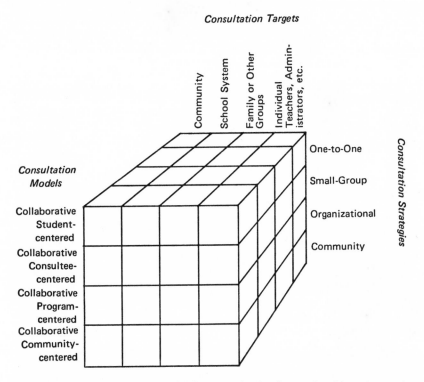

FIGURE 1.1.   Conceptual model for consultation by a school-based consultant

tional change as a major goal of consultation and, at least occasionally, the community will be the target of their efforts. These persons, groups, and organizations become of interest to the consultant whenever influencing change can result in improving the effectiveness of the educational enterprise. *Effectiveness* is roughly defined here as meaning any outcome that has a favorable impact upon the student.

Strategies of Consultation

A *consultation strategy* can be defined as an approach or a process designed to influence a target group. A one-to-one strategy is perhaps easiest to conceptualize, with a community strategy being the most difficult. In reality, school-based consultants will not often be involved with a community strategy that would involve working with influential individuals, organizations, and groups simultaneously to bring about a situation that would increase the quality of an educational program or perhaps the entire educational enterprise. Working within a community to pass a bond issue that would result in new educational programs would require a community strategy.

A group strategy is much like an individual approach except that it involves a small group of consultees, usually eight to twelve. Organizational consultation may require the consultants to work with a number of individuals and groups but within the context of the organization and with the specific purpose of bringing about organizational change.

What is important is that all strategies have common phases, which are entry or relationship, problem identification or diagnoses, goal setting, strategy selection, implementation, and evaluation. These will be discussed in more detail later in this chapter and in the chapters that follow.

Collaborative Models

As was stressed earlier, all the consultation paradigms shown in Figure 1.1 are based upon a collaborative relationship rather than an expert service approach and are an adaption of Caplan's (1970) typology of consultative approaches. As was also noted earlier, we fully realize that the expert service model has limited utility for the school-based consultant. To reiterate our position, though, we believe that those consultation relationships based on collaboration have the greatest potential for producing lasting and meaningful results.

In the collaborative student-centered model, the basic goal of consultation is to assist the consultees to deal more effectively with a particular student and to improve that student's functioning with other similar students. The consultation then is focused on identifying collaboratively those characteristics of the particular client that makes him or her unique and with the consultee determining means of more effectively providing an educational program to the student. An example of this particular approach might be where a learning resource specialist helps a group of classroom teachers to identify the cognitive styles that are unique to the educable mentally retarded (EMR) child and then assists them to generalize current teaching techniques to those EMR students. The assumption underlying this particular model is that consultees already possess the skills needed to deal with a particular student or a group of students, but because of their lack of information are unable to determine how the skills can best be applied.

In contrast, in collaborative consultee-centered consultation, the focus is upon the deficiencies of the consultee. The consultee and the consultant work collaboratively to identify the deficiencies, to draft a plan to remedy the deficiencies, and then, once remediation has occurred, to develop a plan in which the consultee applies the newly developed skills to the educational process. School psychologists and school counselors often find themselves in this type of situation with teachers whose traditional approaches to classroom discipline have failed and who need to acquire more adaptive approaches to classroom management.

In program-centered consultation the focus is obviously upon helping the consultee in program development just as community-centered consultation focuses upon involving the community in accelerating the achievement of educational goals. A learning resource teacher might collaborate with the principal to develop a tutorial program that would use parent volunteers. Similarly, a school counselor might work with a variety of government officials, the local community mental health center, and an association of local clergy for the purpose of developing better treatment and care of unwed mothers. In the situation involving the learning resource teacher, the consultant would use a program-centered model and a one-to-one strategy, with the intent of involving individual parents. The school counselor would use a community model and a community strategy, with the intent of influencing the treatment of pregnant girls. The school psychologist who worked with a small group to plan a parent effectiveness program would be using a program-centered model and group strategy in the hopes of influencing the behavior of a group (families).

An illustration of the way in which consultation services progress through various models, targets, and strategies is provided by the example of an emotionally disturbed child, "Lucille." Lucille exhibited behavior problems from her first day of entry into first grade. She was verbally aggressive and physically assaultive and she twisted bunches of hair from her head, leaving small bald spots. Although a distressed family situation was recognized at the time, the contribution of environmental variables would not be fully understood for a number of years.

In the beginning, *expert* consultation on a one-to-one basis was offered Lucille's teachers. The objective was reduction of the high frequency of unacceptable aggressive and self-injurious behavior. A plan to modify her behavior was outlined with teachers, while other target groups — family, school system, and community — were resorted to for information. During the first half of the school year little progress was made.

Unable to cope with Lucille's disruptive behavior in the regular classroom, the local school moved her to a specially constructed cubicle located in a corner of a hall foyer, together with one other child and a special teacher. The problem had now escalated to the program level. The teacher remained as target while the strategy shifted to small group work. The strategy became one of managing disruptive behavior while facilitating learning in a small group.

While Lucille was being managed at the local school level, the school system had begun to recognize broader needs for a number of children with similar behavior and emotional problems. The result of this work was the establishment of a self-contained classroom unit for emotionally disturbed children. In her second year of school Lucille was transferred to another school, where the class for emotionally disturbed children was located.

During the second year, consultation became collaborative and program-centered, with instructional strategies developed for one-to-one and small group instruction. A rather large child, Lucille appeared at school complaining of pain, with obvious bruises and welts in evidence. During an interview, the mother readily admitted that she "whupped" Lucille regularly with the ironing cord. A final summary conference on this case was held with representatives from more than a dozen community resource agencies, the school system, the mother, and various consultants. Not long after this meeting, mother and daughter moved away from the school system.

As one can readily ascertain by examining Figure 1.1, consultants use a variety of models, employ a number of strategies, and hope to influence many individuals, groups, and agencies. It is perhaps understandable why some have been uncertain about what "really" constitutes the process known as consultation.

DIMENSIONS OF THE CONSULTATION PROCESS

Consultation has thus far been discussed only in general terms. An attempt will be made at this time to put some flesh on the skeleton that has been developed and to breathe life into consultation as a process by discussing the various roles and methods utilized by the consultant. Finally, a step-by-step analysis of the consultation process will be presented.

Goals of Consultation

A number of individuals have discussed the goals of consultation. Some, like Williams (1972), have described the goals very generally as follows:

1. to free energies within the consultee that are not being utilized productively;
2. to help the consultee direct his energies in the most satisfactory ways; and
3. to find ways to sustain the developed and redirected energies [p. 16].

Others, such as Dinkmeyer and Carlson (1973), have discussed goals only in relationship to specific activities, while Fullmer and Bernard (1972) have specific goals that must be classified somewhere between the two extremes represented by Williams and by Dinkmeyer and Carlson. Let us now turn to look at what seems to be appropriate goals of consultation.

First, a goal of consultation should be to develop a situation in which the psychological development of the student is viewed as a high priority. Numerous authors (Kohl, 1967; Postman and Weingartner, 1969; Silberman, 1970; Glasser, 1972) have pointed to the cavalier attitude that American educators take toward the psychological impact of educational processes upon students. The debilitating results of schooling have been described graphically by these authors and will not be further discussed here. However, it should suffice to say that educators need to pay much more attention to promoting psychological health than they have in the past.

A second goal of the consultation process should be to enlist heretofore untapped resources to enhance the development of students. Let us first look at a rather simple example of how this goal can be accomplished and then at some that are more complex. It has long been realized that children from middle-class homes adapt better academically and generally gain more from their educational experience than their lower-class counterparts do. Why does this occur? One reason is certainly because their parents are heavily involved in the educational experience at home. Indeed, Shelton and Dobson (1974) found that when parents were more heavily involved in the educational process, children's attitude toward school improved. Parents, a little used and available resource, can be focused to aid students' development educationally and socially. The relationship between community resources such as the courts, the police department, the welfare system, and the church and student development is not so clear but nevertheless has potential for assisting this process. Consultants should act to focus these resources to this end.

A third goal of consultation is to develop the skills of consultees so they are better able to cope with the difficulties of enhancing student development. Bindman (1964) made this clear in the definition quoted earlier. The inadequacies of teacher education programs to prepare teachers to deal ably with students is a well-known fact. The intention here, though, is not to indict educational preparation programs; it is to develop an awareness that expertise needs to be developed in educational specialists on a continuing basis.

Fourth, consultation should result in increased communication among the various professionals concerned with facilitating the educational and psychological development of students (Fullmer and Bernard, 1972). While most counseling, school psychology, administration, and teacher education textbooks give lip service to the team concept, practice in the school is often somewhat different. In the pupil personnel departments, groups involving professionals whose work should be highly correlated, people often do not coordinate their efforts. Jargon, status concerns, and territoriality are all divisive influences in the pupil personnel team, as well as elsewhere in our schools. Each professional, whether he or she be teacher, administrator, psychologist, or counselor, has knowledge and skills that should be shared with other staff members. Duplication of effort among and between groups must be eliminated if we are to maximize our efforts to promote pupil growth. Skills and knowledge can be shared and duplication avoided through increased communication.

A fifth goal of consultation should be to enhance human relations in schools. The inhumanity of educational processes and their negative effects upon students has already been alluded to. However, at this point the trouble springs only partially from professional practices and techniques. Clearly many of the alienating factors in our educational enterprise lie not in techniques but in the societal hypocrisy students see mirrored in their schools. Accounts of disputes among students of various racial and ethnic groups are almost daily fare in our newspapers. So are the labor-management disputes that occur between practitioners and administrators as adversarial negotiations methods are adopted. Perhaps not so public is the racial tension that can exist among teachers and the discrimination that occurs not only in teacher-student relationships but in professional relationships as well. And only lately has the public had a glimpse of how educational misfits are dealt with by educators. Children less able to cope with the academic demands placed upon them by the typical classroom teacher are shunted aside into special rooms and derided by other students. Students emotionally unable to deal with the pressures of the school are forced out or punished in archaic fashion for their nonconformity. The area of human relations must receive a high priority from all consultants if the increasing cynicism among students is to be stemmed.

A sixth goal of consultation lies in the area of organizational change. Consultation must be able to help the school organization adapt itself in a manner that will enable it to accept methods, techniques, and approaches through planned change. Toffler (1970) made many of us aware of the rapidity of change occurring in our society, but Stiles and Robinson (1973) point out that schools are slow to accept change, at least on a logical basis. Schools do respond to societal pressure, producing a yo-yo effect. An example that has occurred during the last decade is in the area of so-called modern math. At the urging of society and under the pressure to produce scientists, schools abandoned traditional teaching procedures. Subsequently it was found that many children did not possess rudimentary mathematical skills, and public pressure has caused schools to abandon "modern math" for more traditional approaches. The consultant may very well become the locus of the force for planned educational innovation.

Seventh, consultation is aimed at enhancing the educational achievement of students. While this goal is implicit in some of the previously enumerated ones, it must be explicit. Whether we like it or not, most accountability in education focuses upon pupil achievement and not the development of self-concept, communications skills, et cetera. With the "back to basics" movement so obvious in this country, an emphasis on measurable academic achievement is likely to be accentuated. Consultants must then strive to increase educational achievement.

The Consultation Process

In an early article Gibb (1959) enumerated eight steps in the consultation process: (1) entry, (2) diagnosis, (3) data collection, (4) relationship, (5) boundary agreement about roles taken, (6) resource development, (7) decision making, and (8) termination. Some fourteen years later Havelock (1973) provided a similar list with altered steps. These were: (1) relationship, (2) diagnosis, (3) acquisition of resources, (4) choosing an alternative course of action, (5) gaining acceptance for the course of action, and (6) implementation and disengagement. Although the steps listed by either of these authors would be acceptable, here we have adopted Havelock's with some minor changes: specifically, a substep, developing an awareness of the problem and motivation for action, is needed after diagnosis in Havelock's scheme. Second, the acquisition of resources seems to be more appropriately a substage of the implementation process. Third, evaluation of the process must occur before disengagement. Now let us look at this slightly altered paradigm of the consultation process in greater detail.

Relationship The educational and psychological literature is replete with information, both objective and subjective, that supports the importance of the relationship, in a variety of endeavors ranging from teaching to psychotherapy. Many of these statements are based upon the ideas set forth by Rogers (1957) and put into practice by Ivey et al. (1968), Carkhuff (1969 A. and B.), and Gordon (1970). Since the dimensions of the relationship are well known, they will be discussed only briefly here.

Communication is the basis for the consulting relationship as it is for all human relationships. The ability to hear what the consultee is saying and to communicate clearly to that individual or group of individuals what is heard is a prerequisite to any action. Additionally, the consultant must be able to hold his or her own values in abeyance, at least in the initial stages of the relationship with the client. Until the relationship is characterized by open communication and mutual trust, the consultants' ideas and opinions may only serve to threaten the consultee or, perhaps worse, build a dependent relationship in which the consultee is clearly the subordinate. In either case the relationship will be impaired and the possibility of a successful outcome greatly reduced.

Another important aspect of the consulting relationship is a genuine concern for both the individual consultee and the problem at hand. It is difficult to maintain a relationship and involve oneself deeply in the problem of a consultee if there is no basic interest in and/or concern for either. It will of course not be possible to establish a consulting relationship with all prospective consultees. However, if there is a variety of potential consultants available, this will not be a problem.

Diagnosis: Determining the "What" of Consultation As we shall see in subsequent chapters, the actual process of diagnosis varies depending on the theoretical model being followed, the assumptions guiding the consultation process, and whether consultation is being done to assist an individual or an organization.

Generally diagnosis involves the development of a working hypothesis, from which consultants begin to formulate their own plan of action.

Diagnosis in the most simplistic sense is an attempt to understand the present situation of the consultee (Havelock, 1973). The process itself is guided by a set of theoretical assumptions (Lippitt, 1959; Brown and Brown, 1975) about how individuals or organizations should function. Usually, according to Lippitt (1959), the diagnostic theory includes ideas about symptoms that are evidence that something is wrong and assumptions about the underlying causes of these symptoms. Diagnosis then determines the content of the consulting process. When a teacher agrees that instruction is poorly paced or that classroom management could be enhanced by rearranging the seating arrangement, problem resolution can begin. The ability to assess adequately the wide range of problems present in today's schools requires a broad background of knowledge about human behavior, instructional processes, assessment procedures, learner characteristics, and much more.

Awareness and Motivation   Once a diagnosis has been made, awareness of the need for action and motivation to act must be developed. Although this may seem like an easy task, it often proves difficult. A group of teachers may enter into a consulting relationship because of their concern for students. The consultant may come to realize that it is the teachers' own behavior that is largely responsible for the problems they are experiencing. Trying to develop awareness that the teachers need to act to change their own behavior can result in defensiveness and termination of the relationship unless the relationship has become a sound one. Similarly, while consulting with an entire building staff, a consultant may discover that oppressive rules result in both teacher and student dissatisfaction, but find that the principal denies the obvious because of his or her beliefs about school management. Or it may become clear to a consultant that racial disturbance in the school can be reduced only through communication and consciousness-raising workshops dealing with the problems of minority groups. However, when teachers are confronted with workshops and extra work, they may decline and deny either the presence of the situation or its importance.

In a still timely article written in 1959, Bowman discussed the role of the consultant in motivation. He indicated that the consultant's own enthusiasm for action may be contagious and thus produce impetus for action. He also suggested that data about the area in need of change can be gathered as one means of developing motivation. Additionally, it may be necessary to help individuals and groups set priorities before action will occur. The question that must ultimately be answered in the motivational process is: Will the potential outcomes warrant the effort to be expended? Unless the answer is clearly in the affirmative, stimulating action may be difficult. In short, awareness of the need for action can be developed if open communication exists between the consultant and the consultee. Action in the form of problem solving does not necessarily follow, however.

Problem Solving Once an individual or a group has decided that action needs to be taken, alternatives must be delineated and one chosen. Havelock (1973) suggests that the way to choose an appropriate alternative is to look at the implications of the research literature. Unfortunately, educational research often provides little basis for decision making in the area of program design and organizational change (Stiles and Robinson, 1973). Fortunately there are probably some empirical data to guide counselors, school psychologists, and special educators when they are consulting in some areas of concern. Other sources of information typically used in generating alternatives during the problem solving process are authoritative texts, officials of other school districts who have implemented programs that relate to the area of concern, State Department of Education personnel and other consultants, usually external to the school.

Solutions to problems should logically grow out of the objectives that the individual or the organization has set forth. A teacher may wish to have all of his or her students complete their homework or a parent may want to reduce sibling bickering. Students may want to assist other students in their efforts to influence the school, or the school system itself may want to involve students to a greater degree. These objectives, regardless of their nature, must be specified operationally before a choice of alternatives can be made wisely. Too often consultation takes place without considering this important fact.

Implementing Alternatives and Disengagement Once a course of action has been chosen, it should be collaboratively implemented. The consultant should work directly in the situation during implementation to help identify needed resources, meet regularly with the consultee to "brainstorm" or make process evaluations, or, more likely, be involved in all of these activities and more. In some situations, such as those that involve parents, the consultant will be unable to go directly into the home. However, he or she should be available by telephone to the parent on a standby basis. In summary, it will often be mandatory that the consultee take the lead during the implementation stage, but the consultant must be as active as possible in the process.

Implementation of individual practices or organizational change is usually done tentatively and on a relatively small scale so that it can be carefully evaluated prior to adoption as a standard practice. Evaluation practices thus become an integral part of the implementation phase and should be planned before the actual beginning of this phase. Once a practice has been demonstrated to be of worth, the consultant can begin to withdraw from the particular relationship. A common error made by many consultants is not making clear that once the innovation has been installed and tested, termination will occur. Failure to make this stipulation may result in dependence upon the consultant and consequent failure of the consultee to gain the needed knowledge and/or skills to function independently.

In the next chapters the consultation process, which has been so briefly presented here, will be elaborated and focused on as consultation with parents, teachers, administrators, organizations, and the community is discussed.

COMPETENCIES OF THE CONSULTANT

In order for the counselor to achieve the goals of consultation, a variety of skills is required. Concern about these skills has been expressed by several individuals, including Dinkmeyer and Carlson (1973), who put forth a list of competencies required in consultation, and Gallessich (1974), who listed curricular areas that she believes should be included in the preparation of consultants; these areas imply skills or competencies needed by the consultant. One danger in presenting a comprehensive list of needed competencies is that they will seem to be so complex that persons interested in consultation will be overwhelmed to the point of abandoning the thought of consultation because of perceived inadequacies. These perceptions may be intensified by some of the recommendations now being made for the education of consultants. Dinkmeyer and Carlson (1973) have recommended a two-year preparation program for consultants, and Gallessich (1974) recommends that the doctorate be the minimal educational level for school psychologist-consultants. It should perhaps be noted that most persons acting as consultants today have neither the doctorate nor the shorter two-year program. Most consultants have been forced to acquire their skills through personal experimentation, reading, short-term workshops, part-time college course work, or some combination of these approaches. Although this may not be the most desirable situation, it does indicate that one can become a consultant in a variety of ways. It is to be hoped that the following will be a useful list for those seeking to become consultants regardless of the path chosen.

COMPETENCIES NEEDED IN ORDER TO DEVELOP
CONSULTING RELATIONSHIPS
1. Be able to identify personal strengths and limitations.
2. Be able to respond to and clarify verbal and nonverbal components of behavior.
3. Have a knowledge of the backgrounds of individuals from various backgrounds — ethnic, racial, and socioeconomic — and be able to utilize that knowledge in the development of open communication.
4. Demonstrate respect for persons from different ethnic, racial, and socioeconomic backgrounds and be able to communicate that respect in the consulting relationship.

5. Demonstrate through one's behavior emotional stability and independent functioning.
6. Be aware of personal values and how these influence one's behavior in the consulting relationship.
7. Be able to maintain objectivity and personal calmness when dealing with a crisis situation.
8. Be able to gain the confidence and trust of others, as evidenced by their participation, and follow through in consultation.
9. Be able to develop consultee readiness for consultation.
10. Be able to develop a rationale for consultation in terms that the consultee can readily comprehend.
11. Be able to structure the consulting relationship in a manner that clarifies the roles of both the consultant and the consultee, with emphasis upon the development of an independently functioning consultee.
12. Be able to maintain a coequal relationship with a consultee.

COMPETENCIES REQUIRED IN DIAGNOSIS

1. Be able to collect objective data about the unmet developmental needs of students as well as crisis situations that exist.
2. Be able to analyze and diagnose the teaching or learning situation and design strategies necessary to remedy deficiencies.
3. Be familiar with at least one major psychological theory to the extent that individual actions can be described in terms of that theory.
4. Be familiar with organizational theory to the extent that organizational functioning can be described according to that theory.
5. Be able to present hypotheses accurately and succinctly in a manner that does not arouse defensiveness.
6. Be able to present hypotheses along with underlying rationale in a manner that can readily be understood by the consultee.

COMPETENCIES REQUIRED IN DEVELOPING
AWARENESS AND MOTIVATION

1. Be able to communicate the nature of the problem clearly in both oral and written form.
2. Be able to collect objective data to support the need for action.
3. Be enthusiastic and persistent.
4. Be able to develop, without dramatization, accurate scenarios of the future of the situation if change occurs.
5. Be able to develop an entrée into the decision-making power structure.
6. Be able to develop external power bases that can influence organizational decision making.

COMPETENCIES REQUIRED IN DECISION MAKING

1. Be familiar with the decision-making process.
2. Be able to identify materials, programs, and persons with bearing on the development of alternatives and the final selection of an alternative.
3. By utilizing group leadership skills, be able to facilitate group decision-making processes.
4. Be able to provide, on occasion, specific answers, or strategies that may serve as alternatives.
5. Be able to identify and form a change agent team.
6. Be able to develop behavioral objectives.

COMPETENCIES REQUIRED IN IMPLEMENTATION AND TERMINATION

1. Be able, when appropriate, to model solutions that have been chosen.
2. Be able to develop evaluation procedures for the practices, programs, or other changes that have been identified.
3. Be able to teach communication skills.
4. Be able to teach the utilization and understanding of psychological theories.
5. Be able to develop feedback mechanisms so that evaluation data are utilized to improve practice.
6. Be able to develop cohesive groups of teachers and parents that can collaboratively implement solutions.
7. Be able to identify and help secure resources that will implement the chosen alternative.
8. Be able to terminate the relationship once the knowledge base and skills of the consultee are sufficiently developed to carry on the implementation.

OVERVIEW

In Chapter Two the theoretical basis of indivdual and small-group consultation will be examined. This discussion will be followed by two chapters (Three and Four) which deal with the content, process and strategies of teacher consultation. In Chapter Five the consultant's role in dealing with exceptional children will be addressed. Curriculum development will be considered in Chapter Six, and in Chapter Seven a rarely discussed topic, consultation with students, will be explored. Chapter Eight deals with parental consultation and education. Chapter Nine moves from an individual focus to an organizational focus as does Chapter Ten. In Chapter Nine change in the educational organization will receive attention. Chapter Ten looks at the consultant's role in developing and utilizing community resources to assist students. The final chapter, Eleven, deals with the evaluation of consultation.

SUMMARY

In this chapter the idea of consultation has been introduced and contrasted to other intervention strategies, particularly counseling. Consultation has been defined generally as a process involving a consultant and consultee, primarily for the benefit of an uninvolved individual or group. The consultee benefits indirectly from the process because of new knowledge or skills that are acquired if the process is successful.

The process of consultation has been described as involving five phases: relationship, diagnosis, awareness and motivation, decision making, and implementation and termination. The skills required to function in each of these phases have also been presented.

REFERENCES

American Personnel and Guidance Association. *Policy for Secondary School Counselors.* Washington, D.C.: APGA, 1964.

_____. "The Role of the Secondary School Counselor," *School Counselor,* 21(1974): 380–381.

Bindman, A. J. "Mental Health Consultation: Theory and Practice," *Journal of Consulting Psychology,* 23 (1959): 473–482.

_____. "The Psychologist as a Mental Health Consultant." *Journal of Psychiatric Nursing,* 2 (1964): 367–380.

_____. "The Clinical Psychologist as a Mental Health Consultant." In *Progress in Clinical Psychology,* eds. L. E. Cibt and B. F. Reiss. New York: Grune and Stratton, 1966.

Bowman, P. H. "The Role of the Consultant as a Motivator of Action," *Mental Hygiene,* 43 (1959): 105–110.

Brown, D., and D. J. Srebalus. *Contemporary Guidance Concepts and Practices.* Dubuque: William C. Brown Publishing Co., 1972.

Brown, D., and S. D. Brown. *Consulting with Elementary School Teachers.* Boston: Houghton Mifflin Co., 1975.

Caplan, G. *The Theory and Practice of Mental Health Consultation.* New York: Basic Books, 1970.

Carkhuff, R. R. *Helping of Human Relationships,* Vol. 1: *Selection and Training.* New York: Holt, Rinehart & Winston, 1969 (A).

_____. *Helping of Human Relationships,* Vol. 2: *Practice and Research.* New York: Holt, Rinehart & Winston, 1969 (B).

Dinkmeyer, D. C., ed. *Guidance and Counseling in the Elementary School: Readings in Theory and Practice.* New York: Holt, Rinehart & Winston, 1968.

Dinkmeyer, D., and J. Carlson. *Consulting: Facilitating Human Potential and Change Processes.* Columbus: Charles E. Merrill Publishing Co., 1973.

Fullmer, D. W., and H. W. Bernard. *The School Counselor-Consultant.* Boston: Houghton Mifflin Co., 1972.

Gallessich, J. "Training School Psychologists for Consultation," *Journal of School Psychology,* 12 (1974): 138–149.

Gibb, J. K. "The Role of the Consultant," *Journal of Social Issues,* 2 (1959): 1–4.

Glasser, W. *Schools without Failure.* New York: Harper & Row, 1972.

Gordon, T. *Parent Effectiveness Training.* New York: Peter H. Wyden Inc., 1970.

Havelock, R. G. *The Change Agent's Guide to Innovation in Education.* Englewood Cliffs: Educational Technology Publications, 1972.

Ivey, A. E., C. J. Normington, C. Miller, W. H. Morrill, and R. F. Haage. "Microcounseling and Attending Behavior: An Approach to Prepracticum Counselor Training," *Journal of Counseling Psychology,* 15 (1968): 1–12.

Keat, D. B. *Fundamentals of Child Counseling,* 2nd ed. Boston: Houghton Mifflin Co., 1974.

Kurpius, D. J. "A Conceptual Framework for Consultation." In *Psychoeducational Consultation: Conference Proceedings,* ed. D. J. Kurpius and W. L. Lanning. Bloomington: Indiana University Press, 1975.

Kohl, H. *36 Children.* New York: Signet, 1967.

Lamb, J., and R. Deschenes. "The Unique Role of the Elementary School Counselor," *Elementary School Guidance and Counseling Journal,* 3 (1974): 219–223.

Lippitt, R. "Dimensions of the Consultant's Job," *Journal of Social Issues,* 2 (1959): 5–12.

Postman, N. and C. Weingartner. *Teaching as a Subversive Activity.* New York: Delacorte Press, 1969.

Pryzwansky, W. B. "A Reconsideration of the Consultation Model for Delivery of School Based Psychological Services," *American Journal of Orthopsychiatry,* 44 (1974): 579–583.

Rogers, C. R. "The Necessary and Sufficient Condition of Therapeutic Personality Change," *Journal of Consulting Psychology,* 27 (1957): 95–103.

Ruben, A. G. "Will Counselors Ever Be Consultants?" *School Counselor,* 21 (1974): 95–103.

Shelton, J. E., and R. L. Dabson. "Family-Teacher Involvement, a Counseling Key," *Elementary School Guidance and Counseling,* 8 (1974): 190–196.

Silberman, C. E. *Crisis in the Classroom: The Remaking of American Education.* New York: Random House, 1970.

Stiles, L. J., and B. Robinson. "Change in Education." In *Processes and Phenomena of Social Change,* ed. G. Zalman. New York: John Wiley & Sons, 1973.

Toffler, A. *Future Shock.* New York: Bantam Books, 1970.

Williams, D. L. "Consultation: A Broad Flexible Role for the School Psychologist," *Psychology in the Schools,* 9 (1972): 16–24.

Wrenn, C. G. *The World of the Contemporary Counselor.* Boston: Houghton Mifflin Co., 1973.

CHAPTER TWO Theoretical Bases for the Consultation Process

INTRODUCTION

This chapter was included for two reasons. First, in the collection of case material for this book it was decided that consultants holding certain theoretical biases would be asked to provide material. Once this material was examined, it became clear that while the reader could readily discern what a particular consultant did, the more important question of why a particular action was taken could not be ascertained without some insight into the consultant's theoretical view. This chapter was developed to assist the reader to achieve that end.

Second, this chapter was included because of the author's view that good educational and psychological practice should be theory based. Much but not all of the theory base for consultation is similar to that which undergirds counselor theory and teaching, as will be illustrated in this chapter. Since not all of the possible theoretical bases underlying these processes could be included, only three have been chosen for explication here.

These three will provide most of the theoretical base needed to consult with teachers, parents, and students and in the community. However, Chapter Nine contains some theoretical material that is peculiar to organizational consultation.

Let us begin by examining the assumption that a theory should provide the basis for consultation. To the question "Do any of us practice from an atheoretical basis?" must come the reply "Probably not." The senior author recalls the many parental consultation sessions that he has observed and conducted in which parents gave their own explanations of why their children were not functioning as they should. One explanation frequently heard was that the child had rejected God and he and the parents were being punished for the child's sins. One pair of parents was convinced that not only had the child rejected God, but the devil had completely taken possession of the child. In this latter instance the parents forced the child to take strong emetics and placed his head in the toilet bowl, flushing the toilet repeatedly. Both practices were designed to cleanse the child of the evil forces that were present in his body. In another situation, the child, who was thought to be alienated from God, was forced to go to church, sent to religious camps, and involved in other similar experiences. In these cases, parents were acting on personal theories of human functioning based upon their perceptions of religious teachings.

Other explanations of misbehavior that have been heard repeatedly are the child has "bad blood" (inherited tendencies), the child had one or more traumatic experiences such as witnessing violent crimes, or his or her mother or father was not present in the home, thus leading to deprivation of a basic aspect of human nurturance. These explanations are, in fact, a type of theoretical explanation, since they are unverified empirically. Consultants who purport to have no theoretical basis for their practice often use terms such as *poor self-concept, environmental deprivation,* and *instincts.* The point is that most of us have developed ideas about why students learn and behave as they do, although we may not see our ideas as constituting a theory.

The Role of Theory in Consultation

Stefflre and Grant (1972) pointed out that, although we do not have an empirical basis for our practice, we must act as though we do. While this idea may have a disquieting effect on many, the fact is that we must have some frame of reference for interpreting the vast amount of data communicated in a consultation session, must help the consultee interpret that data, and, with the consultee, must be able to design strategies to deal with the situation at hand. Theory can provide the basis for each of these steps.

An important point that deserves emphasis is that theory provides the consultant with a means of interpreting and making "sense" out of a large array of data. Theory, in fact, becomes a perceptual screen, and individuals view data in different ways. Several years ago the senior author participated in a presentation in which an Adlerian and a behavioral counselor gave demonstrations of consultation sessions and then discussed not only their own sessions but each other's. It became very clear that each consultant focused on different types of data, and only by understanding the theoretical perspective of each consultant could an individual truly understand how certain criticisms arise.

Another important role of theory in consultation is that it serves as the basis for communication between the consultant and the consultee. It is perhaps obvious to individuals that a psychoanalytically oriented consultant and a behaviorist would interpret data differently. It does not take a great deal of imagination to realize that the communication problems would be greater if one of the consultants had no systematic basis for interpreting human behavior. Unfortunately, the consultee is very often in this situation. Since communication is vital to the consultation process, effective consultants often find themselves teaching their own theoretical premises to their consultees. It makes little difference, to the author at least, whether the consultee learns to understand fully the meaning of self-actualization, of social interest, or of positive reinforcement, all of which are motivational concepts. What is necessary is that persons involved in consultation understand each other if outcomes are to be meaningful.

Adopting a Theory

The point has been made that consultation should be theory based. Two questions must be answered once this premise is accepted. The first is: Should consultants adopt already existing, systematic theories? Brammer (1969) has rejected this alternative, advocating that each consultant evolve a personal and eclectic position. He has made it clear that he does not view eclecticism as an indiscriminate process where the consultant develops a position without considerable thought. Rather, consultants should develop good observational skills so that they can discern the nature of interactions and draw conclusions from them. They should also study theories for ideas, but should not succumb to the attractive alternative of adopting a theory in its totality. Finally, consultants should understand themselves thoroughly, so that they understand their own personal philosophy, values, and inclinations. The essential question to be answered in this self-searching is: What assumptions, ideas, and techniques can one as a consultant accept and practice (Brammer, 1972)?

The idea of developing a personal theory is appealing, but unfortunately preparation programs do not provide the background experiences, either in the form of academic coursework or opportunities for self-exploration, necessary for this process to occur. Another problem with this concept is that evolving a consistent personal theory is a rather lengthy process. For these reasons it is recommended that the consultant adopt a single theory, learn it extremely well, and then set himself or herself on the path that Brammer has outlined. In this process of evolving a personal theory, Brammer's three steps — developing observational powers, studying theory, and self-exploration — are vital. However, the additional step of studying the empirical verification of theoretical positions seems also to be an important step in the process.

The second question, alluded to earlier, is: Which theory should be adopted? Theories that might support the consultation process with teachers, parents, and administrators in order to help them facilitate individual functioning abound. Grant and Stefflre (1972) presented four theoretical positions. Patterson (1973) discussed fourteen theories, and Corsini (1973) has included twelve theoretical positions in his exposition. Many theories lend themselves nicely to consultation practice. But which ones are most useful to a consultant? We have attempted to answer this question, since this volume is dedicated to both theory and practice. Therefore, we selected three theories for presentation here. The criteria utilized in this distillation process were: (1) the theory has stood the test of time; (2) the concepts are relatively well defined and can be communicated effectively to persons with little background in psychology; (3) an empirical basis for the theory either exists or is emerging; (4) books, articles, and other materials exist that can help the consultant expand upon the limited presentation here; and (5) the theory has demonstrated some practical utility for consultation practice. The three theories that have been chosen are the behavioral, Adlerian, and neo-client-centered models.

NEO-CLIENT-CENTERED THEORY

In 1951 Rogers published his first major statement on client-centered approaches, although some of the concepts had started to emerge in the early forties (Rogers, 1942). Since the publication of *Client Centered Therapy,* Rogers has published numerous other books and articles, including *On Becoming a Person* (1961) and *Freedom to Learn* (1969), which have particular relevance for individuals interested in applying his ideas to educational settings. Robert Carkhuff has also made a substantial contribution to client-centered thought by carrying out many of Rogers' original concepts and extending the original client-centered model by adding a problem-solving dimension (Carkhuff, 1973 A, B.). It is from these and other related sources that this section is drawn.

Rogers (1951) characterized human beings as functioning in a perceptual or phenomenal field that is reality for them. Starting with early experiences and continuing throughout life, a self-identity emerges from the perceptual field; Rogers labeled it the self-concept. The self-concept becomes the basis for personal functioning, since perceptions are experienced directly by the organism in the light of this self-identity. Individuals have one basic life striving: self-enhancement or self-actualization; this is important. As a result, perceptions are experienced in a manner favorable to the individual. This proposition has led some critics of client-centered theory to say that the theory describes human beings as selfish. Combs and Snygg (1959) indicate that to a degree this view does portray individuals as basically selfish, but they further indicate that in order to maintain a sense of adequacy the individual must be able to cope with the world, and he or she cannot do so in a destructive manner. Let us now turn to a more comprehensive look at the theory.

Personal Development A child is born with one basic tendency: self-actualization. The child also has the inborn capacity to discern those experiences that will negatively or positively affect the self-actualizing tendency. As a result, the child "values positively" those experiences that enhance the self and "values negatively" those experiences that detract from the self. This inherent capacity directs the self-actualization process by leading the individual toward perceptions that will be self-actualizing.

The family provides the basic experiences for the developing child, and during the early childhood years the self-concept begins to take shape. Combs and Snygg (1959) identify four basic ingredients in the family structure that contribute to the development of the self-concept. These are experiences of adequacy, experiences of acceptance, experiences of identification, and expectations that emerge later as aspirations. Rogers (1959) seems to subsume these early family experiences and others under the rubric of positive regard, a basic and universal need of all. In short, the experience of positive regard results in positive self-regard, and the individual attempts to experience self-worth in a manner that he or she has learned in significant interactions with others (Meador and Rogers, 1973).

Throughout life the self-actualizing tendency remains as the life-striving. However, because of the need for self-regard and the manner in which it must be experienced (because of previous learning), a conflict may develop (Meador and Rogers, 1973): that is, an individual's actions enable him or her to receive positive regard even though the actions may be at odds with the self-actualizing tendency. The result of this conflict is that the individuals begin to perceive selectively and to symbolize their experiences. This selectivity may result in distortion or complete denial (Rogers, 1959; Snygg and Combs, 1959). Whenever there is an incongruity between self and experience — that is, when experiences are either distorted or denied — anxiety develops, a state of maladjustment exists (Rogers, 1959).

Snygg and Combs (1959) have discussed the circularity of function of the self-concept. They point out that once a self-concept develops it perpetuates itself by accepting only those perceptions that are consistent *with already existing self-perceptions.* The self-concept is composed of all of those thoughts, feelings, and perceptions that an individual has about himself or herself; it includes perceptions about the person's physical and psychological being (Combs and Snygg, 1959). Therefore, if a person perceives himself or herself to be stupid, experiential data to the contrary will be denied. Similarly, a person who is relatively unattractive by societal norms but has self-perceptions of personal attractiveness will deny data that suggest that he or she is unattractive. The formulations of both Rogers and Combs and Snygg suggest that the purpose is experiencing positive self-regard and hence maintenance of the self.

In 1951 Rogers indicated that in order to assist individuals whose perceptions were incongruous, who thus were unable to symbolize their experiences directly into the self-concept, a threat-free climate was a necessity. In 1957 he became much more explicit, saying that certain conditions must be present for personality change. These he identified as (1) two persons in psychological contact, (2) an incongruent client, (3) a congruent counselor, (4) a counselor who experiences unconditional positive regard for the client, (5) a counselor able to experience the inner feelings and attitudes of the client (empathy) and (6) communication of both unconditional positive regard and an understanding of the client's inner frame of reference. These conditions have been redefined more recently by Meador and Rogers (1973) as empathy or experiencing the phenomenal world of the clients as the clients do, positive regard, or unpossessive caring and genuineness. The last condition, genuineness, is described briefly as follows:

> The therapist trusts his own organismic responses in the situation and conveys those feelings which he intuitively believes have relevance in the relationship [Meador and Rogers, 1973, p. 139].

In short, Rogers now sees as one very important part of the therapeutic relationship not only a fully functioning counselor, but one who shares his or her basic reactions with the client.

Robert Carkhuff (1969 A, B) has taken the basic ideas of empathy, positive regard, and genuineness and has arranged them so that they can be more easily taught. He has broken them down into six substages: empathy, respect, concreteness, genuineness, confrontation, and immediacy. However, Carkhuff did not stop with the various substages. From his point of view the behavior-change process may be aided by the introduction of problem-solving skills and so he introduced this dimension (Carkhuff, 1973). His affirmation of the importance he places upon problem-solving skills is contained in the last paragraph of the preface of his book *The Art of Problem Solving:*

> In short, it [the book] is particularly appropriate for responsible human beings who want to nourish the conditions for emergence and growth of their loved ones and their communities and to extinguish the conditions that retard their emergence and growth [Carkhuff, 1973, preface].

Let us look in more detail at Carkhuff's substages and his problem-solving paradigm. Carkhuff (1969 B) indicates that the helping process can be separated into two phases: (1) the downward or inward phase and (2) the upward or outward phase. During the first phase, the counselor would try to assess the nature of the problem and the way the consultee perceives himself or herself. The second phase would be devoted to working with the consultee to determine a direction for problem solving. Let us look in greater depth at phase one of the helping relationship.

Phase I At the outset of any helping situation, whether it be counseling, consultation, or teaching, the relationship is characterized as lacking in depth (Carkhuff, 1969 B). The consultant's function at this point is to demonstrate high levels of warmth, empathy, respect, and concreteness. This is done in two ways. The consultant shows concern for the consultee first by his or her nonverbal behavior. This involves eye contact, bodily posture, and an overall physical involvement with the consultee. The second aspect of this early phase of the helping relationship involves the verbal behavior of the consultant. Essentially the goal here is to respond in such a way that the verbal response to the client contains the essence of the verbal and affective content. It is also important that the consultant suspend judgment during this phase and communicate that the consultee is valued for his or her uniqueness and differences and despite any shortcomings that he or she may personally perceive. The demonstration of personal respect and empathic understanding must be coupled with concreteness: that is, restating consultee communications in a manner that links not only content and affect but also the general themes of the consultee's communications.

To illustrate the foregoing ideas, let us consider a first-year junior-high teacher who came to a consultant with some grave concerns about her teaching ability. Although the teacher discussed her problems very openly, it was still necessary to establish a basic relationship along the lines that Carkhuff describes. The consultant began simply by listening attentively and restating (empathic understanding), as is illustrated in the following excerpt:

T: I just became aware that you were working in the school this year as a consultant to teachers. Believe me I could use some consultation or I'm going to need my own counselor full time.

C: Sounds like things aren't going well for you this year and you're kind of happy to have someone like me around.

T: Yeah ... I'm a first year teacher and to say the least things aren't going as planned. If they don't get better in a hurry I may go back to working in a bank.

C: At this point things have already gone so badly you're beginning to think about getting out ... going back to the bank.

T: Well, I really don't want to do that. What I want to do is teach. But I didn't know that schools could be such a zoo. The kids here are horrible.

C: You want to teach ... but the kids here are really getting to you.

In these opening statements the consultant responds empathically and merely listens. Later in the same session the consultant has an opportunity to demonstrate the respect dimension of Carkhuff's initial phase overtly:

T: There are times when I think I shouldn't be in this school. My ideas about teaching and students are just different from every other teacher in this school. I just feel different.

C: You feel a little odd because your views are different from the other teachers', but they are uniquely yours and that seems important to me.

T: Well I'm glad to hear you say that . . . I get the feeling that nobody else around here cares whether I have any opinions or not.

Usually respect is communicated in the early stages simply through a nonjudgmental attitude, at least initially (Carkhuff, 1969 B). However, direct communications of respect may be used in the early stages and should probably increase as the relationship develops.

Empathy, respect, and concreteness are all utilized to foster increased understanding on the part of the consultee. Concreteness is particularly important in this early phase of increasing self-understanding — is, in fact, pivotal since it sets the stage for the problem-solving period. At the very outset of the helping relationship, the consultant should merely make sure that the cognitive and affective dimensions of the communication are linked together in responses to the consultee. However, as the session moves along and it is apparent that the consultee is grasping better his or her relationship to the situation, the consultant begins to assist the consultee to focus upon the specific dimensions of the problem at hand.

This is demonstrated in the following excerpt:

C: Things just haven't been going too well for you during this year and in fact they are extremely frustrating. Thus far in our session you have raised questions about your choice of a school, about your skills in dealing with students and underlying the whole thing has been your concern about your competency as a person in all areas.

T: That's right. You know it's all so overwhelming. Things just couldn't be worse. (sigh)

C: Things just seem pretty bad now . . . hopeless.

T: Yeah — If I could just get on top of something — particularly my classroom.

C: So right now your classroom discipline seems to be the most important thing to you.

By summarizing and specifying the parameters of the situation, the consultant causes the teacher to focus upon the global nature of the problem. Then, out of this series of communications emerges a primary concern: classroom discipline. The stage is set for problem identification and action. One final note should be inserted here regarding concreteness or specificity. Throughout the helping relationship it is the helper's responsibility to assist the helpee to define and specify not only the nature of the concern, but alternative actions and means of pursuing those alternatives (Carkhuff, 1969 B).

Phase II As was stated earlier, the second phase of the helping relationship is characterized by directionality, a move toward problem resolution. It is important to note that this phase is dependent upon not only the nature of the relationship established in the early phase but the degree of self-understanding attained. It is also important that the dimensions of empathy, respect, and concreteness are continued throughout the second stage and at deeper levels. This continuity is intended to increase the level of self-understanding for the helpee, for without the accomplishment of this objective, problem solving will be meaningless. In fact, problem-solving activities are built upon the self-understanding that the consultee develops (Carkhuff, 1969 B).

Carkhuff (1969 B) identifies, in addition to increasing self-understanding, two other important dimensions of phase two. There are "... (1) an increasing emphasis upon consultee initiation of action-oriented dimensions and (2) a consideration of a variety of courses of action calculated to get the consultee to where he wants to go [p. 59]." In order to improve these three areas, the consultant must become more genuine in his or her own actions, be able to use facilitative confrontation, and be able to focus upon the relationship in a manner that will maximize communication. Carkhuff (1969 B) terms this latter action *immediacy*.

In a very real sense the consultant emerges as a person in this latter stage of helping. In the early stage the consultant suspends judgment and attempts to develop an understanding of the consultee's situation from the consultee's frame of reference. The early focus, then, is on being aware of one's own feelings and attitudes toward the consultee. However, once the relationship has developed, the consultant begins to disclose more of his or her own feelings and concerns, hoping that doing this will lead to greater self-disclosure from the consultee. These early self-disclosures might simply be the consultant's attitudes and ideas that are germane to the consultee's situation. Later, genuineness involves responding authentically to the consultee in both a negative and positive manner, much as one would do in any human relationship (Carkhuff, 1969 B). The following excerpts illustrate some of these ideas.

SELF-DISCLOSURE

T: I have some doubts about my ability to deal with eighth graders. They are much more complex than I ever suspected.

C: You are experiencing some of the same self-doubts that I and others have felt.

LATER

T: Things just aren't what they should be. Schools just aren't doing what they should be for students!

C: I get a little angry about the inadequacies of this school too.

GENUINENESS, EXCERPT 1

T: I just want to pick up every kid that misbehaves and shake them until something comes loose. I actually hate some of those students.

C: Your anger turns into pure hate at times and you just want to get some of those kids . . . to really hurt them . . . but that doesn't seem like a very good idea to me . . . there must be a better way.

T: You are right, but the anger builds anyway and I do want to learn some ways of coping with the students.

EXCERPT 2

T: We've talked three times now and things just aren't going as I had hoped. I'm disappointed.

C: You're feeling a little down because your situation hasn't cleared up as quickly as you would like. Actually, I think things have gone pretty well and that you are making good progress.

T: That surprises me. I thought you expected me to become a super teacher just by talking to me.

C: I'm sorry that I've conveyed that type of expectation. I have no expectations of your becoming a super teacher.

Please note that in both of the foregoing excerpts the consultant felt free to express his or her own feelings, both positive and negative. Confrontation also requires that the consultant express ideas and opinions. Technically, a confrontation is an incident in which the consultant points out discrepancies between consultee verbalizations, verbalizations and behavior, underlying affect and cognitive content, or consultant and consultee experiences (Carkhuff, 1969 B).

The following excerpts illustrate confrontations in each of these areas:

CONFRONTATION: DISCREPANT VERBALIZATIONS

C: You've been telling me two things which I am having a hard time understanding. On one hand you tell me that you have never had any difficulties dealing with people before and then you tell me about a long series of conflict situations starting with your professors and your supervising teacher and ending with some of the teachers here in the building.

T: I guess that would be confusing. I really never thought of it sounding that way. In fact, I really never thought about it at all.

CONFRONTATION: DISCREPANT VERBALIZATION AND BEHAVIOR

C: We've been talking about your classroom for the past several sessions and the last two times we talked about specific courses of action. On both occasions you have not taken any action and I am wondering what is going on.

T: Well to be honest I'm scared to death to try some of the ideas. I'm afraid I'll fall on my face.

CONFRONTATION: DISCREPANCY BEHAVIOR UNDERLYING AFFECTIVE AND COGNITIVE CONTENT

C: Did you know that while you are talking quite calmly about your students you are making a fist and that your facial expression becomes one of anger?

T: Really! You know I do have some strong feelings about those students and I really didn't want you to know how strong. I guess that seeped out anyway. Well, they do make me angry!

CONFRONTATION: DISCREPANT CONSULTANT AND CONSULTEE EXPERIENCES

C: You've told me repeatedly that the parents in this school encourage their children to run wild, and that they don't care. My experiences have been quite the opposite. I have found most of the parents to be extremely cooperative.

T: (Defensively) Well try talking to some that I have talked to and besides you don't have to deal with them like I do.

C: You got pretty uptight about what I said and you think I'm being unfair because my experiences are different.

T: That's right! (more calmly) I have to deal with them when there is some problem . . . I suppose you have to do that too.

In the last excerpt the teacher became defensive and the consultant immediately reverted to empathic responses. When confrontation causes defensiveness the best hypotheses about the causes are (1) the consultant had not developed a high degree of self-understanding or (2) a relationship based upon trust and mutual understanding had not been built. In either event the consultant rightly chose to respond to the consultee rather than attempting to defend himself (herself).

In addition to genuineness and confrontation, immediacy is also a part of the action-oriented phase of Carkhuff's model of helping. According to Carkhuff (1969 B), it involves focusing upon the inability of the consultee to communicate some aspects of his or her own concerns. Carkhuff views this inability as indicative of a difficulty that transcends the helping situation, relating to a deficiency in self-understanding and self-acceptance. However, he recommends that the problem be interpreted within the context of the helping relationship. The immediate relationship between the consultant and the consultee can be used to assist the consultee to perceive reality if the consultant can discern and focus upon the inability of the consultee to communicate adequately. The following excerpts may help to clarify the concept of immediacy.

IMMEDIACY, EXCERPT 1

T: Well . . . I am sure you are going to think I'm silly, but I just can't get going before the second period and my first period class suffers.

C: You seem to be afraid of what I'll think about your inability to get started in the morning. Perhaps we should take a look at that.

EXCERPT 2

T: I really do apologize for smoking. It's a nervous habit that I just cannot seem to break.

C: That's the third time you've apologized after I reassured you that it was perfectly o.k. to smoke. You seem awfully jumpy about my reaction to you.

EXCERPT 3

T: I would like to tell you one personal thing about myself but — oh, forget it.

C: That's happened before. I am beginning to wonder if you trust me.

Immediacy is, then, focusing upon the consultant-consultee relationship in the hope of deepening the intensity of the relationship and facilitating self-understanding on the part of the client.

Problem Solving The expected result of phase two is that the primary problem area will be defined and action taken to deal with the situation. In *The Art of Problem Solving* (Carkhuff, 1973), the details of the problem-solving process are elaborated on. The first step, as already outlined, is to help the consultee develop self-understanding, but this must be accompanied by a thorough understanding of the problem. Once both have been accomplished, an operationally defined goal must be established and alternative courses of action listed. After each alternative has been explored thoroughly, including an examination in terms of the consultee's values, one course of action must be chosen, and it in turn must be implemented. After implementation, feedback upon the action should be obtained in order to evaluate the result. This feedback may result in the identification of other problems, the establishment of new goals, and/or the selection of new courses of action, depending upon the nature of the data received. This problem-solving paradigm is summarized in Table 2.1. To supplement this brief overview of the problem-solving aspect of Carkhuff's model, *The Art of Problem Solving* is well worth exploring.

The Implications for Consultation of Neo-Client-Centered Theory

At the beginning of this chapter, Carl Rogers's theories and ideas were presented. Then there followed a presentation of Robert Carkhuff's extension of those

TABLE 2.1. Carkhuff's problem-solving paradigm

Step One	Explore the problem.
Step Two	Define the problem.
Step Three	Establish goal.
Step Four	Develop alternative courses of action and collect data.
Substep	Order values of problem solver.
Step Five	Choose alternative.
Step Six	Implement course of action.
Step Seven	Get feedback on outcome — recycle if necessary.

ideas. In the latter presentation, an attempt has been made to illustrate the concepts utilizing case material. The ideas of both Rogers and Carkhuff have been viewed as sound bases for establishing human relationships, and this is one of the major implications of some of the techniques discussed in this chapter. There are others that will be examined at this point.

Rogers's emphasis upon the importance of expressing positive regard has definite implications for child rearing and therefore for parent consultation. Rogers (1959) indicates that positive regard is a basic need and the individual attempts to experience positive regard as he or she experiences it as a child. If the child learns that conformity and rigidity are the basis for experiencing positive regard, he or she will manifest this behavior for the same purpose as an adult. Unfortunately, this type of behavior will result in negative feedback, which in turn must be distorted. The important point here is that the child needs to experience positive regard in a wide variety of ways and in a multiplicity of settings so that the need can be met in adulthood.

Not only must parents learn to provide positive regard, but so must teachers and other educators. Schools must clearly learn to furnish accepting, nurturing environments if the personal growth of the student is to be facilitated.

The nurturing of the self-concept has long been valued as a goal in teaching. George Gazda, in *Human Relations in Education* (2nd ed., Allyn and Bacon, Boston, 1976), has demonstrated how Carkhuff's ideas can be applied in the classroom setting in order to aid in self-concept development. For consultants to teachers who value teacher-student communication and hope to promote self-concept development, this book is essential. It should also be noted that the Carkhuff ideas have been implemented as teaching strategies in the Alamance County Schools, Graham, North Carolina, for their Heart of Teaching Project. George Gazda has served as the chief consultant in that project.

It is important for parents, teachers, and consultees to experience positive regard in the consulting relationship. In a very real sense the consulting relationship needs to be an affirmation of the consultee's personal dignity and worth, so that personal growth will result. Rogers and Carkhuff make it quite clear that unless there is self-understanding and self-acceptance little else will be accomplished.

The area of communication is an important skill to master if the consultant is effectively to implement the neo-client-centered ideas. Carkhuff (1969 A, B; 1973 A) not only specifies that communication is important but goes on to suggest precise levels of communication that are to be used in various stages of the helping relationship. Teaching, parenting, or administering can be forms of the helping relationship; therefore, the skills advocated by Carkhuff become crucial for all.

Systematic problem-solving skills are needed by all practitioners, including students, parents, teachers, administrators, adults, and consultants. However, these skills are of little use unless the consultee learns how to apply them to resolve the difficulties which confront them, but once that point is reached they can play a vital role in problem resolution. The consultant must be conversant with the systematic problem-solving paradigm.

Carkhuff's (1969 A, B; 1973 A) and Gazda's (1976) books should be used as the starting place for learning the so-called neo-client-centered model. Thomas Gordon, in *Teacher Effectiveness Training* and *Parent Effectiveness Training,* published by Peter H. Wyden Inc., New York, N.Y., has also provided materials that will be useful to the consultant not only in acquiring needed communications skills but also in helping the consultant develop programs for others. However, the best advice to prospective users of the neo-client-centered ideas is to enroll in a systematic training program before actually using these techniques.

THE INDIVIDUAL PSYCHOLOGY OF ALFRED ADLER

In 1911 Alfred Adler broke off his association with Freud (Furtmuller, 1964). However, long before this break he had begun to develop a comprehensive theory of human functioning, which was in most ways dramatically opposed to Freud's. He posited that the personality of human beings must be viewed as a holistic entity rather than as a series of substructures. He also theorized that each individual operates within a perceptual field that is uniquely his or her own. In addition, Adler believed that human beings, far from being goaded by instinctual drives or environmental stimuli, have inherent creativity and a concern for the rest of society. These ideas received great attention in the early 1900s because of their departure from psychoanalytic theorizing and are increasingly popular today. One final note should be inserted here before turning to look at the theory in more depth. The reader is certain to recognize in Adlerian theory many ideas that are similar to those found in other humanistic theories. In fact, Adler's phenomenological theory and his emphasis upon growing, developing, and creative individuals preceded or provided the basis for many humanistic theories (Mosak and Dreikurs, 1973).

Adlerian theory posits that from the beginning the child is confronted with his or her inadequacies because of his or her dependency upon others and because of physical deficiencies. These early feelings of deficiency are intensified to a degree as the individual develops because of the realization of his or her insignificance in the world and the universe. Adler (1931, 1964) indicates that these feelings are not abnormal, since all of us possess them. His view on this subject is subsumed in the phrase "to be human means to feel inferior" (1931, p. 96). Feelings of inferiority, rather than being abnormal, serve as the basis for movement, growth, or, as Adler put it, a striving for superiority. Thus, in considering Adler's model of human beings, we must consider the individual as being in a state of moving from a negative self-view to one that will be a positive perception of self. However, while feelings of inferiority give impetus to the process of movement, the goals of security and perfection become the motivating force (Adler, 1964 B).

Because of the frailties of the human child, all initial interaction takes place in the family unit. Within this context the child begins to develop ideas, concepts, and ideas about self. The child is not, however, a passive recipient of family feedback but is actively involved in trying to find a niche. Each child creatively restructures the family in order to establish a feeling of belonging. If this cannot be accomplished in a useful way, the child will turn to what Adler referred to as the useless side of life, but still will have the same goal: belonging. This striving for belonging is an early manifestation of the child's social interest (Adler, 1935).

Adler often discussed how the family should act in order to assure the child a place, a feeling of belonging. He placed great emphasis upon the importance of the mother in this process and believed that mother love was an important aspect of the humanizing process (Adler, 1964). Adler also believed that as early as possible the child should be made a partner in the family and should be allowed to assume responsibilities commensurate with his or her abilities, being assisted with these responsibilities only when the task exceeds the child's physical abilities.

Child-rearing techniques were of great importance to Adler and to other Adlerians (Dreikurs, 1948; 1967). Children are not to be ridiculed, held up as examples, reminded of their misbehavior or inadequacies, punished, or rewarded for good behavior, for each of these actions reminds the child of his or her inferiority. These traditional methods of correcting the child should give way to the use of natural and logical consequences (Dreikurs, 1967; 1968). Dreikurs (1968) defines natural consequences as "a logical and immediate result of the transgression not imposed on him [the child] by an authority, but by the situation itself, by reality" (p. 75). A child who throws a rock through a window and is cut by flying glass suffers from the natural consequences of his or her behavior.

Logical consequences are less easily defined. They are, in contrast to natural consequences, maintained and administered by the individual in authority.

However, logical consequences, related to the transgression in both nature and severity, are administered only when a rule of long standing has been broken, and when that rule grew out of true social order (Bullard, 1973). An adolescent who is denied the use of the family car after receiving a speeding ticket is being subjected to logical consequences. So is the dilatory child who is left behind when some members of the family leave at the appointed time on a shopping trip. Bullard (1973) emphasizes that logical consequences must be administered with fairness and concern or they are no different from traditional punishment. However, as is the case with all Adlerian techniques, logical consequences are designed so that the individual who has broken a rule or violated a family norm will not feel that his or her place is threatened and will feel that the situation, not a more omnipotent individual, dictates the punishment.

Perhaps the most important aspect of the Adlerian approach to dealing with the development of social interest and meeting the child's inherent need for belonging is the emphasis upon encouragement (Dinkmeyer and Dreikurs, 1963; Adler, 1964; Dreikurs, 1967, 1968). Encouragement is designed to assist the child "to develop courage, responsibility, and industry" (Dreikurs and Dinkmeyer, 1963, p. 50). In order to attain these goals, the children must be valued, be respected, be provided with recognition for their efforts and/or a job well done, and be recognized for their strengths and assets rather than their shortcomings (Dinkmeyer and Dreikurs, 1963).

Children who do not receive encouragement do not meet their need for belonging; they turn to the useless side of life. Dreikurs (1968) has identified the four mistaken goals of this useless behavior as attention getting, power and superiority, revenge, and discouragement. The manifestation of the attention-getting goal is distracting, acting out, and sometimes "cute" behavior. A child manifesting this goal will stop when corrected but may return in a short time to this same activity or related ones. On the other hand, the child with the power and superiority goal will probably not stop and will "push" the individual correcting him or her to anger. Even if the child of this type is physically restrained from performing some activity, he or she still "wins" the struggle for superiority. The revenge goal results in retaliatory behavior, and the discouraged child withdraws from social interactions in order to avoid being defeated again. It should be quickly added at this point that the foregoing are only examples of behavior that may be manifested. Dreikurs (1968) has pointed out that children may act either actively or passively, constructively or destructively, in pursuing their goals. However, only when the child has been accepted does he or she act constructively.

An important aspect of the family environment is the family constellation (Adler, 1928, 1929). Mosak and Dreikurs (1973) point out that family constellation is not to be confused with birth order or the position of the child in relation to other siblings. Rather, it is a much broader concept related not only to birth order, but to number of years between and among children, influences from grandparents or other relatives, and the relation of parents both to each other and to the children. Even though all of the foregoing facts are known, one other factor must be considered: the child's subjective view of the situation. In other words, it is an error to assume that because a child was born first, certain types of characteristics will develop (Mosak and Dreikurs, 1973).

Certain factors, either physical, physiological, anatomical, or environmental, may heighten a child's inferiority feelings and lead to the development of an inferiority complex. Adler (1964) identifies these factors under three general rubrics: inferior organs, pampering, and neglect. Adler first wrote about organ inferiority in 1907 and throughout his writings he used the term rather broadly. Essentially "organ inferiority" can refer to a deficiency in a basic body organ, a physical deformity, a low energy level, or some similar condition. Pampering or spoiling, for Adler, was giving in to the child and never allowing the child to develop his or her own personal potency. Neglect had the same connotation for Adler as it does today; it involves child abuse and depriving the child of physical necessities. The resultant development of an inferiority complex is viewed by Adler (1964) as an abnormal state of affairs. The manifestation of the inferiority complex is frequently the establishment of goals of conquest that, according to Adler (1904), "are in contradiction to the welfare of the individual and also to the progressive development of humanity" (p. 101). In addition, the presence of an inferiority complex can be detected by the lack of social interest emanating from an individual.

Children develop a view of the world based upon their experiences in the family and perhaps tempered by factors such as organ inferiority. Since these perceptions are not true approximations of the objective world they are referred to as "fictions." However, the child acts upon the perception "as if" it were reality. Similarly, children develop fictions about themselves, views based upon experiences and feedback. It is the self-perceptions and perceptions of the world that serve as the basis for the style of life. Adler defined life-style in a variety of ways (Ansbacher and Ansbacher, 1956), such as our attitude toward life, the theme or unity of personality, and/or our method of facing or solving problems. Mosak and Dreikurs (1973) define life-style as the cognitive organization of the person. Although these definitions are broad, they tend to give emphasis to Adler's idea of the unity of personality, to its holistic nature.

In a very real sense the life-style or approach to life is the method of striving for superiority. The underlying basis or motivation for the life-style is either largely or totally awareness; thus the individual who has an inferiority complex is unaware that his or her means of attaining superiority is through defeating other people. Mosak and Dreikurs (1973) point out that individuals are more aware of their behavior than of their motivations.

Adler (1931) believed that the style of life developed in early childhood, probably by the age of five or six. From that point on, the individual's direction became fixed, that is, the achievement of superiority through the implementation of a life-style. Adler did not intend that this should be interpreted to mean that behavior was fixed, however. He theorized that individuals make choices that are consistent with the life-style and that may take many forms. For example, an individual may choose a variety of occupations, any of which will lead him or her toward the same goal.

The life-style is implemented in a social context and, in this context the individual must deal with three life tasks: work, love, and friendship (Adler, 1931). For Adler work was one of the means through which an individual could demonstrate his or her interest in society. He stated, "The person who performs useful work lives in the midst of the developing society and helps advance it." Friendship is essentially the task of recognizing the value of others and adapting ourselves to their worth. Friendship should be characterized by cooperation and social feeling, a genuine concern for other human beings. The third task, love, is the affirmation that the individual is a member of a given sex and the successful fulfillment of a sex role is vital for the continuation of humankind.

Social interest is for Adler an innate component of the human being. Born small and helpless, the human being develops feelings of inferiority. These feelings of inadequacy motivate the individual toward superiority — a movement that, if accompanied by the right training, can benefit humankind. The early manifestation of social interest is seeking a place, belonging in the family, and then it later generalizes to work, friendship, and love. Indeed, Adler (1931) believed that these three tasks were highly related aspects of social interest. The person who contributes to others through work, develops unselfish empathic friendships, and implements a sex role successfully has a high degree of social interest.

The alteration of a life-style once it is formed is a matter of great concern to counselors. Mosak and Dreikurs (1973) outline a four-step process in psychotherapy: (1) relationship, (2) understanding the dynamics of the life-style, (3) disclosure, and (4) reorientation. The relationship is for the Adlerians much as it is for other psychologists. The second phase of the change process is actually an investigation stage, where the therapeutic agent tries to understand and interpret the life-style of the individual. For children, particularly if the investigator uses the schema developed by Dreikurs (1968), this is not especially difficult. However, for individuals above the age of ten to twelve, the determination of life-style takes a great deal of skill. In Table 2.2 there is an outline used by some Adlerians as a guide for life-style detection.

After the life-style is ascertained, it is disclosed to the individual and reorientation begins. The expectation of the Adlerian psychologist is that person whose life-style is disclosed will gain insight into his or her fictitious goals and, once they are fully understood, will be able to act to make changes. The reorientation process can be enhanced if the change agent can act as a model, if specific tasks can be set for the individual, and in a variety of other ways such as homework assignments and role playing. As the behavior change process progresses, the individual has a series of "aha" experiences in which there is a realization that new thoughts, ideas, and behaviors do work and are beneficial. There is also an increase in self-confidence and an increased willingness to confront life's problems (Mosak and Dreikurs, 1973).

Implications for Consultants

It is obvious first of all that great emphasis is placed upon the family by Adlerians. This emphasis has led to the establishment of child guidance clinics and family study groups designed to teach families Adlerian principles. Consultation with family members would be an important aspect of the Adlerian consultant's role.

Democracy in the family and in our educational institutions is also a very important concept in Adlerian thought. In addition to working with families to establish egalitarian structures, the Adlerian consultant would work to establish democratic classrooms and educational organizations. Through democratic structures the individual can gain a place and meet the need for belonging.

The Adlerians have been instrumental in eliminating corporal punishment in the classroom and replacing it with the use of natural and logical consequences. Rudolf Dreikurs's book *Psychology in the Classroom* (Harper and Row), has sold well since its publication. Dreikurs advocated throughout his life that teachers must learn to determine the fictitious goals of children's behavior, disclose the goals to children, and redirect the children's behavior using natural and logical consequences. He also asserted that democracy in the classroom would lead to the type of teacher-learner relationship that would engender personal growth. Thus, the teacher's role of relationship, investigations, disclosure, and reduction parallels exactly the psychotherapeutic process that occurs in counseling or therapy. This is not to imply that they are the same, but the Adlerians believe that many human problems can be handled by relatively untrained persons who understand the dynamics of human functioning.

The consultant must be able to interpret life-styles of children, adolescents, and adults and teach others to do the same. As was pointed out earlier, doing so is not extremely difficult in children under age twelve, but becomes much more complex after that age. This complexity serves as one of the real barriers to utilizing Adlerian ideas with older students.

An Adlerian consultant also needs to be able to assist parents and teachers to utilize the encouragement process and natural and logical consequences instead of rewards and punitive methods. Again, doing this calls for a complete understanding of the concepts and an ability to transmit them to other persons. These ideas, when coupled with democratic principles, should lead to a family and/or educational institution that will nurture the individual and that would nurture the social interest that Adler posited to be the essence of humankind.

TABLE 2.2. A guide to life-style analysis

I. *Family Constellation*
    List all siblings in descending order, including the patient in his posi-
    tion. Give patient's age and add after each sibling the years of age
    difference with patient, with plus and minus sign. Include siblings now
    dead.
    A. *Description of Siblings as They Were When Patient Was a Child*
        1. Who was most different from you? In what respect? (Ask
            patient to elaborate.)
        2. Who was most like you? In what respect?
        3. What kind of kid were you?
        4. Describe the other siblings.
    B. *Ratings*
        List highest and lowest sibling for each attribute, and, if patient is
        at neither extreme, give his position as to similarity to either.
        1. Intelligence
        2. Hardest worker
        3. Best grades in school
        4. Helpful around the house
        5. Conforming
        6. Rebellious
        7. Trying to please
        8. Critical of others
        9. Considerate
        10. Selfish
        11. Having own way
        12. Sensitive — easily hurt
        13. Given to temper tantrums
        14. Having sense of humor
        15. Idealistic
        16. Materialistic
        17. High standards of achievement, behavior, morals, etc.
        18. Who was the most athletic? Strongest? Tallest? Prettiest?
            Most masculine? Feminine?
        19. Who was the most spoiled, by whom, how, and for what?
        20. Who was the most punished, by whom, how, and for what?
        21. Who had the most friends? What kind of relationship —
            leader, exclusive, gregarious?
    C. *Sibling Interrelationship*
        1. Who took care of whom?
        2. Who played with whom?
        3. Who got along best with whom?
        4. Which two fought and argued the most?
        5. Who was father's favorite?
        6. Who was mother's favorite?

D. *Description of Parents as They Were When Patient Was a Child*
1. How old is father? Mother?
2. What kind of person is father?
3. What kind of person is mother?
4. Which of the children is most like father? In what way?
5. Which of the children is most like mother? In what way?
6. What kind of relationship existed between father and mother?
    a. Who was dominant, made decisions, etc.?
    b. Did they agree or disagree on methods of raising children?
    c. Did they quarrel openly? About what? How did these quarrels end?
    d. How did you feel about these quarrels? Whose side did you take?
7. What was more ambitious for the children? In which way?
8. Did any other person (grandparent, uncle, aunt, roomer, etc.) play a role in the family? Describe them and your relationship to them.

II. *Early Recollections*

How far back can you remember? (Obtain recollections of specific incidents, with as many details as possible, including the patient's reaction at the time. Make sure that this is a recollection and not a report. Childhood dreams are early recollections.)

BEHAVIORAL THEORY

In the most simplistic terms, a behaviorist is an individual who believes that the way to understand human beings is to examine that portion of functioning that is observable behavior. We have seen in earlier sections of this chapter that neither the Adlerians nor neo-client-centered proponents would accept this premise. There are other major differences between the humanistically oriented and the behavioral theorists. Perhaps most basic among these is the concept of how behavior develops.

For the behaviorist, all behavior is learned as a direct result of environmental consequences. Human functioning, then, must be understood in terms of these environmental factors that contribute to the acquisition of learning and those that retard the learning process, causing unlearning of behavior. This somewhat simple statement perhaps belies the actual complexity of behavioral learning theory and its application with students. However, few behaviorists recognize personality concepts or constructs such as life-style as important to either the understanding of why individuals function as they do or the process of changing human behavior.

Unlike the advocates of neo-client-centered and Adlerian theory, behaviorists take a molecular view of human beings. That is, instead of looking for the guiding themes that govern the personality, behaviorists look at the specific aspects of malfunctioning and try to correct those. When a child develops poor work habits, the behavior involved in completing tasks will be addressed rather than assessing and reorienting personality.

Let us turn now to look at the acquisition of human behavior.

Acquisition of Behavior B. F. Skinner (1936, 1953) believes that all higher-order behavior is emitted by the organism: that is, that there are no antecedent conditions for human behavior such as drive states or personality structures. Skinner (1936, 1953) does recognize that some behavior is acquired as the result of respondent conditioning, a learning paradigm first demonstrated by Pavlov. In the Pavlovian paradigm, an unconditioned stimulus becomes paired with a conditioned stimulus, with the result that a conditioned stimulus will produce the same response as the unconditioned stimulus. The reader may recall that Pavlov found in his experiments that when food (unconditioned stimulus) was presented, the dog salivated (response). However, after a bell had been rung for a period of time when the food was given, the bell alone (conditioned stimulus) would produce the response of salivation. Skinner (1953), however, believes that this paradigm is not sufficient to explain the acquisition of the broad range of human behavior. In order to explain this process, he developed the idea of operant conditioning (Skinner, 1963).

Higher-order behavior — that is, behavior that operates upon the environment — is emitted and results in certain types of consequences (Skinner, 1953). If an emitted response is followed by positive consequences, the response is strengthened and as a result is more likely to occur under similar conditions in the future. A high-school boy who speaks to an attractive girl in the hall and in turn is greeted warmly is more likely to use that response in the same or similar circumstances in the future. This entire process is called positive reinforcement and is, for Skinner at least, the keystone to the acquisition of behavior. There are two broad types of positive reinforcers: primary reinforcers, which include food, water, and sexual contact, and secondary reinforcers, stimuli that have acquired reinforcing properties. Primary reinforcers were originally thought to have universal reinforcing properties, and in a general sense perhaps they do. However, not all individuals respond to the same types of food, water cannot be considered a reinforcer for all, and certainly sexual contact is a not a universal reinforcer.

Perhaps the most important subset of secondary reinforcers contains those involved with human contact, such as smiles, pats on the back, winks, nods of the head, and so on. These are termed social reinforcers. Skinner (1953) believes that the basis for becoming influential, in the sense of having one's behavior be reinforcing, is to attend to another person. This, he believes, occurs because most of us have been reinforced by individuals who have attended to us. Attending to an individual involves eye contact and listening, much like what Rogers and other humanistic psychologists term communication processes.

There are other important secondary reinforcers such as money, tokens, grades, gold stars, plaques, and awards. It is difficult to determine which of the primary and secondary reinforcers listed here will in fact be reinforcing for a given individual. One way, the only real way, is to provide some item or some type of contact and then discern the impact upon behavior. Premack (1959) has also suggested that reinforcement can be determined by observing the individual and determining those behaviors frequently engaged in by that person. These high-probability behaviors such as playing ball, working a puzzle, or drawing can be used as reinforcers for such low-probability behaviors as attending class, getting along with peers, or completing homework assignments.

Just as a positive reinforcer strengthens a response, so does a negative reinforcer. While positive reinforcement is somewhat synonymous with reward, negative reinforcement is quite different. Essentially, negative reinforcement is the process of removing an aversive or unpleasant stimulus, thus increasing the probable repetition of the behavior that terminated the unpleasant situation. An individual may seek shelter from a cold rain, thus removing an aversive stimulus (cold rain). In doing this, the individual has increased the probability of seeking shelter in rainstorms. A teacher who screams at his or her students' unruly behavior with the result that they stop their misbehavior is similarly reinforced.

In addition to positive reinforcement, the concept of shaping must be considered. Technically, shaping is the development of complex behaviors from approximations of that behavior and at times seemingly unrelated behaviors. The human child comes into the world with a zero level of learned behavior. As the child grows and develops, certain aspects of his or her behavior are reinforced, leading to the development of complex behaviors.

It is perhaps apparent that it would be difficult to account for the acquisition of all human behavior with just the concepts of positive and negative reinforcement and shaping. To these ideas must be added several other ideas, among which imitative learning is of utmost importance. For Skinner (1953), imitation is the result of the individual's being differentially reinforced: that is, reinforcement occurring in the presence of certain circumstances. Skinner (1953) provides as an example that an individual learns that approaching another person for social purposes is more likely to be rewarding when that person is smiling than when he or she is frowning. Similarly, individuals learn as a result of their reinforcement history that imitation in a given situation is likely to result in reinforcement. To go back to our high-school student, he, because of his reinforcement history, may imitate a friend in approaching a girl not because the friend is successful, but because he has been reinforced under similar circumstances. Behavior, then, is the result of shaping and imitation, both of which are under the control of differential reinforcement.

Albert Bandura (1969, 1971) has presented some compelling evidence that Skinner's ideas about imitative behavior may be incorrect. Skinner, in short, believes that we imitate others in situations that produce reinforcement, thus strengthening the imitative behavior. Bandura (1971) believes that imitation can result in new behavior even in the absence of direct reward. A child who observes another child being reinforced for class participation can develop a new approach to class recitation because of that observation. The observation of the reinforcement process increases the child's attention to the model (the other child) and increases the likelihood that the observer will respond as the model did because of anticipated reinforcement. Here we are involved in a rather technical debate about whether or not cognition is an important component of the imitation process. However, both Skinner and Bandura would see imitation as an important means of acquiring new behavior.

Reinforcers are obviously the key to the development of new behavior. At this point two important factors that influence the use of reinforcers will be discussed. The first of these is a construct known as schedules of reinforcement. Although there are many types of schedules of reinforcement, only three will be considered here: ratio reinforcement, interval reinforcement, and what is essentially a special case of the first two, intermittent reinforcement. A ratio schedule of reinforcement is one delivered in accordance with the number of responses. For example, a child may be given a dollar for each A, and thus the ratio of response to a reinforcer is one-to-one. A big-league baseball pitcher with a clause in his contract that stipulates that he will receive five thousand dollars if he wins twenty games is on a one-to-twenty ratio. It is important that one-to-one ratios are effective in the development of behavior. Interval reinforcers are provided on a time basis. A child who receives a gold star at the end of the day for staying in her seat is on an interval schedule of reinforcement. So is a schoolteacher who is paid once a month irrespective of performance. Both ratio and interval schedules of reinforcement are important. However, intermittent reinforcement has a special significance.

Although a one-to-one ratio schedule of reinforcement is a good way to initiate a response, behavior developed in this way extinguishes relatively quickly whenever reinforcers are withdrawn, as does behavior developed with the use of any reinforcement schedule that follows a set pattern. The most effective way of developing behavior that is resistant to extinction is to use an intermittent reinforcement schedule. These reinforcers are delivered in such a way as to approximate a random pattern. Let us return to our high-school student. He will not be reinforced each time he approaches a member of the opposite sex. In fact, what may occur is that he may be greeted warmly once or twice, then ignored several times, then rebuffed, and so forth. This is an intermittent schedule of reinforcement in a natural setting.

In addition to the schedule of reinforcement used, the contiguity of the response and the reinforcer are of considerable importance. The principle here is that the closer in time the reinforcement is to the response, the greater the effectiveness of the reinforcer (Skinner, 1953). Parents, teachers, and others often forget promised rewards, and so the reward loses much of its potency.

Two final concepts must be introduced when considering the acquisition of new behavior: generalization and discrimination. A small child may be taught to use the screwdriver in his toy toolchest to assemble and disassemble the building blocks that accompany the chest. The child's parents may be quite surprised to discover that the child has used his father's screwdriver to dismantle a large portion of the family's radio. Obviously the knowledge learned with the toys transferred to another situation. This happened because there are common elements in the two situations. Similarly, a child who has learned that 2 + 2 + 2 = 6 should find learning 3 X 2 = 6 easy to master, and once this is learned, dividing six by three should not be a difficult task. The important point about generalization is that even though a student may appear to have difficulties in a variety of areas it is possible to work on one area at a time and expect that the behavior learned will have utility in all areas of the individual's life.

Discrimination is the process by which an individual learns to respond differentially to environmental stimuli. The small child who uses the same table manners in a restaurant that he does at home may also find that the type and volume of verbal interchange acceptable at home are unacceptable in the restaurant. The student who cannot discern when the teacher is teasing and when that same teacher is serious has not learned to discriminate among certain auditory and visual stimuli. Discrimination, like generalizations, comes about as the result of differential reinforcement.

Punishment Punishment may be defined as either the withdrawal of a positive reinforcer or the presentation of an aversive stimulus (Skinner, 1953). For the moment, we are concerned with the latter definition, for it fits into the more popular conception of punishment. The former definition will be taken up in the section that deals with unlearning behavior.

Skinner (1953) asserts that punishment — that is, the use of aversive stimuli — does not do what it is expected to do: contribute to the unlearning of behavior. Punishment does temporarily reduce the incidence of a behavior (Skinner, 1953; Bandura, 1969; Buckley and Walters, 1970), but the behavior may occur again and in fact be accelerated (Buckley and Walters, 1970). Additionally, there are many undesirable side effects that may occur with the use of aversive stimuli, such as reprimanding, the inducement of pain through hitting, or other physical means to eliminate behavior. Buckley and Walters (1970) specify these as follows:

1. The individual may strike back.
2. The punishing agent may be avoided.
3. Effects are short-lived.
4. The undesirable behavior may be reduced only when the parent, teacher, or other punishing agent is present.

Skinner (1953) and Bandura (1969) have pointed out that punishment may also give rise to emotional responses that may interfere with the functioning of the individual. A child punished for not going to sleep may develop an intense fear of the dark, a condition that will cause additional problems for the child. In conclusion, punishment using aversive stimuli has dubious value, both because of the impact upon behavior and because of its possible side effects.

Unlearning Behavior Whenever a response is emitted and fails to find reinforcement, it gradually drops from the behavioral repertoire. This process is called extinction and is the primary means by which behavior is unlearned. In a natural setting some responses are reinforced and some are not, so that certain behavior patterns develop. When an individual attempts to alter behavior, it often becomes necessary to withdraw reinforcement from responses that are maladaptive and to increase reinforcement for adaptive ones. This process can be arranged by a teacher, a parent, or another significant figure in a person's life or by the individual (Watson and Tharp, 1972).

Counterconditioning has also been shown to be an effective means of unlearning undesirable behavior (Wolpe, 1969). Counterconditioning involves the reinforcement of responses that are incompatible with existing but maladaptive behavior. Buckley and Walters (1970) describe a situation where an individual with a relatively short attention span was systematically reinforced for not attending to distracting stimuli, and Wolpe (1969) induces a deep physical and psychological relaxation, then has individuals systematically explore anxiety-provoking events. Obviously one cannot attend and not attend at the same time, just as it is impossible to be anxious and relaxed simultaneously.

An additional means of assisting individuals to unlearn behavior is through stimulus change (Buckley and Walters, 1970). Watson and Tharp (1972) assert that most operant behavior comes under the control of antecedent stimuli or cues. These cues indicate whether or not a behavior will receive reinforcement. If cues that have elicited maladaptive behavior are removed, that behavior is less likely to occur. Educators have used this principle as a disciplinary measure without knowing the underlying rationale for their actions. Principals have transferred students from one class to another and teachers have altered seating arrangements as a means of eliminating undesirable behavior. These are stimulus-control techniques. So is the avoidance of situations that will lead to overeating or excessive drinking.

Implications for the Consultant

Behavioral principles have been applied in a wide variety of settings, and the educational and psychological literature abounds with books on classroom management, precision teaching, self-management procedures, contracting, child rearing, et cetera.

Behavioral psychology provides teachers with a variety of techniques that can enhance classroom discipline (time out, contracting, systematic verbal reinforcement, counterconditioning). It can also provide a basis for individualizing instruction through precision teaching approaches and the development of programmed learning modules. Finally, behavioral psychology can provide some insight into the motivational process, a perennial teaching concern. These uses alone make a knowledge of behavioral principles important for anyone concerned with consulting with teachers.

A number of books on the use of behavioral principles in child rearing have appeared, including *Families* by Gerald Patterson. For the most part they have been based upon techniques that are empirically derived and that therefore can be provided with some confidence by the consultant.

Behavioral principles are now being widely used by business and industry to increase worker satisfaction and productivity. The authors could come up with no specific instances where these principles are being used on a widespread basis in bringing about change in educational personnel, however.

The behavioral consultant will need to be able to set up systematic observation procedures in order to ascertain the occurrence of carefully defined behaviors, establish operational goals for altering target behaviors, design interventions, and evaluate outcomes. It perhaps goes without saying that the principles of learning and unlearning must govern the development of interventions and that these principles must be applied systematically when designing and altering interventions. Fortunately there is a variety of programmed materials dealing with most of the skills needed in this area, although some systematic training in this area would also be helpful.

SUMMARY

In this chapter three theories with the potential to serve as the foundation for the consulting process have been introduced. These theories, Adlerian, neo-client-centered, and behavioral, are by no means the only theories that might provide a guide for this process, but each has some empirical support, has been widely discussed in the literature, and provides a comprehensive view of human functioning. Each theory has been presented in the briefest form, since the objective of this chapter was not to teach theory. Nevertheless, the implications of each theory for the consultation process were drawn so that the potential consultant could perhaps better visualize how each theory would be placed into practice.

REFERENCES

Adler, A. *Problems of Neurosis*. London: Kegan Paul, Trench, Truebner and Company, 1925.

_____. "Characteristics of the First, Second, and Third Child." *Children*, 3 (1928): 14, 52.

_____. "Position in Family Influences Life Style." *International Journal of Individual Psychology*, 3 (1929): 211–227.

_____. *What Life Should Mean to You*. Boston: Little, Brown and Co., 1931.

_____. "The Prevention of Delinquency." *International Journal of Individual Psychology*, 1 (1935): 3–13.

_____. *Social Interest: A Challenge to Mankind*. New York: Capricorn Books, 1964.

_____. "The Advantages and Disadvantages of the Inferiority Feeling." In *Superiority and Social Interest: A Collection of Later Writings*, ed. H. L. Ansbacher and R. R. Ansbacher. Evanston: Northwestern University Press, 1964.

Ansbacher, H. L., and R. R. Ansbacher. *The Individual Psychology of Alfred Adler*. New York: Basic Books, 1956.

Aubrey, R. F. "Misapplication of Therapy Models to School Counseling." *Personnel and Guidance Journal*, 48 (1969): 274–278.

Bandura, A. *Social Learning Theory*. Morristown: General Learning Press.

_____. *Principles of Behavior Modification*. New York: Appleton-Century-Crofts, 1969.

Brammer, L. M. "Eclecticism Revisited." *Personnel and Guidance Journal*, 48 (1969): 192–197.

Brown, D., and S. T. Brown, *Consulting with Elementary School Teachers*. Boston: Houghton Mifflin, 1975.

Buckley, N. K., and H. M. Walker. *Modifying Classroom Behavior*. Champaign: Research Press, 1970.

Bullard, M. L. "Logical." In *Alfred Adler: His Influence on Psychology Today*, ed. H. H. Mosar. Park Ridge: Noyes Press, 1973, pp. 171–174.

Carkhuff, R. R. *Helping of Human Relations*, Vol. I. New York: Holt, Rinehart & Winston, 1969 (A).

_____. *Helping and Human Relations*, Vol. II. New York: Holt, Rinehart & Winston, 1969 (B).

_____. *The Art of Helping*. Amherst: Human Resource Development Press, 1973 (A).

_____. *The Art of Problem Solving*. Amherst: Human Resource Development Press, 1973 (B).

Combs, A. W. and D. Snygg. *Individual Behavior*, 2nd ed. New York: Harper & Row, 1959.

Corsini, R. (ed.) *Current Psychotherapies*. Itasca: F. E. Peacock Publishers, Inc.

Dinkmeyer, D., and R. Dreikurs. *Encouraging Children to Learn: The Encouragement Process*. Englewood Cliffs: Prentice-Hall, 1963.

Dreikurs, R. *The Challenge of Parenthood*. New York: Duell, Sloan, and Pearce, 1948.

_____. *Fundamentals of Adlerian Psychology*. Chicago: Alfred Adler Institute, 1953.

_____. *Psychology in the Classroom*. 2nd ed. New York: Harper & Row, 1968.

_____, and V. Soltz. *Children the Challenge*. New York: Duell, Sloan, and Pearce, 1967.

Fürtmuller, C. "Alfred Adler: A Biographical Essay." In *Superiority and Social Interest: A Collection of Later Writing,* ed. H. L. Ansbacher and R. R. Ansbacher. Evanston: Northwestern University Press, 1964.

Meador, B. D., and C. R. Rogers. "Client Centered Therapy." In *Current Psychotherapies,* ed. R. Corsini. Itasca: F. E. Peacock, 1973, pp. 119-166.

Mosak, H. H., and R. Dreikurs. "Adlerian Psychotherapy." In *Current Psychotherapies,* ed. R. Corsini. Itasca: F. E. Peacock, 1973.

Patterson, C. H. *Theories of Counseling and Psychotherapy,* 2nd ed. New York: Harper & Row, 1973.

Premack, D. "Toward Empirical Behavior Laws: I—Positive Reinforcement." *Psychological Review,* 66 (1959): 219-233.

Rogers, C. R. *Counseling and Psychotherapy.* Boston: Houghton Mifflin, 1942.

_____. *Client Centered Therapy.* Boston: Houghton Mifflin, 1951.

_____. "The Necessary and Sufficient Conditions of Therapeutic Personality Change." *Journal of Consulting Psychology,* 21 (1957): 95-103.

_____. "A Theory of Therapy, Personality and Interpersonal Relationships, as Developed in the Client-centered Framework." In *Psychology: A Study of Science,* vol. II, *Formulations of the Personal and Social Concept,* ed. S. Koch. New York: McGraw-Hill, 1959.

Skinner, B. F. *Behavior of Organisms: An Experimental Analysis.* New York: Appleton-Century-Crofts, 1936.

_____. *Science and Human Behavior.* New York: Macmillan, 1953.

Stefflre, B., and W. H. Grant (eds.) *Theories of Counseling,* 2nd ed. New York: McGraw-Hill, 1972.

Watson, D. L., and R. G. Tharp. *Self Directed Behavior: Self Modification for Personal Adjustment.* Belmont: Wadsworth, 1972.

Wolpe, J. *The Practice of Behavior Therapy.* New York: Pergamon Press, 1969.

CHAPTER THREE **The Content and Process of Teacher Consultation**

INTRODUCTION

Increasingly those working within educational settings are recognizing that for mental health and/or educational interventions to have any lasting value they must be adopted by the classroom teacher. Unfortunately, this realization has come only after considerable effort has been expended to convince teachers that the most effective means of providing help to students is to remove them from the classroom and provide them with counseling, therapy, or some type of special educational program. We are now faced with the task of reversing our stand and attempting to persuade teachers that in many instances the most effective milieu for making successful educational and psychological interventions is the regular classroom.

There are indicators that teachers may be difficult to convince that they should join in a collaborative, classroom-based effort to attack students' problems. One Long Island, New York, teachers' group wanted their contracts to contain a clause that guaranteed that their classrooms would contain "no special students." Teachers in a North Carolina community petitioned the administrators to create special classes for what they termed the "emotionally disturbed students," who were in reality the students who caused discipline problems. These incidents and others are disturbing in that they graphically illustrate how far we have traveled away from the concept that most difficulties should be handled within the classroom and toward the practice of referring all problems to a specialist of some type.

There are, of course, in our society and in our educational institutions forces at work that, one hopes, will help to counter attitudes against designing and implementing interventions for students within the classroom. The practice of returning educable mentally retarded students to regular classrooms, which is increasingly being mandated, is one of these. The increased pressure from parents and boards of education for teachers to deal more effectively with discipline problems is another. Finally, the small but growing body of literature that demonstrates that teachers can effectively ameliorate a variety of problems that in the past would have been referred to a specialist must also be considered as a driving force toward classroom intervention.

Although it must be admitted that the empirical basis for teacher intervention is limited, the generally positive nature of the data is encouraging. In a study without adequate controls, Moon and Wilson (1970) reported gains in reading scores, a reduction in classroom discipline problems, and greater classroom cohesiveness as a result of teacher-counselor collaboration. In another study, Lewis (1970a) compared teachers' ratings on the Achievement-Oriented Behavior Scale for groups of students who had received counseling and were the subjects of consultation and those in three different control groups. He found that teachers perceived students in the consultation group to have made the greatest gain in achievement-oriented behavior. In still another study, this same investigator (Lewis, 1970b) looked at the impact of counseling and consultation upon sociometric status and personal adjustment of third grade pupils. In this study no significant differences were noted between these groups and the controls. Other research has demonstrated that teacher consultation can improve classroom behavior (Engelhardt, Sulzer, and Altekruse, 1970), have a favorable impact on teachers' ratings of behavior problems (Palmo and Kuzniar, 1972), and can improve academic performance (Randolph and Sabu, 1973). While the results of the research have been generally favorable with regard to teacher consultation, most research has concentrated on consultation relationships with elementary school teachers. McAllister et al. (1969) did demonstrate that incidence of inappropriate high-school classroom behavior can be decreased as a result of teacher consultation, and Farber and Mayer (1972) found that the frequency of completing assignments can be increased by the classroom teacher after consultation had been provided. Even though the data regarding the outcome of consultation with high-school teachers are less plentiful, there appears to be no reason to doubt that secondary-school teachers can develop effective intervention when appropriate assistance is made available.

In the authors' view, the teacher consultation function is central to the success of the overall consultation program. In order to develop an effective program in this area, consultants must understand the process of teacher consultation as well as knowing means for overcoming the resistance to consultation that is certain to be present.

THE PROCESS OF TEACHER CONSULTATION

The Relationship

There can be no doubt that a mutually satisfying relationship is basic to the consultation process. Dinkmeyer and Carlson (1973) have gone so far as to indicate that the consultation process must have the same characteristics as those often associated with counseling and therapy — mutual trust, open communication, genuineness, and positive regard — a premise that we accept with few reservations. However, one concern that should be stated is that the exact nature of the consulting relationship has received little attention from investigators and thus is open to some question.

A variety of procedures and techniques for and theories about establishing human relationships could be presented at this point. However, Robert Carkhuff (1973) has developed what is perhaps the most comprehensive model for establishing human relationships. Carkhuff believes that attending is first and perhaps the most basic of the steps in establishing relationships. Attending involves bodily posture, eye contact, and listening. In short, we are attending to a person whenever our body is turned and leaning toward that person, when we establish eye contact and are able to note the person's nonverbal behavior, and we are able to hear both the content and affect inherent in the communication.

Hearing and understanding another person and being able to interpret mentally what is being said is not sufficient, however. The consultant must be able to communicate effectively that what has been said has been understood. On a very simplistic level, this can be done merely by repeating verbatim what has been said (Carkhuff, 1973 A; Ivey, 1970). However, the development of the relationship can best be facilitated if the helper is able to identify the affective portion and the content of what has been communicated (Ivey, 1970; Carkhuff, 1973 A). The ability to experience thoughts, feelings, and ideas and communicate them has been labeled as *empathy* by Rogers (1957).

During the early stages of developing relationships, the helper needs to suspend his own judgment, according to Carkhuff. During this phase the focus is upon listening and communication. However, once rapport begins to develop, the nature of the helper's role begins to change. Instead of merely mirroring what the helper has said, the helper (consultant) begins to put together the themes of the consultee's statements, begins actively to confront the helped when discrepancies occur, and responds to the helped more as a genuine person. The following excerpts from a typescript of a teacher consultation session may help to illustrate some of these ideas.

EXCERPT 1

T: I really am interested in doing something about some of the kids in my classroom. Many of them simply are not getting anything from school — at least not what they should. I am at my wits' end.

C: You're highly concerned about several of your kids and at the same time frustrated because you don't know what to do about it.

T: Yeah! It's a shame too because I am really neglecting many of my students. They deserve better than they are getting. There are times when I would really like to get rid of the slow trouble makers and get on with it. They aren't really going to get much anyway.

C: I see. Your frustration goes deeper than just not helping the slow ones. You feel that they are beyond help and your concern is really for the brighter kids.

T: No! That's not it. Oh, shit — yes it is. I don't like teaching the slow kids. They just don't move fast enough. Things are much worse you know — since they started mainstreaming. The resource teachers don't help either. I'm really not interested in helping the slow kids because basically it is a lost cause.

The consultant helped the teacher verbalize her prejudices about slow kids. Now the real concern can be addressed.

EXCERPT 2

C: How have things been going this week with the two boys we discussed?

T: Oh, o.k. I guess — things are a little better.

C: You don't sound too sure how things are really going.

T: Well really things are about the same.

C: So things aren't any better. Can you account for that in any way?

T: No — not really. I tried the ideas we developed but they haven't helped. Maybe we should just give up.

C: You are a little frustrated at this point and tired of trying.

T: That's right.

C: Well, the basic decision to continue is certainly yours. I personally would be very disappointed because I have enjoyed working with you. I also believe you can handle the situation.

Note: The consultant shows disappointment here and affirms belief in the consultee. Also, there is immediate acknowledgment of the teacher's privilege of ending the consulting relationship.

EXCERPT THREE

C: You know we have met several times and while I have enjoyed our sessions I'm beginning to wonder if anything is really coming of them — if students are benefiting.

T: Well — Yes a lot of good things have happened. I've enjoyed our sessions immensely. They have been very helpful!

C: Perhaps we could explore some of these at this time because I am frankly concerned that I am wasting your time.

T: Well — to be honest with you I have been reluctant to tackle some of the problems we've been discussing during the past few weeks. Frankly, I'm a little scared that I'll mess them up and you'll think I'm an idiot. We've gotten to be good friends and well I wouldn't want you to think I am well you know incompetent.

C: Trying new things seems awfully frightening to you and particularly because of what I might think if you mess up. Let me assure you that my role here is to help you and not judge your performance.

Note: Here the consultant used confrontation to deal with a teacher who was resisting. Not surprisingly the resistance was tied up in both the teacher's own insecurity and fear that the consultant would evaluate or judge the activities which might result from consultation.

There is a good deal more to establishing a consulting relationship than attending and communication, although without these components the other ideas to be presented here would be of little value. One of the important aspects of the consultation process is structuring role relationships. Gaupp (1966) asserts that the authority components of consultation have not been fully addressed. Gaupp's position, which seems to be a viable one, is that power is ascribed to the consultant even when no formal power exists. This power is derived from his or her perceived expertise and competence, and this perception can lead to a relationship that is essentially a leader-follower one. Initial structuring should be done so that the relationship is egalitarian, not one involving a superior and a subordinate. This latter arrangement can lead to dependency, resistance, and heightened defensiveness because of personal insecurity.

Another important part of structuring in teacher consultation involves establishing an agreement for action. Consultation is not a therapeutic relationship aimed at assisting the teacher with his or her personal problems or in-service education aimed at merely imparting knowledge. The consultation relationship is aimed at change, which will require action on the part of both the consultant and the consultee. This expectation should be developed early.

Finally, the development of the initial relationship should take place in such a way that termination is an expected result. While it may seem somewhat strange to talk of termination in the initial phase, it seems important to start immediately to work toward the goal of developing a fully functioning, independent consultee.

Determining the Teacher's Problem-Content

Caplan (1964) described four types of problem that may be encountered in teacher consultation: lack of skill, lack of objectivity, lack of confidence, and inability to understand the nature of the student's problem. Let us look at each of these areas in some detail, starting with the last concern, inability to understand the student's problem.

Teacher education often focuses almost exclusively on the process of instruction while ignoring the development of a basic understanding of human behavior. To be sure, some courses in educational psychology are included in most teacher preparation programs, but even these courses focus on cognitive processes and learning styles. This information would be useful in dealing with the broader range of student problems if teacher trainees were given assistance in generalizing it beyond the informational aspects of classroom activity. Unfortunately, this often is not the case. Because of this deficiency in preparation, teachers are at a loss to explain why students function as they do. One clue that teachers may be unable to conceptualize students' problems adequately is that the teacher uses stereotypical rather than theoretical or empirically based concepts in describing students. Or the teacher may use psychological terms such as *self-concept* and be unable to explain fully the implication of the term. Some of the following statements were selected as representative of situations where the teacher is clearly unable to understand the nature of the students' difficulties.

STEREOTYPICAL STATEMENTS
He comes from a bad family. No one from that family has ever amounted to anything and neither will he.
I know that I should be reaching these kids, but they are so poor. They don't have a chance in life. What can we do?
He's a discipline problem because he has a poor self-concept. He has a lot of friends outside the classroom, though, and his parents don't seem to have any problems with him.

USE OF PSYCHOLOGICAL JARGON WITHOUT UNDERSTANDING
She has a low I.Q. It's impossible to motivate kids like that.
Of course, all children want reinforcement and should have it. I can't see the value of paying attention to her work until it's better, however.
I know that we are in a power struggle, but I just am not going to give in. It's him or me.

Lack of skill is also a contributing factor to the inability of some teachers to function effectively with students. We have been involved with many teachers who were given a strong theoretical foundation but no companion skill training in the use of the theory. For example, many school districts have hired consultants to conduct workshops in the theory of behavior modification but little follow-up has been conducted in the classroom to insure that teachers were using reinforcement procedures, extinction, behavioral contracting, and other techniques appropriately. We have also observed the reverse situation, where communications skills have been taught but the conceptual base has not been provided. One teacher indicated that she thought that the communications skills she had learned needed to be used only for the first few weeks of the semester because after that period everything would be "all right." Clearly the development of a theoretical base and the skills necessary to implement the theory are necessary components of any effort to improve the functioning of teachers.

Objectivity is an essential ingredient in teaching, counseling, and consulting. Teachers will often admit that they literally despise the student because he or she is dirty, black, white, or obnoxious, or for a variety of other reasons. Neither theory nor skills are of use to teachers of this type because their perceptual state simply will not enable them to develop an unbiased view and utilize their knowledge and skills. The consultant can be of assistance in this situation by providing objective data through observation and feedback. Indeed, the determination that a teacher lacks objectivity may come through observation of the child as well as data collected from sources other than the teacher. Clearly, when lack of objectivity is the difficulty, confrontation procedures will need to be utilized at some point in the consultation process.

Caplan (1964) indicates that lack of confidence may very well stem from perceived personal deficiencies and therefore the consultants may find themselves involved in providing encouragement, reinforcement, and, at times, referral for outside therapeutic assistance if the teacher (a) is unable to overcome these personal inadequacies and/or (b) requests such assistance. The consulting relationship is undoubtedly the key to understanding teachers who have self-doubts, for without mutual trust and open communication it is doubtful that difficulties of this type will actually surface.

Generally, as Caplan indicates, difficulties experienced by teachers can be attributed to lack of skill, lack of objectivity, lack of confidence, or inability to conceptualize students' problems. However, these four categories can serve only as the beginning point in assessing a teacher's problem since they lack specificity. Let us look at some rather concrete problems that teachers experience in the instructional/educational process and pose a series of questions that should be useful in diagnosing them.

Classroom Management Discipline is probably the number one problem confronting America's teachers. There can be little doubt that lack of parental support for teachers has contributed heavily to this situation, but the fact remains that teachers must become more proficient in disciplining students. Fortunately, classroom management is an area about which we know a great deal, and our knowledge is increasing steadily.

It is suggested that whenever a consultant is asked by a teacher to assist with correcting a disciplinary problem, the following questions be used as means of determining the nature of the problem.

1. Has the teacher planned? Although most teacher education programs stress the importance of developing good lesson plans, many teachers ignore this process. Poor planning can result in an incoherent presentation of subject matter, time gaps in the presentation, inability to develop salient points, and so on. Obviously, all of these situations can distract students from the learning task and thus cause discipline problems.

2. Does the teacher possess good communication skills? Communication is the essence of good teaching, and unless the teacher is able to understand both verbal and nonverbal communication, the result is likely to be chaos. It should be stressed that perhaps the key communication in teaching is still recognizing nonverbal cues that materials are not understood or that attention is waning.

3. Is there constant monitoring of student behavior? Does the teacher maintain eye contact during presentation? When students are working alone or in small groups, is the teacher alert to the interactions that are occurring? Without continuous monitoring, much behavior goes unnoticed and unfortunate situations can develop.

4. Is a group focus maintained? Many teachers make the mistake of posing questions as follows: "Johnny, who discovered America?" This type of question shifts the focus to an individual and cues the other students that they no longer need to be involved. If the teacher had asked, "Class, who discovered America?" every student would have been involved. Asking questions to maintain a group focus is important. So is calling on students in a truly random basis. Most teachers call on the same few students most of the time. Teachers cannot afford to allow students to relax mentally if they are to maintain attentiveness.

5. Is the teacher consistent? Students react negatively to differential treatment of students. Although it is difficult to maintain an unbiased approach to disciplining students, doing so is essential if one is to maintain their respect. Further, students expect a teacher to act consistently in areas such as grading, giving extra credit, and involvement of students in class activities. Relationships with students are a key to good discipline, and consistency in all areas of behavior is one basis of good relationships.

6. Does the teacher model the type of behavior he or she expects from students? Students will not accept "Do as I say, not as I do!" dicta. Teachers who belittle, physically abuse, and scapegoat can expect students to imitate that behavior. Conversely, teachers who communicate effectively and treat students fairly can expect that students will act in the same manner. It is a truism that we teach in many ways, but in the area of discipline the teacher's own behavior becomes an important way of influencing students.

7. Is an attempt made to develop a student-centered norm through effective rule setting? A common bit of advice given to beginning teachers is to go in and

"lay down the law." Although this may be an effective procedure for suppressing some negative behavior in the beginning, the long-run benefit to be derived from establishing a normative structure based solely on teacher expectations is probably minimal. It is undoubtedly more effective to begin the process of rule setting by determining student expectations. Some teachers are surprised to learn that students' concerns about classroom behavior are similar to their own. Since this is usually the case, students' perceptions of needed rules and regulations may be used as the basis for classroom rules, thus establishing norms that are student-centered.

8. Is the teacher enthusiastic? Little needs to be said about the importance of being enthusiastic. Students soon learn that a teacher is working only until her or his husband or wife finishes graduate school or until a better job comes along. In these situations, their attitude quickly becomes "Why should we care when you do not?" Monotonous presentations, poor eye contact, poorly prepared lessons, spending large amounts of time on noneducational activities, and not staying on schedule should be avoided, for they demonstrate lack of enthusiasm.

9. What is rewarded in the classroom? Most teachers are unaware of the process of vicarious reinforcement. The author has often seen teachers inadvertently lose control of their classes by focusing exclusively on the negative aspects of behavior. Students, realizing that the only way to get the teachers' attention was through misbehavior, misbehaved. Teachers must learn to emphasize the positive and, whenever possible, ignore the negative.

10. How is punishment used? To be effective, punishment should take place early in the sequence of events, "fit the crime," be administered as close to the act as is possible, and be humane. It is better to stop two boys who are beginning a fight and punish them than it is to punish them after the fight. Thus the teacher must constantly be aware of students' behavior in the classroom.

Students who do not complete homework should not be physically abused. Rather, some punishment should be devised which relates to the homework or to schoolwork itself, such as staying after school. And, if parents can be contacted, the student should stay after school that same day.

Finally, the student should never be dehumanized. Most psychologists recognize that severe punishment is met with resistance and rebellion or, even worse, withdrawal. Teachers want to correct problems, not create them in the disciplinary process.

11. Does the teacher pace classwork appropriately? Classroom teachers have a serious dilemma. They must present material in a manner that will maintain the interest of the most able student while communicating effectively with the least able individual. This problem has led to a greater emphasis upon individualization and less upon group-centered instructional approaches. However, economy demands that some material be presented in the group, and thus the concern for pacing. If either the fastest or slowest is ignored, attention will wane and misbehavior is likely to result.

12. Is the classroom arranged to facilitate instruction and discipline? The teacher should have easy access to students and should be able to monitor all behavior. The actual arrangement of the furniture will be dependent upon the teaching approach to be used, however. It is suggested that *Individualizing Instruction* by C. M. Charles, published by C. V. Mosby Co. of St. Louis, Missouri, in 1976, or *Educational Psychology: A Realistic Approach* by Thomas L. Good and Jere E. Brophy, published by Holt, Rinehart and Winston in 1977, be consulted for more specific information in this area, however.

It should also be noted that students simply should not be placed randomly in seats. Antagonists should be separated. So should close friends who cannot control their urge to talk and disrupt. Disruptive students should be placed so they will receive as little attention as possible for their antics and shy students where they are certain to be noticed. All in all, arranging a room and the students in the class so that both contribute to rather than detract from the classroom atmosphere is not difficult but is an often overlooked factor in classroom management.

13. Does the teacher have a good repertoire of disciplinary techniques? It is a sad fact that many teachers can rely only upon reprimands and corporal punishment to control students. They know nothing of contracting procedures, counterconditioning, communications skills, logical and natural consequences, time out, and other more positive approaches to discipline. The consultant should ascertain the approaches used by the teacher and work to enhance the available repertoire of disciplinary techniques.

In summary, there are a number of ideas associated with the teaching process itself that can enhance classroom discipline. These are adequate planning, communication, enthusiasm, the maintenance of a group focus, monitoring through eye contact, and appropriate pacing. Disciplinary procedures that will enhance classroom management involve modeling appropriate behaviors, emphasizing the positive, involving students in rule setting, using punishment effectively, and having a variety of more positive disciplinary measures at one's disposal. This is not an exhaustive list of ways to improve classroom discipline, but it can serve as a basic list for consultants to teachers.

The Observation of Learning Principles Many of the principles governing the acquisition of knowledge and skills have been empirically validated. To the extent that we have this information, it should be applied in the design and implementation of classroom instruction. The following is a list of questions that should be asked in the process of determining whether or not teachers are adhering to learning principles.

1. Is attention gained through instruction using multiple sensory channel communication? Student attention is maintained most effectively when all senses — sight, hearing, touch, smell, and taste — are involved in the learning process. Teachers depend most upon the auditory and visual channels of com-

munication, thus requiring students to use only two senses. Some elementary school teachers bring in the senses of touch, smell, and taste in certain units on shapes, fabrics, foods, textures, and so on, but usually these senses are ignored. Generally all senses should be included when feasible, but whenever certain students are failing to learn through the modalities of sight and hearing, these should be supplemented with learning experiences involving the other senses.

2. Is the teacher aware of the importance of stimulus salience? It is an obvious fact that we learn those things that are most important to us. It is also true that students are likely to learn those facts, ideas, and concepts that the *teacher* deems most important if they know what those are. It is the teacher's responsibility to develop stimulus salience: that is, through cuing, giving directions, and the use of advanced organizers, teachers should help students recognize which material should be accorded the greatest importance.

Middle-class, bright students are able to determine stimulus salience — that is, recognize what is important — because they often have better verbal skills and they have been in a teaching-learning situation at home. However, for all students the old public speaking law, "Tell them what you are going to tell them, tell them, and then tell them what you told them," is applicable. Teachers can present written, verbal, and oral advance organizers, then begin to develop a perceptual set about what is to be learned. They can cue students through statements such as "What is important here?" or "What is the principle involved?" or by reinforcing certain types of response from students. Teachers can also refrain from making critical presentations whenever external distractions are great or students are agitated, in order to insure that students focus on the major points. Teachers can also continuously "check out" communication with students in order to determine that main points are being made. These and other procedures will enhance the learning process.

3. Is the teacher aware of satiation? Students have different abilities to stay on the task and absorb information. Teachers must monitor student reactions to insure that exercises are not meaningless.

To a certain extent, ability to maintain attentiveness and stay on the task is associated with physical condition. Therefore, most elementary schools schedule reading when students are physically fresh. Ability to maintain attention is also based on motivation, a fact that most teachers recognize but sometimes ignore. Both physical alertness and motivation level need to be considered in planning an instructional program, for the amount of time to satiation is critical. However, after the plans are made, a teacher still must gear teaching to student reaction.

4. Has the teacher planned for incidental learning? Much learning occurs outside the formal setting, and a good teacher arranges centers, group activities, games, and other activities that will enhance the formal classroom work.

5. Is repetition used? While some learning occurs on a one-trial basis, material that is retained is usually acquired through some type of repetitive practice. This

is not to suggest that teachers should return to the mindless rote-learning exercises that characterized instruction at the turn of this century. However, students need to repeat multiplication tables and the proving of geometric theorems. This repetition can have its greatest benefit when it takes slightly different forms. Nevertheless, repetition must be a part of any good instructional program.

6. Is feedback/reinforcement used systematically? Students need to know what kinds of mistake they have made and what principles they have mastered. As a result, teachers must give systematic oral and written feedback regarding performance. The teacher who does not correct math problems or English themes is not providing students an opportunity to correct their mistakes.

When providing feedback, teachers need to stress what students have done correctly. For too long we have stressed what is done wrong, but we can build students' academic skills better when emphasizing their strengths rather than their weaknesses.

7. Are learning tasks sequenced appropriately? It is perhaps obvious that reading must precede other types of learning tasks. It is also true that counting should precede addition, and addition, subtraction. The fact that this type of sequencing must occur makes the classroom teacher's chore a particularly difficult one, because in a class of thirty students only a very few are actually at the same learning level. Most teachers are aware of the appropriate sequencing of their subject matter (although there are enough who are not to make it a problem for the consultant) but ignore or overlook the individual in planning instruction.

8. Is overlearning encouraged? The very word *overlearning* is a paradox. Can anything be overlearned? *Overlearning* is used to denote the process by which material is made relatively resistant to forgetting. Overlearning is probably best accomplished through repetitive practice, particularly repetitive practice that occurs in different circumstances. The author once observed a teacher having children recite historical dates during a dodgeball game. The teacher would ask a question and then, when a student was struck with the ball, he or she had to give the answer. Unlike most dodgeball games, if the student knew the answer to the question, he or she was allowed to continue playing, even after being hit.

9. Are students assisted in the transfer of knowledge to other relevant areas? Ultimately students should be helped to transfer the knowledge, which they live. Reading serves valuable functions in leisure, work, and in good citizenship. Most subject-matter areas have been developed so that they will transfer to the "real world." By helping students generalize their knowledge, the teacher enhances motivation, for students realize the value of their learning experiences.

It is also important that teachers assist students to transfer information and skills from one subject matter area to others. Addition and subtraction are obviously related and involve related principles. Mathematics can also contribute to performing certain scientific functions: for example, chemistry equations are solved using algebraic principles. Teachers should not assume that pupils automatically make this type of transfer, however. Each lesson should consider what students have learned previously and develop means for helping students transfer that knowledge to the present situation.

10. Is spaced practice encouraged? Spaced practice is more effective than bunched or concentrated practice in insuring that material will be retained. Most college students who have acquired material for a midterm examination by "cramming" realize the working of this principle by final examination time. Teachers need to plan for spaced practice.

11. Is modeling provided when appropriate? Teachers should show students how to conjugate verbs, prepare a slide for the microscope, weld cast iron, and how to operate in many other areas. Teachers who ignore the importance of modeling are depriving students of one of the most valuable learning situations available: observing others. "Show them, don't tell them" should be the rule.

A teacher who is not having the desired impact either upon an entire class or an individual in that class may be ignoring certain basic principles of learning. The consultant to teachers must be able to review these principles systematically and assist the teacher in making corrections when appropriate.

Individualizing Instruction Throughout the section on learning principles, allusions were made to the importance of individualizing instruction. Perhaps no single skill is more needed for being a successful teacher. The following list of questions can be useful in describing a teacher's ability in this vital area.

1. Can the teacher diagnose learner difficulties using standardized tests, teacher-developed devices, or observation? Obviously, the key to adequate individualization is to determine the characteristics of the learners involved and then build instructional packages to match those characteristics. Through observation a teacher should be able to ascertain which students have attention problems, are unable to transfer knowledge, and have difficulty understanding oral directions. More systematic devices will often be needed to determine reading level, vocabulary deficiencies, and mathematical skills. Without skills in assessing learner characteristics, individualization cannot succeed.

2. Can the teacher develop objectives and design instructional packages that correspond to learner characteristics? Much has been made of writing instructional objectives, and that point will not be belabored here. It should suffice to say that teachers must have the ability to write these objectives. The term *instructional packages* is used here to mean any lesson plan, unit, learning center, or autotutorial device developed by the teacher or purchased by the school district to meet an instructional need. In whatever fashion the teacher wishes to provide instruction, the major point remains: "Does the approach consider individuals?" If some individuals are left out, the answer is obviously "No," and that should be cause for concern.

3. Do instructional approaches provide for feedback/reinforcement based on individual rather than group performance? Individualized instruction requires ideographic grading approaches. It is not enough to individualize the instruction

if one then fails a student who does not meet some arbitrarily established group norm. Slower students will not be motivated by this system and teaching will fail for this group.

4. Is progress monitored carefully? An individualized approach to teaching requires careful and detailed record keeping. Yet, unless the progress of each student is carefully monitored new material will not be introduced as appropriate, and pacing will be either too fast or too slow. When accurate records are not kept and, as a result, progress is not monitored, an individualized approach is no better than a group-oriented instructional program.

5. Are student interests considered in the planning? We all have greater and less interests. It was stated earlier that motivation is at least partially based upon interest. The teacher who can use Tommy's interest in butterfly collecting to teach reading will be more successful than one who ignores these interests. While it is not always possible to capitalize upon each student's interests in the instructional process, it is helpful to do so.

6. Is reteaching planned? One of the maddening aspects of teaching, to some teachers at least, is that instruction must be repeated for some students. Theoretically, whenever reteaching is called for, there was a problem in the original teaching paradigm. Practically, regardless of the care and concern with which teaching is conducted, some students will not learn. Individualization requires a recycling if the process of assessment, planning instructional units, designing instructional packages (including teaching), and monitoring progress is carried out. If reteaching is not planned, individualized instruction will fail.

Many teachers do not adequately individualize their instruction. There are times when they simply lack skill in this vital area. The consultant can use the foregoing list as a basis for determining whether or not the teacher is approaching the matter of individualization appropriately.

Individual Differences   To a certain extent, the discussion that follows could have been included in the previous section, for individualization and individual differences are intimately related. However, the section on individualizing instruction focused upon mechanical issues, whereas here we discuss the physical, psychological, cultural, and sexual differences that must be considered in the instructional process. When consultants to teachers ask, "Can the teacher assess individual characteristics?" they are asking about their ability to consider the factors to be discussed here.

1. Is the physical development of the students considered in the design of the facilities and in instruction? Desks and chairs should be appropriately sized for students. Left-handed chairs and equipment should be provided. Bookshelves, work tables, hangers, and other equipment should fit the student. Uncomfortable chairs can lead to premature satiation, and chairs that are too big or too small can add to what may already be a frustrating situation. Overlooking these factors may make difficult situations harder for the student to cope with.

2. Is the anxiety level of students considered? Anxiety has shown itself to be an important variable in learning. Highly anxious students are self-disparaging, often are unable to discriminate which of the teacher's communications are most significant, and may even develop physical symptoms in threatening situations. These students can be effectively dealt with by reducing ambiguity, minimizing risk, and breaking assignments up into smaller units.

Teachers need to realize that test results rarely are adequate measures of the ability or knowledge of highly anxious students. They also need to realize that the physical symptoms (stomach cramps, diarrhea, and so on) are real. A lack of sensitivity to these issues can only worsen the psychological distress and decrease academic performance.

3. Are sex differences considered? Is sexual stereotyping obvious? We have come a long way in our society toward providing equal opportunities for men and women. Most of us realize that there are few if any sexual differences that must be accommodated in our instructional programs. It is particularly a disservice to girls and young women to stereotype poor performance in mathematics as simply representative of women. It is also unfair to stereotype occupational or other societal roles. It is to be hoped that schools will contribute to equalization of opportunities, not the perpetuation of stereotypes.

4. Are socioeconomic differences considered? Good and Brophy (1977) indicate that socioeconomic differences among students are among the most important factors to consider. Status in the community, differing orientations to education, and differential family income all lead to learner characteristics that must be considered. For example, differences in language patterns have led some educators to suggest that books be furnished that are written in the language indigenous to the student's locale, and further that teachers speak this language (Good and Brophy, 1977). Deficiencies in background experiences must also be considered along with the language deficits already mentioned. Not only do learner characteristics need to be considered in planning instruction but so do differences in the support environment. Lower-class parents are often less willing to become involved in the educational process and often less able to provide help when they do become involved. This discussion could continue, but the point should have been made: instructional planning should consider socioeconomic background.

5. Are ability levels considered in instructional planning? Teachers should not overlook intellectual ability, yet they persist in doing so, probably because of the increased workload inherent in planning for varying ability levels. It is clearly the consultant's job to encourage this type of planning, however.

Individual differences, of course, should be considered. Consultants to teachers will obviously be involved in collaboratively planning instruction that will consider those differences. The consultants will often find themselves securing more materials, assisting in setting up learning processes, establishing cross-grade tutoring programs, and carrying out a host of other activities that transcend the usual consultation role.

Teacher Expectations We know that what the teacher expects students to do influences what will happen in the classroom, particularly in the area of academic performance. As a consultant to teachers, we must concern ourselves with these expectations and their influence upon students. In assessing teachers' expectations we should ask the following questions.

1. Does the teacher have realistic expectations? Each student comes into a classroom with a history, much of which the teacher has learned. Test scores, previous grades, other teachers' comments, and community contacts serve to set expectations. To the extent that these sources can be faulty — and there is considerable room for error — expectations can be faulty. But let us consider the situation where initial expectations are realistic, but the student has a typically poor first few weeks in school, either academically or behaviorally. Again, negative or inappropriate expectations can be developed. These in turn are communicated to the student and in a sense become a self-fulfilling prophecy. In this case, the role of consultant to teachers obviously becomes one of correcting expectations.

2. Are expectations communicated on a regular basis? Students need to know expected academic and behavioral standards. These need to be communicated positively and continuously. Doing so eliminates much of the ambiguity that has already been identified as a debilitory factor for highly anxious students. It also enables students to judge their own progress and make adjustments where appropriate.

3. Do all students experience success? Inordinately high expectations can result in a situation where some students do not receive positive feedback. Since experiencing success is crucial to emotional and academic development, the results are disastrous for these individuals. Consultants need to help teachers with extremely high expectations to make those more realistic. The use of objective data about abilities and past performance can be useful in this area. Teacher expectations influence student performance. Consultants must work to insure that realistic expectations develop and that they are communicated regularly and clearly. Learning will be enhanced and ambiguity lowered if expectations are made known.

Group Dynamics Individualization of instruction, cross-grade tutoring, and many other instructional techniques require the use of small groups. This entire volume could have been devoted to small groups and group dynamics in the classroom. However, a small number of questions will be listed to assist the consultant in determining whether or not a teacher is using small groups appropriately.

1. Does the teacher retain "control" of the group whenever he or she is involved? Good small-group interaction requires that some semblance of a democratic atmosphere be established, that communication be directed to the group rather than to a group leader, and that, at least to some degree, rules and regu-

lations (norms) be established by the group itself. It is easy to discern when a group is leader-centered. When this is the case, the students talk to the leader rather than to each other and eye contact is made with the leader rather than with group members.

It is probably true that the best way to "teach" small-group leadership is to demonstrate the techniques. This means that the consultant may very well be called on to co-lead or co-teach a small group in order to demonstrate effective techniques.

2. Are the groups composed appropriately? A variety of mistakes can be made in composing small groups. A common one is basing a group on behavioral type. It is impossible to have much meaningful group interaction when all participants are acting-out, aggressive types. It is also difficult when a group is comprised entirely of low-risk-taking, shy individuals. Groups should be comprised heterogeneously, at least with regard to their behavior. Conversely, it is probably useful to have somewhat homogeneous grouping with regard to academic level. Of course, this has been traditional educational practice.

3. Is the size of the group appropriate for the age group involved? Typically, small groups should not exceed ten to twelve in size. However, with younger children who have shorter attention spans, it may be wise to reduce this number from six to eight. The main factor in determining size is the amount of interaction that can occur and the number of times each child can participate. Specifically, students should be able to participate often enough to insure that their attention is maintained.

4. Is the teacher aware of the developmental stages of groups? Groups move through specific stages: socialization, norm setting, and problem solving. Teachers need to recognize that in the early stages (socialization), students do not share as readily or take risks as freely. Some effort needs to be undertaken that will allow students to become acquainted, develop some feeling of trust, and establish patterns of communication.

The norm-setting stage is actually a work–no work decision-making stage. Some groups adopt a no-work norm, while others decide to work. Teachers can enhance the possibility of a work norm's being developed by reinforcing working behavior and modeling task-oriented behavior. Groups should contain a preponderance of students who are interested in working.

The problem-solving stage is a task-oriented one where pupils attack everything from mathematics problems to Keats and Shelley. In this stage, members should be supportive of each other, assisting in the teaching-learning situation.

Teachers often make the mistake of expecting groups to solve problems without passing through the socialization or norm-setting stages. The consultant can be of assistance in correcting this oversight.

5. Does the teacher use good leadership techniques? Good leadership techniques are little different from good teaching procedures. Teachers need to learn to monitor the group through good eye contact, to recognize contributions to

the group, to model appropriate behaviors, to involve the group in rule setting, and so on. Not using these techniques will greatly reduce the effectiveness of the group and minimize the learning that results.

The use of small groups requires skills not possessed by some teachers. Developing these skills calls for more than a collaborative effort. It requires the consultant to become involved in modeling the procedures and techniques. This means that the brief background provided here will not suffice. The book *Group Processes in the Classroom* by Schmuck and Schmuck, published by William C. Brown, Dubuque, Iowa, 1975, can fill some of the gaps in the foregoing presentation. However, systematic course work dealing with group dynamics and small-group leadership will be more helpful in developing needed skills.

Self-Concept Conversations with most teachers about students' problems will often turn to self-concepts. Because of the humanistic bias of much teacher education literature, teachers often blame learning and disciplinary problems on the students' poor self-images. While this is not always the case, there is empirical support for the idea that self-image and behavior are related and that a negative self-concept does in some cases deter the student from achievement and attainment of mental health (Charles, 1976). Several questions may be asked when helping teachers facilitate self-concept development in the classroom.

1. Is the teacher familiar with measures of self-concept? Psychometric devices have been designed which specifically assess self-concept. The Piers Harris Children's Self Concept Scale and the Tennessee Self Concept Scale (Counselor Recordings and Tests, Box 6184, Acklen Station, Nashville, Tennessee 37212) are two commonly used inventories. The Bills Index of Adjustment and Values and the Coopersmith Self Esteem Inventory are also widely used. There are in fact dozens of self-concept inventories available, and the consultant needs to be familiar with at least half a dozen of these so that assistance can be provided to teachers in the selection of a self-concept scale that possesses reliability and validity.

2. Does the teacher communicate well? To theorists like Rogers (1957), communication is the key to the maintenance and enhancement of self-concept. As was asserted earlier, teachers must have good communications skills if they are to promote self-concept development. *Human Relations in Education* by Gazda can serve as a basic guide to teaching and learning communications skills.

3. What is the atmosphere in the classroom? Negative, threatening climates result in poor self-concepts. When the teacher uses divisive, negative approaches to discipline, emphasizes competition rather than cooperation, and holds the threat of failure over students' heads, the result is likely to be low self-images among students.

4. Is there democratic decision making? Charles (1976) stresses that involvement of students in their own learning is an effective way of improving self-

concept. He advocates open-ended class meetings and other opportunities for students to participate openly in classroom rule setting and decision making.

5. Are affective education approaches incorporated in the curriculum? One means of enhancing self-concept is through the development of self-awareness and personal skills. Clarification of values, developing decision-making skills, friendship classes, and achievement motivation groups are a few of the many affective education techniques that can be used for this purpose. As we shall see in chapters to follow, curriculum revision is not an easy chore, but it is essential if affective concerns are not included in classroom offerings.

Other Areas The preceding discussion has listed what is viewed here as the likely content for most teacher consultation sessions. These sessions may include the development of teacher-made tests, decision-making skills, and referral procedures. They may also include staff relationships, dealing with parents, and a myriad of other concerns. No book or set of experiences can prepare a consultant to teachers for all eventualities. Perhaps the best preparation for teacher consultation, in addition to a good solid preparation program and a variety of experiences, is a well-stocked library and one or two personal consultants. Even with this type of background, however, the consultant from time to time is going to have to say, "I don't have the answers!"

GOAL SETTING

Goal setting, at least in specific operational terms, has generally been associated with behavioral psychology. However, humanistic psychologists such as Carkhuff (1973 B) and Adlerian psychologists such as Dinkmeyer and Carlson (1973) also subscribe to this idea, as do many others. To put it simplistically, it is necessary to specify the goals of consultation so you will know when you get there. Stated somewhat differently, unless goals are operationally defined, it is extremely difficult to evaluate the effectiveness of the consultation process (Brown and Brown, 1975). Let us look briefly at some general descriptions given of students by teachers and some of the objectives that emerged as a result.

PROBLEM 1
Ron seems to be totally unable to get along with the other children. He stays away from those who are his size and bullies the smaller children. He has no friends and has admitted to me that he would like to be accepted by the other children.

OBJECTIVE 1
Ron will be asked to participate in small group activities by one or more of the other children at least 90 per cent of the time within six weeks.

PROBLEM 2

Susan is a shy, sensitive seventh grade girl. Although she is extremely bright she never takes part in classroom activities. When called on in classes she blushes and drops her head.

OBJECTIVE 2

Susan will by the end of the semester be able to participate in classroom activities without visible signs of embarrassment.

PROBLEM 3

John is an eleventh grade boy who simply will not complete his home-work. During class he fidgets in his seat and pays little attention to class activities.

OBJECTIVE 3

Within nine weeks John will complete his homework at least 85 per cent of the time.

While the goals listed here are not in the strictest sense behavioral, they are adequate in that they identify target behavior and they do set a target date. Specification beyond this point may be desirable in certain cases.For example, for John it may become necessary to state not only how often homework will be completed but with what degree of accuracy. Setting target dates is always somewhat risky since it involves some guesswork. It is of particular importance to develop the understanding that time limits are approximate estimates and behavior change may take more or less time than anticipated.

Warner (1975) has pointed out that we can establish operational objectives for groups as well as individuals. One example of this type of objective is cited by Warner:

> At the conclusion of a drug abuse prevention program, each participant without the aid of reference material, will be able to answer correctly 90% of the items on a drug knowledge test [p. 11].

The purpose of this illustration is to point out that several students in a class-room may share a common problem, and objectives and appropriate evaluation procedures must be established for the group.

Selecting Strategies for Goal Achievement

The selection of strategies must be divided into two categories: those designed to assist the teacher overcome deficiencies and those specifically aimed at achieving the established goal. Let us look first at strategies aimed at assisting teachers.

Signell and Scott (1971) recommend role modeling as an important means of influencing consultee behavior. Techniques that are to be used in the process designed to help the student can be modeled by the consultant, or, if he or she is unable to do so, a third party may be asked to demonstrate the necessary skill. Modeling is but one process by which teachers can be assisted to ready themselves to help students, and it probably has its greatest utility in skill development. Direct teaching or the identification of reading materials may be a necessary step when working with teachers who lack a conceptual frame of reference. For those who lack objectivity, data collection to illuminate the problem may be a satisfactory approach, just as encouragement and support are necessary for the teacher who lacks the confidence to proceed independently. The question of how a consultant is to deal with the teachers so as to enable them to proceed in a successful fashion is a difficult one. In all likelihood, the ideas introduced here and others that each practitioner will develop will be utilized.

The collaborative relationship model of consultation requires that the strategies that are to be utilized to achieve the outcome specified in the objective should be developed by the teacher and the consultant together, although it is likely that one or the other will play a dominant role. Lauver (1974) has outlined a process in which the consultant makes suggestions regarding techniques or strategies, and these are modified in accordance with the teacher's wishes. It is perhaps obvious that the reverse of this situation could occur. The point to be made here is that the collaborative relationship model does not demand that both parties have the same amount of input, only that both agree on final decisions.

Since strategies are to a certain extent specific for each of the theoretical perspectives presented in this book, let us consider each separately, starting with the neo-client-centered theory. Since for this group the key to behavior change is the human relationship, achievement of this end should be emphasized. The key to the relationship is communication, and thus the consulting session might very well focus on learning to communicate more effectively. The ability to systematically solve problems is also deemed by humanists as a critical skill for human functioning. Therefore the teacher may wish to develop problem-solving skills in addition to developing better communications skills.

Behavioral psychology has been labeled as technique-ridden, and this may in fact be true. However, behaviorists do have a greater variety of techniques in their repertoire than those persons with other theoretical perspectives have. The selective use of reinforcement of ignoring maladaptive behavior to achieve extinction would be a basic strategy suggested by the behavioral consultant. Time out, behavioral contracting, assertiveness training, desensitization procedures, and others might also be suggested for use (Brown and Brown, 1975). Observation procedures would also be suggested, along with companion recording systems, to insure that the progress of consultation can be carefully plotted.

Adlerian consultants would accept some of the ideas from the foregoing lists. Certainly the relationship is important to Adlerian consultants as would be systematic problem-solving and contracting procedures, although reinforcers would not be included as a part of the contract. Further, Adlerian consultants would suggest means of encouraging children, provide teachers with the skills and techniques necessary to avoid power struggles with students, and, perhaps more important, suggest that teachers learn to use logical and natural consequences in the disciplinary process (Dreikurs, 1968). A table summarizing some of the techniques utilized by Adlerians, neo-client-centered consultants, and behavioralists follows.

Evaluation

The evaluation process can be described succinctly. The extent to which the goals established are realized is the degree of success of the consultation procedures. No sophisticated evaluation procedures are required if goal setting has been conducted adequately. The first objective stated in an earlier section was that Ron be chosen to participate in small classroom groups at least 90 percent of the time. By simply counting how often the student has been chosen we can ascertain our success. Similarly, we can determine if a student can participate in classroom discussions without visible signs of embarrassment, and we can go one step further: we can ask the student about his or her degree of comfort during classroom participation. We can also determine if a student is completing homework, how often that work is done, and with what accuracy. The ability to conduct this type of evaluation is, of course, the major advantage to setting specific goals.

TABLE 3.1. Strategies employed by consultants

Neo-Client-Centered	Adlerian	Behavioral
1. Communications training	1. Training in theory	1. Systematic observation
2. Systematic problem-solving strategies	2. Use of encouragement	2. Use of reinforcement
3. Contracting	3. Contracting (no reward)	3. Ignoring (extinction)
	4. Withdrawal from power struggles (ignoring)	4. Time out
	5. Logical consequences–natural consequences	5. Assertiveness training
		6. Behavioral contracting
		7. Token economy systems

SUMMARY

This chapter has examined the content and process of teacher consultation. No attempt was made to provide an exhaustive discussion of the various problems that will ultimately face consultants to teachers; rather, the primary emphasis was upon depicting the total process and discussing the major problems facing the consultant.

REFERENCES

Brown, G. D., and D. Brown. *Introduction to Social Science.* New York: Mc-Graw-Hill, 1975.

Caplan, G. *Principles of Preventive Psychiatry.* New York: Basic Books, 1964.

Carkhuff, R. R. *The Art of Helping.* Amherst: Human Resources Development Press, 1973 (A).

_____. *The Art of Problem Solving.* Amherst: Human Resources Development Press, 1973 (B).

Charles, C. M. *Individualizing Instruction.* St. Louis: C. V. Mosby Co., 1976.

Dinkmeyer, D., and J. Carlson. *Consulting: Facilitating Human Potential and Change Process.* Columbus: Charles E. Merrill, 1973.

Dreikurs, R. *Psychology in the Classroom.* New York: Harper & Row, 1968.

Engelhardt, L., B. Sulzer, and M. Alterpruse. "The Counselor as a Consultant in Elementary Out of Seat Behavior," *Elementary School Counseling and Guidance,* 5 (1971): 196-204.

Farber, H., and G. R. Mayer. "Behavioral Consultation in Baro High School," *Personnel and Guidance Journal,* 51 (1972): 273-279.

Gaupp, P. G. "Authority, Influence and Control in Consultation," *Community Mental Health Journal,* 2 (1966): 205-210.

Gazda, G. M. *Human Relations in Education.* 2nd ed. Boston: Allyn & Bacon, 1976.

Good, T. L., and J. E. Brophy. *Educational Psychology: A Realistic Approach.* New York: Holt, Rinehart & Winston, 1977.

Ivey, A. E. "Attending Behavior: The Basis for Counseling," *School Counselor,* 18 (1970): 117-120.

Lauver, P. J. "Consulting with Teachers: A Systematic Approach," *Personnel and Guidance Journal,* 52 (1974): 535-540.

Lewis, M. D. "Elementary School Counseling and Consultation: Their Effects on Teachers' Perceptions," *School Counselor,* 18 (1970a): 49-52.

_____. "The Effects of Counseling and Consultation upon the Sociometric Status and Personal and Social Adjustment of Third Grade Pupils," *Elementary School Guidance and Counseling,* 5 (1970b): 44-52.

Lippitt, G. L. "The Consultative Process," *The School Psychologist,* 21 (1967): 72-74.

McAllister, L. W., J. G. Stachowiack, D. M. Baer, and L. Conderman. "The Application of Operant Conditioning Techniques in the Secondary Classroom," *Journal of Applied Behavior Analysis*, 2 (1969): 277-285.

Moon, M., and D. Wilson. "Teacher-Counselor Cooperation: Building Self-Concepts and Confidence in Children," *School Counselor*, 17 (1970): 364-366.

Palmo, A. J., and J. Kuzniar. "Modification of Behavior through Group Counseling and Consultation," *Elementary School Counseling and Consultation*, 6 (1972): 255-262.

Randolph, D. L., and R. G. Saba. "Changing Behavior through Modeling and Consultation," *Elementary School Guidance and Counseling*, 8 (1973): 98-106.

Rogers, C. R. "The Necessary and Sufficient Conditions of Personality Change," *Journal of Consulting Psychology*, 21 (1957): 95-103.

Schmuck, R. A., and P. A. Schmuck. *Group Processes in the Classroom.* 2nd ed. Dubuque, Iowa: William C. Brown Company Publishers, 1975.

Signell, K. A., and P. A. Scott. "Mental Health Consultation: An Interactional Model," *Community Mental Health Journal*, 7 (1971): 288-301.

Warner, R. W., Jr. "Planning for Research and Evaluation: Necessary Conditions," *Personnel and Guidance Journal*, 54 (1975): 10-11.

CHAPTER FOUR Teacher Consultation: Some Issues and Case Material

In this chapter two important issues in teacher consultation will be discussed: group versus individual consultation and overcoming resistance. In addition, two case studies will be presented in an attempt to illuminate teacher consultation further.

GROUP VERSUS INDIVIDUAL CONSULTATION

Up to this point, consultation has been discussed as though it were a one-to-one process. In fact, consultation with teachers may be conducted either on a one-to-one basis or in groups (Mackey and Hassler, 1966; Altrocchi et al., 1969; Dinkmeyer and Carlson, 1973). The obvious positive feature of group consultation is the additional efficiency that is gained from working with more than one teacher. There are some difficulties with group consultation, however. Among these are achieving group cohesion (Mackey and Hassler, 1966), getting high rates of attendance, a greater need for coordination by the consultant, increased problems in drawing out insecure consultees, inability to deal with crisis situations, avoidance of student problems that require confidentiality (Altrocchi, Spielberger, and Eisdorfer, 1969), and generally, the necessity for greater skill on the part of the leader in the group situation. Let us discuss the problem of group leadership first, since it is intertwined with other problem areas.

Leaders of Consulting Groups

Consultation groups are as subject to the principles of group dynamics as other groups are. In a general sense they are task groups, the task being learning to deal more effectively with the students. Accordingly, consultation groups go through the stages of (1) socialization, where members get to know each other and develop mutual trust, (2) norm setting, where the group decides that they will indeed tackle the problem at hand, (3) problem solving, where the problem at hand is actively pursued, and (4) termination (Shaw, 1976). The fact that task groups organized as consultation groups evolve through the same stages as other groups means that consultation group leaders must possess leadership skills that include a knowledge of group dynamics and the ability to facilitate group development. Although it is outside the scope of this book to discuss the many facets of group leadership, some of the skills necessary to lead consulting groups successfully will be discussed here.

Leadership Skills

Brown and Jacobs (1975) have identified the skills needed by a successful group leader as structuring, recognizing nonverbal behavior, interrelating group communication, and maintaining focus on either the group or an individual depending upon the stage of development of the group. In addition, the leader must be able to energize the group and facilitate problem-solving activities.

At the outset of the consulting group, regardless of communication prior to the first session, there will be a certain amount of confusion about the nature of the task, the role of the group members, and the responsibilities of the leader. The effective leader must be able to clarify the purposes of the group, establishing that the group is involved in a collaborative effort to learn new approaches to deal more effectively with facilitating student development. The purpose of the group may at times be more specific: for example, learning to deal with aggressive students. This purpose should be clearly stated. This statement of purpose should be followed by a structuring of roles. Essentially all members have identical roles: that is, to contribute to the learning process of the members. This general rule is true of the leader as well as the members. However, group leaders have an additional role to play: that of group facilitator.

The consultation group leader will quickly recognize that although only one person can talk at a time, all individuals in the group can communicate non-verbally simultaneously. For this reason the technique of maintaining eye contact utilized in one-to-one consultation must be abandoned, and the leader should constantly scan those members who are not talking in order to seek nonverbal communication cues. In this way the leader can determine who is ready to speak, agreement and disagreement with what is being said, and the degree of involvement by group members.

Observing the nonverbal behavior of group members is crucial for maintaining an appropriate focus for the group. In the early stages the focus should be on the group and topics that group members view as common. Many group leaders have erred by allowing one member to dominate the session by talking for long periods of time and discussing topics that are not germane to the entire member-ship. For example, if the group has met to discuss new methods for individualiz-ing instruction, and one of the members spends a great deal of time discussing difficulties that he or she is having with the building principal, it is likely that the interest in the group will dissipate. When this occurs, the leader must remind the group of the topic at hand and work to generate discussion on this topic. Once the group has developed a high degree of cohesiveness, a feeling of "we-ness," the focus can shift to individual members and their concerns.

One important way to keep all group members involved and facilitate group cohesiveness is by pointing out the relationships among what has been related in the group. This technique is simply tying verbal relationships together through statements such as "It seems that several of you have a common concern," and then identifying that concern. Differences in points of view can also be identi-fied in a similar manner.

Facilitating problem resolution is also a key aspect of the group leader's role. The advantage of group approaches to problem solving is that they provide a multiplicity of potential solutions (Shaw, 1976). The leader must become familiar with the knowledge, skills, and practices of the individual members, and must draw into the problem-solving process those persons who can make contributions. However, group consultation does not preclude the leader from making direct suggestions or engaging in the same approaches to problem solving that he or she would in dealing with an individual. The leader should be careful not to provide solutions or alternative courses of action and, by doing so, to stifle the creativity of the group. What often occurs when the leaders are too quick to offer ideas is that the group becomes dependent upon them and merely sits back and waits for "answers" to be given.

One important concept in leading consultation groups is that actions speak louder than words. Leaders may verbally structure a group by defining their role as participant-facilitator, but then immediately may start to dominate the group by talking for long periods of time, thus placing the focus on themselves.

Or the leader may immediately make suggestions regarding situations that arise, thus enhancing his or her power base in the group and failing to include all members in the group by not interrelating the communications of group members. When behavior is contrary to verbal structuring, the group will respond to the behavior. In the situation just described, the leader would probably effectively destroy all opportunities for the development of group cohesion and problem solving, with the result that instead of group consultation, there would be one-to-one consultation in a group.

The energy level of a consulting group can be immediately determined by observing the degree of participation of group members, the intensity of their involvement, and the pace or rapidity of communications. It is impossible to develop high energy level in groups where members are uninterested and uncommitted to the process of the consulting group. However, the enthusiasm of the leader, the ability of the leader to involve all members in the group process, and, of course, the selection of interested, committed members are crucial factors in assuring that a consulting group will have a high energy level. The ability to energize a group through one's own behavior and to select groups that have a high level of energy is another important skill of the consultation group leader.

Coordination of Group Activities

An increase in the number of consultees who are to meet at one time leads to a direct increase in the number of coordination activities required. Problems that arise are meeting time, finding an appropriate place to meet if the group meets during the school day, and conflicting activities interfering with attendance in the group (Altrocchi, Spielberger, and Eisdorfer, 1969). Obviously, the problem of attendance can have a significant bearing upon the cohesion in the group and thus the overall potential of the group for achieving its goal, and therefore attaining a high degree of attendance must be considered carefully. Many attendance problems can be avoided by careful planning, scheduling, by including members in consulting groups who have a reasonably high commitment to the activities of the group, and by establishing effective devices for communication about group activities. Someone in the group should check the schedules of all participants to determine the best possible meeting time, make sure that an appropriate room is available, establish a schedule, and inform group members of the time and place of the meetings. Often the consultant will be involved in these activities, but it is highly desirable for the teachers in the group to take the lead in these activities, for doing so establishes from the outset that they have a primary responsibility for the group and, to a degree at least, involvement in the routine work of the group is an indicator of commitment.

Confidentiality in Groups

It is probably unrealistic to expect that information disclosed in consultation groups will be kept in confidence. For this reason teachers may be reluctant to discuss situations involving material that might be embarrassing or damaging to the student if it were divulged outside the group. Many teachers who have the confidence of their students learn about drug abuse, premarital pregnancies, child abuse, crimes that have been committed by students, and many other situations. Because of the likelihood that the material will not be held in confidence, group consultation lends itself less well than individual consultation to dealing with problems of this type. However, consulting groups are typically established for the purpose of assisting teachers to cope with more mundane problems where confidentiality is not a problem.

Setting norms on confidentiality should be done on a group-to-group basis. The topic should be broached by the consultant near the beginning of each consultation group. Essentially, what the group must decide is whether material will be kept in confidence, thus opening up the possibility that all topics can be discussed, or whether there will be no attempt to keep the material in confidence. Here, the recommendation is for the group to take the latter course of action. This suggestion is made because of the negative impact on the consulting group and the resulting reverberations outside the group when one of the teachers does break the confidentiality rule.

Some consultants have attempted to get around the confidentiality issue by insisting that all direct discussion of students be done in such a manner as to insure anonymity for the student. In large schools where teachers know only a few of the students, this technique may prove to be effective. However, in small schools this is a highly risky approach, since teachers are often able to discern which students are being discussed even when names and other identifying characteristics are deleted from the discussion.

Insecure Consultees in Groups

In an earlier discussion it was pointed out that one of the problems that some teachers have in dealing with students is their own insecurity. This type of teacher requires a highly supportive, reinforcing atmosphere as one of the basic factors in facilitating his or her growth. Unfortunately this environment cannot be guaranteed in group consultation. Since there is some risk that insecure teachers will be confronted with their inadequacies and thus have their concerns heightened, the consultant should either omit them from groups or structure the groups so that little confrontation occurs. In the latter case, it may be well to suggest at the outset that all criticism be constructive and attempt to have the group adopt this as a guideline for group discussion.

Crises and Groups

It is undoubtedly already evident that because of scheduling problems and potential scheduling conflicts it is difficult for a group to meet quickly to deal with various crises that might arise for individual group members. As a result, these types of situation usually must be handled on an individual basis. However, the group does provide one advantage: that whenever the consultant is not available on a full-time basis, the teachers may contact other members of the group for help. This possibility will provide a degree of security emanating from the group situation.

There are no rules of thumb to determine whether individual or group approaches to consultation should be used with teachers. Groups have the obvious advantage of efficiency and enhanced potential for creative problem solving. Group consultation sessions also provide teachers with an opportunity to learn about the difficulties of others, which may have a reassuring effect. On the other hand, individual consultation requires less coordination, is more adaptable to crisis situations, probably can accommodate teachers who have a high degree of self-doubt, may be a better method of dealing with material that requires confidentiality, and probably requires less skill to structure and conduct. Ultimately the decision to conduct individual or group consultation must be decided upon by individual consultants based upon their knowledge of their own skills, the constraints placed upon them by the administrative structure of their school, and their knowledge of the teachers with whom they work.

OVERCOMING RESISTANCE

There is perhaps too great a tendency among educators and psychologists to take a psychological perspective by focusing upon the individual forgetting about sociological variables that influence human functioning. In considering the prob-

TABLE 4.1. Individual versus group consultation

Individual Consultation	Group Consultation
1. Can incorporate the insecure teacher.	1. More efficient.
2. Requires less coordination.	2. Probably will result in more creative solutions.
3. Confidentiality not a problem.	3. Group members can be available when crises arrive when consultant is unavailable.
4. Probably requires less skill to conduct.	
5. Scheduling easier.	
6. May be better in coping with crises.	

lem of overcoming teacher resistance to consultation, it is imperative that we consider teachers within an ecosystem that has formal and informal communication patterns, norms that heavily influence behavior, and a status leader, the principal. While members of this group (teachers) in some instances act independently of the group (staff), we assume that much of their behavior, including the decision to participate in consultation, is and will be influenced by the group. Consultants must deal with each group member separately and at the same time be aware that their actions with individuals may influence the group. Resistance must be considered both an individual and a group phenomenon.

Watson (1966) has discussed both the individual (intrapersonal) and the group (extrapersonal) sources of resistance to the consulting relationship. He noted that resistance to consultation, in all likelihood, comes about because of an interaction pattern between these so-called intrapersonal factors and group considerations.

Watson (1966) went on to list five types of resistance that stem from the social system of which the individual is a part. These he labeled as conforming to norms, protecting vested interests, concern for the sacrosanct, the rejection of outsiders, and attempts to maintain coherence within the group or organizational structure. Needless to say, these are interrelated ideas, but let us look at them individually.

Norms are behavioral standards that develop within a group. Norms that may be present in an individual school may deal with handling one's own discipline problems, belonging to certain professional groups, and using certain titles such as Mr., Miss, and Dr. Further norms may influence out-of-school activities such as use of leisure time or personal habits such as drinking alcoholic beverages. These norms will most certainly influence the degree to which teachers interact with consultants and the nature of the consulting relationship. Obviously, whenever norms within a school are contrary to the acceptance of a consultative relationship, these norms must be overcome.

Another source of resistance, vested interests, must too be identified and overcome. Ruben (1974) indicated that principals have not yet given their unequivocal support to the consultation process; he posits that this is a major barrier to the consultation function. Many principals do in fact view themselves as instructional leaders, and the idea of the consultant infringing upon this role may lead to overt or covert attempts to deter the consultation function with teachers. Certainly the possibility exists that special educators, school counselors, and school psychologists may occasionally find themselves attempting to guard their own vested interests, thus hampering the consultation process.

From the outset, an attempt has been made to make clear that one of the goals of consultation is to promote change. Although it has been emphasized that this change is to be collaborative in nature and carefully planned, the fact is that any attempt to change the status quo can lead to resistance. At no time is this more true than when teachers become aware that time-honored techniques and practices are contributing to student difficulties and thus are in need of change. For example, consultants have often discovered that the combination of grading practices, disciplinary procedures, and lack of individualized instruction leads to the alienation of pupils. These same consultants have also found that some or all of these same practices are viewed by the teacher as untouchable, sacrosanct, and, as a result, not open to discussion. Even broaching these topics can result in resistance to consultation.

Being viewed as an "outsider" can also raise resistance to teacher consultation. Most new counselors, school psychologists, and special educators experience this phenomenon, at least in the beginning. This of course means that as a newly employed person, one must work for acceptance before involving oneself in activities that are potentially threatening. A prospective consultant who is not assigned to a particular building may have greater difficulty in overcoming the "outsider" label than one who is assigned to a particular school. The implication is that the individual may need to spend time getting acquainted or entering the system before launching an intensive effort to consult with teachers.

Finally, resistance stems from a concern for maintaining institutional equilibrium, or, as it was labeled earlier, organizational coherence. Teachers are concerned about their relationship to other professionals, principals, school psychologists, resource teachers, and so on. They recognize that involvement in a consultation relationship will in some way affect their relationship with others in the system. The uncertainty resulting from this realization will keep some teachers from participating in the consultation relationship, particularly if some of the other factors already listed are also operating.

Before considering ways of overcoming the various sources of resistance that result from participation in a group or social system, the other major source of resistance, personality (Watson, 1966) will be addressed briefly. One of the most perplexing problems confronting consultants is that many teachers, principals, and, for that matter, other consultants have (depending upon one's point of view) poor self-concepts, behavioral deficits, or other personality deficiencies. These intrapersonal deficiencies inhibit these teachers' relationships with pupils and generally retard their functioning as professional educators. Unfortunately these persons create situations that need alteration, but, because of their personal deficiencies, they resist change. Some consultants have entered into therapeutic relationships with these individuals. However, providing counseling or therapy is not a viable alternative for all teachers with personal problems. In fact, many of these individuals should be dismissed from teaching, but without the cooperation of school administrators this is not possible, and in fact no solution exists. The inevitable conclusion is that some teachers will remain aloof from, and unaffected by, the consultation function. While no accurate information exists about the number of teachers with personal problems, it is probably true that only a small portion of our teachers fall into this category.

Developing an Influence Network

Perhaps the first chore of consultants who hope to be effective is becoming accepted members of the faculty in their schools. Watson (1966), Havelock (1973), and others suggest that resistance will be lessened if there is an atmosphere of mutual trust, acceptance, and confidence. The development of these conditions is emphasized by most programs that prepare special educators, psychologists, counselors, or other consultants and will therefore be mentioned only briefly here. First, and perhaps obviously, teachers and counselors must have interpersonal contact. Too many consultants shut themselves off from relationships with teachers by working with students in their offices or own classrooms and not venturing into the hallways and certainly not into the other classrooms. Once contact is established, open communication must be developed. Fullmer and Bernard (1972) summarized the importance of communication when they stated, "Communication is the central concern in all helping relationships" (p. 67).

Although interpersonal contact and communication are important means of overcoming the outsider image, they are not enough. The consultant must also express a genuine concern for the problems that teachers are experiencing and demonstrate the ability to assist the teacher to develop resources to deal with them. We have often heard teachers indicate that certain consultants are just like another teacher. Once the teachers make those types of inference the label of "outsider" no longer exists and will not be a source of resistance. The opposite of this situation is one in which the consultant is viewed as an "evaluator," a perception that must be avoided.

Making oneself available and developing communication patterns are of course necessary, but to and with whom is a major problem. To be more specific, where should the consultant begin to develop an influence system that will ultimately result in widespread teacher involvement in consultation? Havelock (1973) identifies three major types of individuals in the schools: innovators, leaders, and resisters. To this list could obviously be added the followers, but for our purposes there is a need to focus on the innovators and the leaders.

Innovators appear to be less affected by the normative systems in the school, tend to be intelligent, and are generally unafraid of risk-taking behavior. What is also important is that this group is also susceptible to those who would initiate change through the consultation relationship (Havelock, 1973). Although the consultant may be able to effectively establish consulting relationships with them, these individuals may have little influence on others in the school.

Status leaders are not as likely to accept change as quickly as innovators. However, according to Havelock (1973) status leaders are more likely to accept an idea that is clearly going to be effective. Importantly, whenever these status leaders accept a practice or an idea, others within the social structure of the school are likely to follow. Teachers who are status leaders must be enticed into the consulting relationship in a variety of ways. One obvious means is for the consultant to demonstrate the worth of certain techniques or to have them initiated by innovators. Once the risk is reduced, the status leaders are much more likely to involve themselves with the consultant.

Another technique that can be effectively employed to involve not only leaders but others in the consultation process is to set up, in cooperation with the principal, a system that provides recognition for those who initiate or respond to invitations to become involved in consultation. Specifically, it is suggested that the consultant begin a one-page communiqué devoted to his or her work, to be published weekly. However, the major emphasis of this newsletter would be to provide recognition for teachers who have started effective programs or had effectively adopted new procedures as a result of the consultation process. The principal should also be enlisted to provide positive feedback to collaborating teachers through his or her daily contacts and in regular staff meetings. It is important that the teachers, not the consultant, be given credit for the programs.

Still another method of involving teachers in consultation is by establishing inter- and intrabuilding visitation programs, whereby teachers are allowed to visit classrooms that have innovative programs developed as a result of a consultation relationship. Newspaper articles can also spotlight teachers who have developed outstanding programs in collaboration with the consultant. Finally, one consultant maintained a bulletin board in the teachers' lounge and another near the front of the building on which he placed pictures taken with a Polaroid camera and other types of data depicting the accomplishments of teachers with whom he had consulted.

It is obvious from the foregoing discussion that the consultant hopes to benefit, through referrals from previous consultees, from the programs outlined. It should be noted that one elementary school counselor was able to develop consulting relationships with 70 percent of her teachers within a one-year period using many of the procedures outlined here. In a case study outlined at the end of this chapter a school psychologist also made effective use of these techniques.

Coordination of Consultation with Teachers

Resistance to consultation can also occur for a very practical reason: too many consultants. Therefore the matter of coordinating the consultation functions of a variety of persons becomes more than a passing concern. Although the focus of this book has been primarily upon three groups — special educators, school psychologists, and school counselors — there are many others who do consult with teachers. These include school social workers, mental health consultants, reading teachers, and school nurses. In order to make sure that teachers are not overburdened with requests for consultation time and so that teachers will have a channel for making requests for consultation, it is suggested that a pupil services committee be formed.

A pupil services committee is made up of all of the above professionals if they are available and may also include outside consultants, an administrator, and other appropriate persons. The purposes of the pupil personnel services committee are multiple but include the responsibility of designating one or more members of its group to work with a teacher on a specific concern.

The process followed by this group is typically (1) the teacher places a request for assistance with a specific student, an instructional approach, or another problem; (2) appropriate background material is collected, particularly with regard to pupils; and (3) the committee determines who will work with the teacher on the concern. If these procedures are followed, needless duplication of services can be largely eliminated and resistance reduced.

Identifying the Teachers' Problems

Another important step in overcoming teacher resistance is for the consultant to address teachers' concerns. There are some recent publications that may give us some insight into the problems teachers are experiencing. By examining Gallup's (1974) research, which asked the public and junior and senior high students their views on education, we can learn that parents listed lack of discipline, integration problems, need for more financial support, use of drugs among students, and the need to recruit good teachers as the top five problems. Of these, the teacher is directly concerned with discipline and racial tension in the classroom and could be involved in drug abuse prevention programs.

Gallup also asked students what they would do to make the school more interesting. Thirty-five percent replied that they believed that there should be a wider range of subjects, while 14 percent replied that they believed that there should be a smaller variety of subjects, and 11 percent thought teachers could be better and more interesting. Other areas of concern for students were need for more extracurricular activities (10 percent), increased freedom to choose courses (8 percent), and better preparation for college-bound students (8 percent). Clearly the curriculum and teaching methods may be of considerable concern to teachers and thus may be areas of teacher-counselor consultation.

The legal rights of students and teachers is also an area where teachers need more information according to a recent (NEA, 1975) publication. Perhaps more important, teachers need to understand how to insure due process in disciplinary action and how to safeguard the privacy of students guaranteed by the Family Privacy Act of 1974. Through in-service education approaches, consultants can assist teachers to understand information typically found in students' folders. Facilitating the application of this information in the design of student-oriented programs clearly falls into the consultative realm.

Probably the best means of determining areas for consultation is to survey local teachers themselves and to collect data about student needs. Certainly no sophisticated research tools are needed, nor are they desirable, for that matter. All that is necessary is that students and teachers be allowed to voice their concerns. Table 4.2 is a questionnaire that has been used to determine areas of teacher concern.

CASE STUDY 1[1]

Background: Susan S. is a school psychologist who is assigned to three elementary schools with a total enrollment of 2,100 students. In one of the schools 20 percent of the teachers indicated that they wanted assistance in handling discipline problems more effectively. In reality, at least three-quarters of the teachers were experiencing discipline problems, according to the principal.

TABLE 4.2. A survey of teacher needs

Members of the pupil services team wish to make themselves available to work with teachers on areas of mutual concern. We believe that through collaborative efforts students' needs can be better met. The following is a list of areas and activities. Please check those areas that are of concern to you.

　　____ Discipline
　　____ Racial problems
　　____ Values clarification
　　____ Drugs and drug abuse
　　____ Individualized instruction
　　____ Developing student study skills
　　____ Student motivation
　　____ Use of career information in the classroom
　　____ Involving parents in the learning process
　　____ Mainstreaming
　　____ Teaching methods (please specify)_____
　　____ None
　　____ Others (please list)_____

Please return this questionnaire to the principal's office. You will be contacted in a few days regarding your concerns.

---

[1]Case studies have been selected in this and subsequent chapters to depict various professionals in action. The procedure used in these studies could be used by any consultant, however.

While assessment took a large portion of Susan's time in the school under consideration, most of the remainder of her time was spent (1) providing individual and group therapy because of discipline problems; (2) making referrals to mental health agencies; and (3) contacting parents about the behavior of certain children. Both she and the principal decided that an effort must be launched to develop teachers' ability to successfully handle discipline problems.

Step One: Since a number of the students who were classified as having disciplinary problems had previously been in the educable mentally retarded (EMR) class, Susan S. contacted the resource teacher to determine if she wished to engage in a collaborative effort to involve teachers in developing more effective classroom discipline techniques. Nancy K., the resource teacher, indicated that she wished to participate. Nancy went on to indicate that many of the teachers were opposed to the mainstreaming effort and as a result had not individualized their instruction to the degree that she deemed desirable. As a result, many of the lower-ability students were unable to complete much of the assigned work, resulting in frustration and concomitant discipline problems.

Step Two: Susan and Nancy met with the school principal and decided that she should express her concern about the nature and extent of the disciplinary techniques. Further it was decided that the principal would request the faculty's assistance in locating and disseminating exemplary disciplinary techniques being practiced within the school and outside it.
Finally, Nancy and Susan decided that they would follow up on the survey that had been conducted and establish consulting relationships with the four teachers who had requested assistance.

Step Three: Nancy and Susan initiated consultation relationships with the four teachers. It was decided that the six of them would meet after school for one hour each week and that these meetings would be followed up by a one-hour classroom observation and consultation session by either Susan or Nancy. Susan suggested that the first step in the group meetings should be to identify the scope of the problem. This, she suggested, should be followed by some discussion on the principles of behavioral modification, the selection of a target student, the design of an intervention, and a follow-up of the effectiveness of the intervention. Teachers were warned not to attempt to deal with too many students at one time, a warning that both consultants found later was unnecessary.

Step Four: The number of students identified as being discipline problems ranged from two out of twenty-seven to nine out of thirty. Some teachers were quite surprised at what others considered to be a discipline problem. In some instances teachers seemed relieved that problems that they considered serious, such as a student leaving his or her seat without permission, was not viewed as a problem by others. This discussion in itself eliminated some so-called discipline problems from the list.

Step Five: Each teacher selected a student with some common problem: hitting, pinching, shoving, or other aggressive behavior. Then with the help of the consultants they collected baseline data about the incidence of the target behaviors. After that, each designed a behavioral contract with the student as a means of attempting to ameliorate the behavior.

Step Six: Once the interventions were instituted, the outcomes were reported regularly in the *School Psychologist's Memo,* Susan's weekly publication, which was sent to all staff members in the three schools. In addition, the principal made weekly announcements about the progress being made by the four teachers in the consultation group and suggested that if other teachers were interested in the techniques being utilized, they should contact the teachers involved.

Several teachers from other buildings made requests about the contracting program that was being instituted. Susan and Nancy arranged for them to visit with the teachers in the consultation group, which had after five weeks expanded to include six teachers. In addition, one teacher was being seen individually by Nancy.

Step Seven: The consultation group discussed a number of other disciplinary techniques, including time out and counterconditioning. During one meeting Nancy suggested that perhaps some of the students were discipline problems because they were bored; she suggested that contracting be used as a technique to individualize instruction. Specifically Nancy offered to provide the teachers with individualized materials for the slower students, help them write contracts that would direct their educational activities, and assist them to evaluate the work of the students. Five of the six teachers in the group agreed to this idea, but the sixth terminated her work with the group.

Evaluation: After one year, ten of the fifteen teachers identified by the principal as having problems in disciplining students adequately had been involved in consultation with either the school psychologist or the resource teacher. Nine of these had made significant progress in reducing the incidence of aggressive behavior in at least one child, and eight reported that their classroom discipline was greatly improved. Susan and Nancy planned to continue this activity as a part of their program for the following year.

CASE STUDY 2

The following is a report of a teacher consultation session conducted by an elementary school counselor. The consultant initiated the consultation process after conferring with the parents of the child. The material has been edited for presentation.

Session One: The teacher quickly indicated that she was unable to cope with one of her first graders. The student refused to participate in group activities, often hit the other children, and was generally uncooperative. This was the teacher's third year of teaching and she admitted that this was the first time that she had felt completely helpless when dealing with a child. The teacher also reported that her conference with the parents had not helped her to understand the child any better. The parents had suggested that the teacher be very strict with him and to spank him hard if necessary to correct his behavior. The parents indicated that this was their strategy at home and they had no problems with the child. The counselor requested permission to observe the child in the classroom, and they scheduled the second session for later in the week.

Classroom Observation Report: I visited the classroom on four occasions for varying lengths of time before making the observations reported here. I wanted to make sure that the children were accustomed to my being in the classroom, thus insuring that my observations represented a typical sample of the behavior of the child. The following is a report of my observations.

In a one-hour period the student was out of his seat eight times. On three of these occasions the student went over to other children and attempted to start conversations with them. When one student refused, she was nearly pushed out of her chair. At other times the student left his desk to play with games in the classroom, watch the fish in the aquarium, or to go to the bathroom. During this particular time the teacher was working with another group, but interrupted her work three times to reprimand the student or to remind him that he should be working. Other students also reminded the student that he should be working.

The second observation occurred during the reading period. As soon as the teacher requested group two to form for reading, the student put his head down on his desk. The teacher came over and took him by the hand and led him to the reading group. Several students made comments such as "Look at him; he has to be led by the hand." The out-of-seat behavior observed in the earlier session was reported six times during this thirty-minute session, and each time the teacher asked, "Will you please get into your seat?" The student refused to read when it became his turn. Both the teacher and the students pleaded with him to read.

As one bit of follow-up to this session I went into the classroom and during an activity period asked the student to read to me. He read willingly and with only a few mistakes.

Session Two: At the beginning of this session a summary of the observations was made to the teacher, which essentially confirmed her own report. The teacher was then asked if she had any systematic rationale for the behavior, to which she replied that she did not. The teacher was then asked if she knew anything about behavioral approaches. She indicated that she had some vague understanding about behaviorism but was not sure about all of the principles. At this point the consultant introduced the concepts of positive reinforcement, extinction, schedules of reinforcement, and shaping behavior.

After the behavioral principles had been reviewed, the teacher was asked to identify possible reinforcers for the student's present behavior. She immediately identified her own attention and the attention of the other students. The teacher was also asked if any reinforcers were provided when the student behaved appropriately, to which the teacher replied, "Rarely, but that needs to be changed."

The next step in this consultation session was to identify adaptive and maladaptive behaviors which the student was exhibiting. The following chart was constructed:

Maladaptive Behaviors Which Need Extinguishing or Reduction in Incidence	Adaptive Behaviors Which Need Strengthening
1. Out-of-seat behavior	1. In-seat behavior
2. Hitting, pushing, etc.	2. Skills in relating to peers
3. Putting head on desk	3. Listening
	4. Participation in groups

The initial goal that was established was to decrease out-of-seat behavior to two times per hour. The strategy adopted was the selective use of reinforcement for in-seat behavior and ignoring out-of-seat behavior. The counselor suggested and the teacher agreed that the student should be made aware of the procedure.

Third Session (One Week Later): The teacher reported that no improvement in the student's behavior had been observed. When asked if she had been utilizing reinforcement and ignoring as planned, she responded that she thought so. The counselor asked if she could observe the teacher, to which the teacher responded affirmatively.

Teacher Observation: The teacher's interaction with the student had changed somewhat. She did ignore his out-of-seat performance, but she failed to provide reinforcement immediately after the student had sat in his seat for a period of time. The student was still receiving reinforcement for his out-of-seat behavior from his peers.

Session Four: The first item addressed was to review the principles of positive reinforcement and particularly the importance of immediate reinforcement. It was decided that if the student sat in his seat for ten minutes the teacher would tell him how pleased she was with his behavior and that expected in-seat behavior would gradually be increased to thirty minutes.

The next problem discussed was how to reduce the student reinforcement of out-of-seat behavior. It was decided that the counselor would work with the entire class to identify certain types of behaviors which the students considered to be helpful in the classroom and behaviors which they considered as not helpful. The counselor would then work with students to help them learn to reinforce helpful behavior and to ignore behavior that was not helpful to students.

Session Five (One Week Later): The teacher reported that she could see marked improvement in the student who had been of great concern. She indicated that she was now ready to start working on developing social skills in the child, using the same techniques. At this point the counselor suggested that the teacher consider one additional idea, modeling. Modeling was explained as simply showing the students, through role playing, certain ways of behaving, mainly because some students never had had the opportunity to learn behaviors that are appropriate in many situations. The teacher agreed that she would involve the entire class in the activity, since many of the students needed improvement in this area.

Subsequent Sessions: As a part of regular classroom visitations inquiries were made about the student's progress. The teacher reported that she was now experiencing no particular difficulty with this student and that in fact she was using some of the ideas she had learned to deal with other students.*

Comment: There is really no such thing as a typical consultation process. Perhaps one atypical aspect of this series of reports is that the teacher accepted the idea so readily, but the teacher had obviously reached the end of her resources once she came to the counselor. This "end of the rope phenomenon" often accounts for the speed in adoption.

One additional suggestion that we would make is to involve the parents. Obviously force and negative approaches have been used with this child. It can be extremely helpful if the parents can provide positive feedback to students about progress in school. One technique that has been used successful is to prepare mimeograph notes such as the following:

_____has made progress in his/her effort to pay attention in class. I hope that you will congratulate him/her.

There will be more discussion about parental consultation in a later chapter.

SUMMARY

This chapter has focused on two key issues in consultation: resistance and individual versus group consultation. Group consultation has the advantage of being more efficient and providing a more supportive environment, but organizational and leadership problems make group consultation difficult. Overcoming resistance to consultation is also difficult because teachers often are concerned that their work loads will be increased. Being an insider and demonstrating a willingness to collaborate can be of assistance in overcoming resistance, however.

---

*This technique will be discussed in Chapter Eight.

REFERENCES

Altrocchi, J., C. D. Spielberger, and C. Eisdorfer. "Mental Health Consultation with Groups." In *Perspectives in Community Mental Health*, ed. A. J. Benliman and A. Spiegel. Chicago: Aldine Publishing Company, 1969, pp. 276–284.

Brown, D., and E. Jacobs. "Group Leadership Skills." Unpublished paper, Chapel Hill, N.C.

Brown, G. D., and D. Brown. *Introduction to Social Science.* New York: McGraw-Hill, 1975.

Caplan, G. *Principles of Preventive Psychiatry.* New York: Basic Books, 1964.

Carkhuff, R. R. *The Art of Helping.* Amherst: Human Resource Development Press, 1973 (A).

_____. *The Art of Problem Solving.* Amherst: Human Resource Development Press, 1973 (B).

Dinkmeyer, D., and J. Carlson. *Consulting: Facilitating Human Potential and Change Process.* Columbus: Charles E. Merrill, 1973.

Engelhardt, L., B. Sulzer, and M. Alterpruse. "The Counselor as a Consultant in Elementary Out-of-Seat Behavior." *Elementary School Counseling and Guidance,* 5 (1971): 196–204.

Farber, H., and G. R. Mayer. "Behavioral Consultation in Baro High School." *Personnel and Guidance Journal,* 51 (1972): 273–279.

Fine, M. J., and M. M. Tyler. "Concerns and Directions in Teacher Consultations." *Journal of School Psychology,* 9 (1971): 436–445.

Fullmer, D. W., and H. W. Bernard. *The School Counselor Consultant.* Boston: Houghton Mifflin Co., 1972.

Gallup, G. H. "Sixth Annual Gallup Poll of Public Attitude toward Education." *Phi Delta Kappan,* 56 (1974): 26–32.

Gaupp, P. G. "Authority, Influence and Control in Consultation." *Community Mental Health Journal,* 2 (1966): 205–210.

Havelock, R. G. *The Change Agent's Guide to Innovation in Education.* Englewood Cliffs: Educational Technology Publications, 1973.

Ivey, A. E. "Attending Behavior: The Basis for Counseling." *The School Counselor,* 18 (1970): 117–120.

Lauver, P. J. "Consulting with Teachers: A Systematic Approach." *The Personnel and Guidance Journal,* 52 (1974): 535–540.

Lewis, M. D. "Elementary School Counseling and Consultation: Their Effects on Teachers' Perceptions." *School Counselor,* 18 (1970): 49–52.

_____. "The Effects of Counseling and Consultation upon the Sociometric Status and Personal and Social Adjustment of Third Grade Pupils." *Elementary School Guidance and Counseling,* 5 (1970): 44–52.

Lippitt, G. L. "The Consultative Process." *The School Psychologist,* 21 (1967): 72–74.

Mackey, R. A., and F. K. Hassler. "Group Consultation with School Personnel." *Mental Hygiene,* 50 (1966): 416–420.

McAllister, L. W., J. G. Stachowiack, D. M. Baer, and L. Conderman. "The Application of Operant Conditioning Techniques in the Secondary Classroom." *Journal of Applied Behavior Analysis,* 2 (1969): 277–285.

Moon, M., and D. Wilson. "Teacher-Counselor Cooperation: Building Self-Concepts and Confidence in Children." *School Counselor,* 17 (1970): 364–366.

National Education Association. "Let's Get the Record Straight on Students' Rights." *Today's Education,* 64 (1975): 69–70.

Palmo, A. J., and J. Kuzniar. "Modification of Behavior through Group Counseling and Consultation." *Elementary School Counseling and Consultation,* 6 (1972): 255–262.

Randolph, D. L., and R. G. Saba. "Changing Behavior through Modeling and Consultation." *Elementary School Guidance and Counseling,* 8 (1973): 98–106.

Rogers, C. R. "The Necessary and Sufficient Conditions of Personality Change." *Journal of Consulting Psychology,* 21 (1957): 95–103.

Ruben, A. G. "Will Counselors Ever Be Consultants?" *School Counselor,* 21 (1974): 376–378.

Shaw, M. E. *Group Dynamics: The Psychology of Small Group Behavior,* 2nd ed. New York: McGraw-Hill, 1976.

Sherman, R., and I. Shapiro. "Teacher-Counselor Communication." *School Counselor,* 17 (1969): 55–62.

Signell, K. A., and P. A. Scott. "Mental Health Consultation: An Interaction Model." *Community Mental Health Journal,* 7 (1971): 288–301.

Warner, R. W., Jr. "Planning for Research and Evaluation: Necessary Conditions." *The Personnel and Guidance Journal,* 54 (1975): 10–11.

Watson, G. "Resistance to Change." In *Concepts for Social Change,* ed. Goodwin Watson. Washington, D.C.: NTL, 1966.

CHAPTER FIVE Consultants and Exceptional Children

Marvin D. Wyne

INTRODUCTION: AN OVERVIEW

The primary purpose of this chapter is to provide an information base and a conceptual perspective needed by the consultant for establishing working relationships with special educators, classroom teachers, and parents of exceptional children. This chapter is not intended as nor can it be a substitute for good solid course work and experience in the area of exceptional children.

Historically, counselors and school psychologists have not been specifically trained in special education. It is only recently that moderate-sized and smaller school districts have employed directors or coordinators of special education, whose background of professional training and experience lies in the education of exceptional children. Of these three groups of professional educators — counselors, school psychologists, and special education coordinators — counselors have been available to serve a consultative role for a longer period of time and in greater numbers than have either of the other two.

Until very recently, counselors have not been assigned, nor have they assumed, responsibility for handicapped pupils in the school (Wyne and Skjei, 1970).

Administratively, schools have generally been organized and staffed in ways that tended to keep the counselor and the special educator apart. Another major factor that has precluded the interaction of these two support systems is that although until recently counselors have been almost exclusively assigned at the secondary level, special education has been primarily an elementary-level service. The professional preparation of counselors has generally not included course work or field experience with exceptional children, their teachers, or parents. Likewise, the training of special educators has given short shrift to counseling concepts and techniques.

School psychologists have always worked with exceptional pupils and their teachers, but the relationship has tended to be a narrowly prescribed one. The responsibility of school psychologists for identification and placement of exceptional children has often precluded a broadening of their role to include consultation with children, teachers, and parents.

The heavily administrative and supervisory nature of the special education coordinator's role has tended to mitigate against serving effectively as a consultant. In addition, the lack of training and the nature of the training available have not included very much in the way of professional consultation for the special educator.

A number of events have taken place within and outside education that permit, encourage, and even mandate these helping professionals to greatly expand and extend their potential as consultants to the school and community.

1. The rapid growth and popularity of elementary counseling. By far the largest amount of activity on behalf of exceptional children occurs at the elementary and preschool levels. School counseling began and continued for many years as a supportive resource available only in high schools and some junior high schools. The growth in the number of elementary counselors makes available much-needed consultation services to classroom teachers, children, and parents of exceptional children.

2. The shift away from the psychological testing model toward a consultative model of school psychology. Most modern school psychologists have labored long and hard to change the traditional conception of school psychology held by educators. Many of the leading school psychology training programs now teach courses or units on the consultation process. Well-trained school psychologists are now prepared to work closely with administrators, curriculum coordinators, teachers, counselors, and parents in ways that go well beyond giving tests and writing psychological reports.

3. The mainstreaming movement has changed the nature of responsibility for exceptional pupils on the part of all school personnel. With the mainstreaming of mildly handicapped pupils back into the regular program of the school, both front-line and support personnel have responsibilities to assist these students in making the best possible adjustment — academically, socially, and personally. Mainstreaming and its implications for consultation will be discussed in greater detail later in the chapter.

4. *The "right-to-education" child will place new and complex demands on the schools.* Pupils once excluded from the public schools because of the nature and severity of their handicaps are now, once and for all, the educational and training responsibility of the schools. Providing an appropriate, nonrestrictive education for these pupils will call upon the entire school community to work together. Some of the salient implications of the right-to-education mandate are discussed in the concluding section of the present chapter.

5. *The passage of Public Law 94-142.* Without question, the most important, all-encompassing event affecting the role of consultation with exceptional children was the passage of P.L. 94-142. Since this landmark legislation was signed into law by President Ford on November 29, 1975, much has been written and said about the bill and its implications. Many misconceptions and misinterpretations have followed the passage of the Education for All Handicapped Children Act of 1975 (P.L. 94-142). This law actually represents the culmination of a series of state and federal laws and court decisions begun in about 1970. P.L. 94-142 has come to be called the Bill of Rights for the Handicapped. A brief summary of the "rights" guaranteed under this law will acquaint the reader with its major provisions.

Right to Education. In its statement of purpose, the Act specifies:

> It is the purpose of this Act to assure that all handicapped children have available to them, within the time periods specified, a free appropriate public education which emphasizes special education and related services designed to meet their unique needs [P.L. 94-142, 1975, Section 3].

The right to education means that handicapped children may not be excluded from an appropriate education at public expense on the grounds that they are unable to learn, that their handicap is too severe, that services do not exist, or for any other reason. If you assumed that this was already being done, you will be surprised to learn that at the time of the bill's passage, nearly two million of our nation's children with handicaps were being entirely excluded from receiving a public education because of their handicaps (*U.S. Congressional Hearings, Subcommittee on the Handicapped,* 1975).

Right to Nondiscriminatory Testing. The act extended earlier federal statutes that protected exceptional children and their parents from the effects of discriminatory evaluation. For helping professionals responsible for pupil evaluation and assessment, this provision of P.L. 94-142 means essentially that: (a) testing materials and procedures used to assess and evaluate children with known or suspected handicaps must not be culturally discriminatory; (b) test materials and procedures must be provided in the child's native language or dominant mode of communication (for example, sign language, for the deaf); (c) no single procedure or test may be the unilateral criterion for determining eligibility or for establishing the appropriate educational program for a child.

Right to an Appropriate Education. For the consulting professional, this provision is extremely important. Limitations of space preclude a detailed treatment here, but the consultant is legally and ethically obligated to be thoroughly familiar with what has come to be known as the "IEP" provision of P.L. 94-142. The *individualized educational program* is the heart of the right to an *appropriate* education.

Weintraub (1977) states that:

> The term "individualized educational program" itself conveys important concepts that need to be specified. First, "individualized" means that the IEP must be addressed to the educational needs of a single child rather than a class or group of children. Second, "education" means that the IEP is limited to those elements of the child's education that are more specifically special education and related services as defined by the Act. Third, "program" means that the IEP is a statement of what will actually be provided to the child, as distinct from a plan which provides guidelines from which a program must subsequently be developed [p. 27].

Already many sins are being committed in the name of IEP. Experts on writing IEPs have come out of the woodwork, some of whom cannot possibly even have read, let alone understood, this provision of P.L. 94-142. The consultant must know and be able to explain the approved plan of the local school unit and the approved plan of the state education agency. These documents spell out the specific procedures for carrying out the IEP provision of the act.

The Foundation for Exceptional Children has developed *A Primer on Individualized Education Programs for Handicapped Children* (Torres, 1977) which spells out in specific terms ways in which general principles of special education theory and practice can be implemented to conform with requirements of P.L. 94-142. Abeson and Zettel (1977) have written an excellent summary of the act, which appeared in *Exceptional Children,* the official journal of the Council for Exceptional Children (CEC). CEC has also produced a useful multimedia (filmstrip-tape) package to orient groups to the background and provisions of P.L. 94-142.

In addition to the IEP aspect of the right to an appropriate education, it is the "least restrictive alternative" principle that is of central relevance. This principle holds that exceptional pupils must be placed in the least restrictive setting in which the most appropriate education can be provided. It means that handicapped and nonhandicapped children will be educated together to the maximum extent appropriate.

The least-restrictive-placement clause has been incorrectly taken by some to mean that *all* handicapped children, including those with severe physical and behavioral impairments, must be "mainstreamed" into regular classrooms. This is not the case, however. Neither was it intended that all handicapped children be placed in self-contained special classes.

Right to Due Process of Law. Over the past decade, several precedent-setting court cases produced evidence concerning the manner in which handicapped children were identified, evaluated, and placed. In these cases, the courts ordered procedural due process as guaranteed by the United States Constitution. These legal opinions and decisions formed the basis for the due-process components of P.L. 94-142. The aim of this provision of the act is to account equitably for the rights and interests of all parties concerned with the child's education, child, family, and school. Some of the specific aspects of the due process provision of P.L. 94-142 are:

1. written notification prior to evaluation,
2. written notification of any change in educational placement,
3. access to all public records,
4. opportunity to obtain an independent evaluation, and
5. opportunity for an impartial due-process hearing.

In actual practice, the implementation of the due-process provision organizes and ensures more effective home-school communication and cooperation. As Abeson and Zettel (1977) quite correctly point out, the communication is what has been missing. The responsibility for building a communications and public relations system around this provision of P.L. 94-142 is often given to one or more of the consulting professionals in the school. In any case, the implementation of due process will necessarily affect policies and procedures in areas of responsibility assigned to counselors, school psychologists, special educators, and others who provide consultative support to the system.

One of the aims of the present chapter is to assist the consultant in gaining a perspective of special education and in placing this rapidly changing field in an appropriate context. Following a discussion of growth trends, the second part of the chapter sets forth a synthesis of definitions of and interventions with exceptional children. The reader will note that the theoretical bases for consultation discussed earlier (Chapter 3) — that is, humanistic, Adlerian, and behavioral — have also been important influences in developing intervention strategies with handicapped and youth. The traditional categorical approach to special education will be contrasted with current changes in the field that have brought about a fundamental restructuring of administrative organization, curriculum, instructional materials, and teacher roles. The chapter concludes with some implications and suggestions for the practice of consultation.

A PERSPECTIVE ON THE EDUCATION OF EXCEPTIONAL CHILDREN

The education of handicapped children is a responsibility only recently taken on by the public schools. The extremely rapid growth of special education and its generally elevated profile in the past few years have caused many educators and laymen to ascribe to this field a maturity that it does not yet possess. Figures published by the United States Office of Education (1971) show that, with the exception of children with speech impairments, it was nearly 1950 before public schools began to serve handicapped children in appreciable numbers. Even then, the focus was heavily on the area of mental retardation at the elementary level. Attention to emotional disturbance and neuromuscular and other crippling and health disabilities did not show a notable increase in public schools until the 1960s. The areas of learning disabilities and multiple handicapping conditions did not begin to attain focus until the late 1960s and early 1970s. Concern for the gifted has yet to come into its own. Even more recently, schools have begun to provide special education and training services to moderately and severely handicapped children.

The relative infancy of special education can also be demonstrated by looking at the training of teachers of the handicapped. Wiegerink and Simeonsson (1975) reported that by 1949 only 22 United States institutions of higher education had developed any kind of professional preparation programs for teachers of the mentally retarded. Fifteen years later, 221 colleges and universities sought support for their special education teacher training programs across a wide range of categories. Even by 1964, most special education teacher preparation programs offered only the small number of credit hours needed for minimal state certification, usually nine to twelve. Balow (1971) noted that half of all special educators teaching in the public schools in the years 1968-1970 did not even meet their states' minimum standards for certification.

Seven of the traditional areas of exceptionality will be described in subsequent sections of this chapter:

1. Mental retardation
2. Emotional disturbance
3. Learning disabilities
4. Speech impairments
5. Vision impairments
6. Hearing impairments
7. Giftedness

Omitted from this review of exceptionalities are such areas as orthopedic handicaps, chronic health impairments, and multiple handicaps. The interested reader should consult one or more of the widely available surveys of these conditions (for example, Kirk, 1972; Dunn, 1973; Haring, 1974; Wyne and O'Connor, 1979). At this juncture, it is crucial that the consulting professional gain an understanding of the tremendous growth that has occurred in special education during a very brief period. Dunn (1973) plotted growth curves of the number of school-age children identified as handicapped during the fifty-year period 1922-1972. During the first twenty-five years of that period (1922-

1947), the growth curves (except for mental retardation and speech impairment) are about the same as those for the school population generally. During the next twenty-five years (1947–1972), however, the number of handicapped pupils in special education increased more than 700 percent. As Dunn points out (1973, p. 19), this represents an increase nearly nine times greater than that for the school population as a whole.

This dramatic increase in pupils identified as handicapped has obvious implications for teacher training. This is particularly the case since special education teachers serve only about half to a third as many pupils as regular teachers do. In fact, Gallagher (1971) has projected that it would take at least until the year 2770 to train a sufficient number of special education teachers, given the present categories and current prevalence and training figures.

Table 5.1 shows the estimated number of handicapped children in the United States, according to the most recent figures from the United States Office of Education.

Reference will be made throughout the chapter to this table as specific areas of exceptionality and various issues and trends in special education are presented.

The sheer numbers alone are alarmingly impressive, but there are some facts behind these figures in Table 5.1 that deserve the reader's attention.

1. Of the more than seven million handicapped children between birth and nineteen, fewer than half were being served at the time these data were published. Note that these figures do not even include the area of the gifted.

2. At least two important "biases" are operating to affect both the number and types of children identified as handicapped. First, the sex ratio is strongly overbalanced toward males. In a survey of children referred for special education, Mumpower (1970) reported that, as a whole, 70 percent of the pupils were males compared with 30 percent females. Second, a socioeconomic bias has tended to result in the overidentification of children from poor, disadvantaged, and ethnic-minority families. The area of mild or educable mental retardation has been particularly open to this bias (see especially Mercer, 1973).

3. From at least 1940 on, the largest number of handicapped children identified and served has been the speech-impaired. In nearly all cases, these pupils have not been separated out from their age-mates for their education, but are served by itinerant speech therapists. Further, the average case load for speech therapists was reported in 1970 to be 82 pupils (Martin, 1970). This is in contrast to the small pupil-teacher ratios for nearly all other types of handicapped conditions (about 1:11, according to Martin, 1970).

4. In summary, 1970 prevalence figures published by the United States Office of Education showed that over 12 percent of the United States school population was estimated to be eligible for special education services. Of that number, over 60 percent were not receiving services in 1970 and over half were still not being served by 1972.

TABLE 5.1. Estimated number of handicapped children in the United States (1972)

	Handicapped Children, 5–19	Handicapped Children, 0–19	Handicapped Children Served	Children Still Unserved
Speech-impaired	2,112,600	2,440,500	1,360,203	1,080,297
Emotionally disturbed	1,207,200	1,388,000	156,486	1,231,514
Mentally retarded	1,388,300	1,697,500	872,213	825,287
Learning-disabled	603,600	697,300	166,534	530,766
Hard of hearing	301,800	348,600	43,915	304,685
Deaf	45,300	52,300	35,624	16,676
Crippled or otherwise health-impaired	301,800	348,600	182,636	165,964
Visually impaired	60,400	69,800	30,630	39,170
Multihandicapped	35,800	40,900	9,310	31,590
Total	6,056,800	7,083,500	2,857,551	4,225,949

EXCEPTIONAL CHILDREN: DEFINITIONS AND INTERVENTIONS

Background

The reader may be familiar with the tag line from an old joke that goes "It's tough to analyze critically alternative ways of draining a swamp when you're up to your ass in alligators." An unbiased observer (which the author proudly is not) would surely note the philosophical and theoretical impoverishment of special education. The demand for special education services and for training special educators has been so great since 1950 that little attention has been given to the theoretical and taxonomic basis of the field. A leader in the education of exceptional children for many years, Nicholas Hobbs (1975) edited an important two-volume work that attempts to fill some of this conceptual and taxonomic void. The historical roots of this young discipline are embedded in the biological and behavioral sciences. The first "special educators" were nearly all physicians: Itard, Seguin, Montessori. Until nearly 1950, the term *handicapped* generally referred to persons who had clearly observable physical, sensory, and neurological limitations. It was quite natural to expect that, as public schools began to be heavily influenced by the psychological testing movement and as intelligence testing became popularized, the "mildly" handicapped child would be "discovered." The results of this combination of factors can be seen in the current tangled web of discrete categories of exceptionality. As Quay (1968) suggested, "One hardly need point out that cerebral palsy is a medical entity, mental retardation is a psychometric category, and emotional disturbance is a psychiatric-psychological classification" (p. 26).

Two additional influences on definitional and grouping practices have acted to push special education into a conceptual cul-de-sac. An important, if unintended, side effect of the massive federal role in the education of exceptional children has been to crystallize the boundaries of the discrete categorical areas. State departments of education, through which federal aid to public schools is largely administered, have generally tied their reimbursement requirements to these categorical labels in order to monitor the allocation of funds. In order for a state to be eligible for special education services, it became legally necessary to test, identify, label, and place or group the child. The use of group labels was found to be administratively simple for public schools (and for teacher preparation programs). These factors came into play at a time when the widely held belief was that if we could only identify these "handicapped" children and provide them with special teachers, special classes (with small teacher-pupil ratios and separate from the less controllable, more competitive regular classes), and special instructional strategies, we could eliminate or greatly ameliorate mildly handicapping conditions.

Parent groups leaped enthusiastically aboard the categorical, special-class bandwagon. Their lobbying efforts to influence state and federal legislation were highly successful. Many states passed laws mandating the formation of special classes and the employment of special education teachers for the categorical areas of mental retardation, emotional disturbance, and the neurologically handicapped. By 1970, a huge federal-state bureaucracy was solidly in place with a dazzling array of programs that had largely determined the form and substance of special education in virtually every community in the United States. Simply put, it had become necessary to categorize, label, and, usually, isolate children in order to provide special education services to them.

TRADITIONAL CATEGORIES OF EXCEPTIONALITY

Mental Retardation

Of all the categories of exceptionality, mental retardation is best known and the most publicized. It remains one of the least understood handicaps despite the voluminous literature on the subject.

1. *Definitions and Descriptions.* Easily the most widely used definition of mental retardation is the one proposed by the American Association on Mental Deficiency (AAMD). This professional organization is comprised of physicians, psychologists, lay persons, lawyers, educators, and sociologists who share a common interest in the field of mental retardation. On six occasions between 1921 and 1973, the AAMD has published manuals on classification and terminology. The most recent manual (Grossman, 1973) contains the current attempt at operationally defining mental retardation:

> *Mental retardation refers to significantly subaverage general intellectual functioning existing concurrently with deficits in adaptive behavior, and manifested during the developmental period.*

Perhaps the most important change in the 1973 revision is that the subcategory of "borderline retardation" has been eliminated from the definition. The previous AAMD definition (Heber, 1961) stated that "MR refers to subaverage general intellectual functioning . . . ," which included children within the 70–85 IQ range. In the revised definition, "significantly subaverage" refers to intelligence test performance that is two or more standard deviations below the mean. In order to be classified as retarded, the child must now have an IQ of 68 or below on the Stanford-Binet and 69 or below on the Wechsler scales. The implications of this fundamental lowering of the psychometric standard of mental retardation are yet to be realized.

2. *Identification and Classification.* In order to identify properly and legally children who meet the current AAMD criteria for mental retardation it is necessary to provide evidence of *both a significantly subaverage IQ and deficits in adaptive behavior*. The "existing concurrently . . ." part of the 1973 definition

means that if either low IQ or problems in adaptive behavior are found in isolation, the term *mental retardation* may not be applied to that child.

Adaptive behavior is a term with a great deal of surplus meaning. In general, it refers to the extent to which the child meets the standards and expectations of his age or cultural group. The AAMD has attempted to make the term operational by developing a measure of adaptive behavior (AAMD Adaptive Behavior Scale, 1974). There are other instruments, some standardized, some not, purporting to measure independent functioning, language, social skills, and so on (Vineland Social Maturity Scale, Doll, 1965; San Francisco Social Competency Scale, Cain and Levine, 1961; TMR Profile, DiNola, Kaminsky, and Sternfield, 1963; Behavior Maturity Check List, Soule, 1973). Some of these devices assess adaptive behavior across a wide range of mental retardation. Others are intended exclusively for the moderately and severely retarded. For the most part, the measurement of adaptive behavior still awaits the development of trustworthy instrumentation.

Table 5.2 shows the AAMD classification system, which has been adopted by most of the helping professions concerned with mental retardation.

Mild Mental Retardation   Peterson (1974) has raised a number of important considerations that were spawned by the elimination of the *borderline mental retardation* classification (Grossman, 1973).

1. The 1973 AAMD reclassification reduces from around 16 percent to 2.3 percent (using the normal probability curve of IQ scores) the percentages of children psychometrically eligible to be identified as mentally retarded.

2. Who is to assume primary responsibility for children previously classified as educable (that is, IQ 70–85) — special education or general education or both?

3. What are the educational implications of the "new" EMR classification: that is, the less intellectually able group of children (IQ 55–69) who continue as a special education responsibility?

4. Is it now feasible to eliminate the concept of "educable mental retardation" altogether and move toward a classification of the milder handicaps based upon adaptation in the learning environment?

Dunn (1973) and Peterson (1974) have suggested a classification system based on the concept of *general learning disabilities*. Table 5.2 permits the comparison of the current AAMD classification with the revisions suggested by Dunn (1973) and Peterson (1974).

Whether or not the notion of *general learning disabilities* will come to replace the concept of *educable mental retardation,* one thing is clear. The most pressing problems for schools will continue to be the large number of children who do not perform academically as well as their classmates. Children whose barriers to successful school adaptation run the range between cultural-language differences to cultural-familial differences will require a variety of regular classroom supportive services.

TABLE 5.2. A comparison of mental retardation classification systems — AAMD, Dunn (1973), Peterson (1974)

AAMD	IQ Range	Dunn	IQ Range	Peterson	IQ Range
Borderline*	70–84	Mild general LD	40–70	General underachiever	100+
Mild MR	55–69	Moderate general		Slow or low average	85–100
Moderate MR	40–54	LD	35–65	learner	
Severe MR	25–39	Severe general LD	25–35	Marginal GLD	70–84
Profound MR	Below 25	Mental retardation	20–65	Mild GLD	52–69

*Remember that the 1973 AAMD definition does away with this borderline MR category.

3. *Educating the Mildly Retarded.* Disenchantment with the whole spectrum of policies and procedures surrounding mild (educable) mental retardation has been visible in the special education literature for a number of years. It was an article by a pioneer in United States special education, Lloyd Dunn (1968), "Special Education for the Mildly Retarded: Is Much of It Justifiable?" that brought to the surface widespread dissatisfaction with labeling, self-contained special classes, discrete categories, indiscriminate testing and identification, and the apparent failure of special classes to outproduce regular classes in the achievement performance of EMR pupils.

Since the appearance of Dunn's watershed article, the controversy over educating the mildly retarded has spread to definitions, terminology, classification, etiology, characteristics, procedures for grouping, methods of instruction, legal right to be educated, and due process. Current intelligence and achievement tests are said to discriminate against minority-group children who manifest cultural and language differences. The theme of the 1970 President's Committee on Mental Retardation was "The Six-Hour Retarded Child," obviously implying that *educable* mental retardation was conceived and nurtured in the school setting between 8:30 A.M. and 2:30 P.M.

Moderate and Severe Mental Retardation The child, youth, or adult who meets the criteria for inclusion in one of these two AAMD classifications (see Table 5.2) is likely to be intellectually, socially, and psychomotorically very different from the "mildly" retarded individual. Until after 1950 or so, the moderately and severely retarded were usually not served by the public schools in classes for the *trainable mentally retarded* (TMR). Today, TMR classes in most schools (where they are available) usually serve the *moderately* retarded pupil. However, the *TMR* label is actually not simple to define, since at times it tends to include the upper-level, severe MR, the moderate MR, and in some cases, the lower-level, "mild" or "EMR" classifications.

Where the mildly retarded child is almost exclusively a charge of the public school, the TMR child attracts a multidisciplinary audience of helping professionals. As a consequence, the TMR population is often defined in a discipline-specific manner. *Medically,* moderate to severe mental retardation ordinarily involves developmental factors such as disease, infections, trauma, and genetic or metabolic aberrations. The TMR child is often necessarily viewed as a medical entity, particularly early in life. By school age, the view shifts more to social and *educational* frames of reference. Increasingly, as parents' alternatives widen beyond the painful dilemma of institutionalization versus home care, such services as day care, infant stimulation, and special classes in the public schools allow TMR children to remain with their families. As TMR children develop into young adulthood, sheltered workshops, vocational rehabilitation work placements, and group homes are alternatives to residential institutions. Much remains to be done to make these community and school programs available to TMR children and their parents. P.L. 94-142 guarantees the right of the TMR child to public educational services and has already begun to accelerate the development of community-based programs.

Causes It has been common in textbooks on the exceptional child to find lengthy lists of clinical types or syndromes associated with moderate and severe mental retardation. There are two major etiological factors which include the great majority of children who become classified as TMR.

1. *Central Nervous System (CNS) Damage.* There are many ways in which the brains of developing fetuses and infants can be injured or damaged: maternal infections (for example, rubella or syphilis), maternal injury through direct damage to the fetus (home or auto accidents), or indirect injury through ingesting toxic agents (for example, drugs, alcohol, lead particles). The extent and location of the damage does much to determine the developmental expression of the damage. Comprehensive damage to the brain results in various combinations of multiple handicaps, including blindness, deafness, lack of motor control and balance, convulsive disorders, speech defects, cognitive deficits, and so on.

The development of the brain and ultimately its functioning capacity may be seriously affected by such cranial anomalies as *hydrocephalus,* caused by increased pressure on the brain due to large quantities of cerebrospinal fluid that is either blocked from circulating normally or may be inefficiently absorbed by the brain's cavities.

Self-arrested cases (nearly 40 percent are) or surgically treated (implantation of a drainage tube or shunt) cases of hydrocephalus may result in only mild losses in intellectual and academic functioning. In situations where more extensive CNS damage has been sustained, the child may be moderately, severely, or even profoundly retarded.

Microcephaly, characterized by a smaller than normal skull, may be caused by genetic or environmental factors (for example, X-ray radiation of the pregnant mother). Usually, the child with microcephaly is born severely or profoundly retarded.

There are literally hundreds of additional sources of CNS damage: *kernicterus,* related to maternal-infant blood incompatibility or Rh factor; *phenylketonuria* or PKU, one of many metabolic disorders that, if untreated, damage the brain; *encephalitis* and *meningitis,* infection of the brain or lining of the brain; *falls* and other accidents resulting in direct injury.

2. *Down's Syndrome (Mongolism)* has been described as the most common cause of mental retardation (Masland, 1963). Children with Down's syndrome account for about one-third of the population in TMR classes (Kirk, 1972). Although many terms have been suggested for this syndrome (for example, "unfinished children," "Kalmuk idiot"), the original name, "Mongolian idiot," used by Langdon Down in 1866 became abbreviated to "mongoloid" and has been the most widely used of the terms put forward. Down was the first to

describe the syndrome in the clinical literature. The term *Down's syndrome* is now the most popular in current use.

Children with Down's syndrome manifest a number of physical characteristics that render diagnosis a simple matter in most cases. The formation of a loose fold (epicanthal fold) of skin over the eyes, short stature, and dark hair combine to give ample reason for Langdon Down's inference about the Asian look of this clinical type.

Children with Down's syndrome vary from near normal to severely retarded in classification. Most are assumed to function in the moderate range of mental retardation. Only future research evidence can help determine the influence of early stimulation and training, well-organized special education classes, and parent training on the adaptability of these children.

There is considerable room still remaining for conjecture about the *etiology* of Down's syndrome, although genetic research has provided some solid answers. The majority of children diagnosed with this syndrome are known to have 47 chromosomes rather than the normal 46. Heredity (Penrose, 1963) and advanced maternal age (Polani, 1963) both show a relationship to this clinical type, although unknown causes still account for a large number of cases.

Cantor and Girardeau (1960) reported that children with Down's syndrome did not differ from their mental-age mates in *learning characteristics*. Bricker and Bricker (1970) reported impressive success of young children with Down's syndrome in learning fundamental language-communication skills. The scarcity of acceptable research leaves the question of learning potential open, however. Very little is known about the effectiveness or even the appropriateness of TMR intervention programs and curricula.

Consulting professionals may find their human relations skills called forward to aid parents and families of moderately and severely retarded children. The birth of a handicapped child has the potential for creating family disorganization and stress that can seriously affect emotional adjustment in siblings and parents. As more programs for moderately and severely handicapped pupils are developed, consultants are likely to be asked to help support school-family and intra-family communication and adjustment.

Emotional Disturbance

This brief description of emotional disturbance is written with two basic assumptions. First, the emphasis will be upon behavioral deviance identified in "normal" children. Second, the discussion will focus on disordered or maladaptive behavior in the school setting. These two assumptions necessarily omit any treatment of severe behavioral disorders under any label: schizophrenia, autism, psychosis, and so on.

1. *Definitions and Descriptions.* By whatever label, there have always been

children who present management problems for educators and parents. These management problems take many forms: aggression, withdrawal, anxiety, impulsiveness, feigned illness, immaturity, extreme sensitivity, rejection, refusal. When school-based programs for emotionally disturbed pupils first appeared over fifty years ago (principally in larger city systems), they were characterized by psychoanalytic, therapeutic, and clinical approaches. By 1972, of the number of emotionally disturbed children estimated to need special education, very few were receiving such supportive services (see Table 5.1). Despite the bleak record of service delivery over that period of time, important changes in approaches to conceptualizing emotional disturbance did take place. The change may be described as a shift in emphasis from a Freudian psychosexual pathology model of emotional disturbance toward a sociological-learning point of view. By no means is there universal agreement on *the* definition of emotional disturbance today. But, maladaptive behavior on the part of school pupils is seen by many as *learned* behavior. Behaviorists, in particular, suggest that maladaptive behaviors are learned by the child because he or she has been (and is being) reinforced for behaviors (responses) that impede school performance and social adjustment.

Probably, the most influential point of view currently expressed is the *ecological* position. One of its principal proponents is William Rhodes (1967). He was an early advocate of the notion that emotional disturbance does not reside in the child, but is symptomatic of a disturbance in the "ecosystem" surrounding the child. This approach posits that it is the *interaction* between the individual and his environment which produces the disturbance. Obviously, the ecological point of view implies a very different concept of intervention than the traditional "something is wrong with the organism" model.

The reader who is interested in an intensive study of the nature and theory of emotional disturbance as seen from medical, social, behavioral, psychodynamic, and ecological perspectives should examine the University of Michigan's Conceptual Project in Emotional Disturbance. Its multivolume publication, *A Study of Child Variance* (1972-1974), is the product of that important project.

2. Classification and Identification. There are two broad categories of disturbed behaviors that encompass most classifications: personality deviations and conduct deviations. Once again, the surplus meaning of the terms used to describe the various dimensions of personality problems clouds our understanding. *Neurotic, overinhibited, shy, hypersensitive, fearful,* and *anxious* are terms applied to personality deviations. Physical and verbal aggression, attention-seeking, hyperactive, disobedient, destructive, and defiant are said to be appropriate descriptions of behaviors that characterize conduct deviations.

Quay (1969) has been influential with his contributions to the classification of emotional disturbance. Stemming largely from his factor analytic research, he has suggested four dimensions of emotional disturbance:

1. Conduct disorder
2. Anxious — withdrawn

3. Inadequate — immature
4. Socialized delinquent

Adherents of the *ecological* position, on the other hand, suggest that any attempt at classifying disordered behaviors distorts further study and understanding of those behaviors.

Identifying Emotional Disturbance For better or worse, the lack of a clear operational definition of emotional disturbance has not kept us from identifying emotionally disturbed children. Considerable attention has been given to developing instruments designed to identify, detect, and predict emotional disturbance. Though a number of these devices are available commercially, few can stand up to rigorous tests of validity and reliability. The interested reader should consult the regularly published critiques of psychological tests for further information.

The most fruitful and pragmatic approach to identifying children whose barriers to school adjustment appear to be emotional in nature is teacher judgment. As long ago as 1957, Bower's research demonstrated the value of structured teacher ratings for identifying behavior disorders in children. Devices such as the *Walker Problem Behavior Identification Checklist* (Walker, 1970) provide simple and practical screening procedures that do not require intensive and costly psychological services. The Walker checklist used in tandem with its companion classroom observation scale has proved to be a useful method for identifying problem behaviors and for monitoring the effects of intervention (Walker and Hops, 1976; Wyne and Stuck, 1977).

3. *Causes.* It seems generally agreed that emotional disturbance can be caused by *biological* or *psychosocial* factors. Haring (1974) has suggested a third view of causation, particularly in the case of mild, school-related emotional disturbance. The *behavioral* explanation attributes a child's behavior problems to the reinforcing contingencies in the environment. Even though severe forms of disturbance are assumed by behaviorists to have a biological origin, mild and moderate behavior disorders are seen as "learned behaviors."

The search for causes of emotional disturbance has not been successful or particularly useful to helping professionals. The biases of the various schools of thought — psychodynamic, behavioral, neurological — have shed very little light on the understanding of emotional disturbance.

4. *Interventions.* The earliest public school efforts at intervening with emotionally disturbed pupils showed a psychodynamic bent. The available research on its efficacy is of poor quality. Hewett (1974) concluded that two-thirds of the pupils labeled disturbed in several studies improved over time without therapy.

Glavin and Quay (1969) reviewed the intervention research in the area of emotional disturbance and observed that interventions are more effective if they involve the parents as well as the disturbed child. Schultz, Hirshoren, Manton, and Henderson (1971), in a nationwide survey, identified twelve types of school services:

1. Special class
2. Resource room
3. Crisis intervention
4. Itinerant teacher
5. Academic tutoring
6. Homebound instruction
7. Guidance counselors
8. School social workers
9. Psychotherapy by school psychologist
10. Psychiatric consultation
11. Public-supported transportation to nonschool agency
12. Public-supported private school placement

The three most common forms of intervention were found to be special class placement, resource room, and homebound instruction. Perhaps the most rapidly expanding service delivery method is the resource room coordinated by a teacher trained to work with children whose learning barriers appear to be emotionally related.

Some school systems maintain or share with neighboring districts separate special schools for emotionally disturbed pupils. Generally this intervention alternative is used when the child's behavior is so intolerable that it cannot be dealt with appropriately in the school setting. Too, there are many cases in which the special residential school is desirable because the home-family setting is exacerbating the child's problem. One of the best-known (Hobbs, 1969) and most successful (Weinstein, 1969) residential treatment efforts is Project Re-Ed.

This approach has been guided by the ecological philosophy as espoused principally by Rhodes (1967, 1970) and Hobbs (1969). The child is removed from the "disturbed" family-school environment and placed in the reeducation residential setting. Intervention, however, is extended to include the child's family. Additionally, a Re-Ed "liaison teacher" brings the other components of the child's ecosystem into active participation — teachers, counselor, and significant others in the neighborhood and community. The goal of Re-Ed is to return the child gradually to his awakened ecosystem and to phase out its own involvement. Follow-up contact and support is routinely maintained after the child's return.

O'Leary and O'Leary (1972) report that many school systems across the country are using behavioral analysis procedures to observe systematically and modify children's behaviors. Even though too many people have become entangled in behavior analysis as a mystique rather than a technique, it is an extremely useful procedure.

Learning Disabilities

Children with learning disabilities (LD) are currently viewed as those having average or above average intelligence who display obvious deviations in academic performance. The reader will note in the brief encounter that follows that the child with learning disabilities is easier to describe than to define. One of the engaging curiosities about these children is that they are usually described in terms of characteristics that they do *not possess*. The LD child has been studied and described by the fields of psychology, medicine, neurology, psychiatry, special education, reading, and education. Each of these fields has approached learning disabilities from its unique perspective and in so doing has too often contributed as much to the problem as to its solutions. The language of each field has given us many terms that relate to learning disabilities — dyslexia, minimal brain dysfunction, perceptually handicapped, brain-injured, neurological disorganization, educational retardation, developmental lag, interjacent child, to name a few.

While LD is the newest categorical area in special education, its history can be traced to the pioneering work of Alfred Strauss and Heinz Werner. Their medical and psychological research with brain-injured children in the 1940s laid the groundwork for two critical trends that led us to the present. First, they promoted the notion that the identification of brain injury and neurological dysfunction in children should be approached through observation of the child's behavior. Second, they did much to shift the focus of intervention from medical-psychological to educational. In their classic textbook, *Psychopathology and Education of the Brain-Injured Child,* Strauss and Lehtinen (1947) pointed out that behavioral characteristics found to be associated with brain injury in children were also present in some children for whom no evidence of brain injury existed.

1. *Definitions and Descriptions.* The Kirk and Bateman (1962) definition provided an early direction for this category:

> A learning disability refers to a retardation, disorder, or delayed development in one or more of the processes of speech, language, reading, writing, arithmetic, or other school subjects resulting from a psychological handicap caused by a possible cerebral dysfunction and/or emotional or behavioral disturbances. It is not the result of mental retardation, sensory deprivation, or cultural or instructional factors.

The "Learning Disabilities Act of 1969" contained a definition put forward by the National Advisory Committee on Handicapped Children (United States Office of Education, 1968):

> Children with special (specific) learning disabilities exhibit a disorder in one or more of the basic psychological processes involved in understanding or in using spoken or written language. These may be manifested in dis-

orders of listening, thinking, talking, reading, writing, spelling, or arithmetic. They include conditions which have been referred to as perceptual handicaps, brain injury, minimal brain dysfunction, dyslexia, developmental aphasia, etc. They do not include learning problems which are due primarily to visual, hearing, or motor handicaps, to mental retardation, emotional disturbance, or to environmental disadvantage [p. 73].

The reader will note the "exclusion" clauses in both of these definitions. Children with subnormal intelligence and emotional or behavioral disturbances are excluded. One strength of the exclusionary definitions is that they force attention upon instructional excellence. Low IQ and emotional factors cannot be used to explain away failure to learn.

2. *Identification.* Many psychoeducational and clinical instruments have been developed to aid in identifying LD in children. The Illinois Test of Psycholinguistic Abilities (Kirk, McCarthy, and Kirk, 1968) purports to measure twelve separate information-processing functions. The Purdue Perceptual Motor Survey (Roach and Kephart, 1966) claims to assess visual, perceptual, and motor development in young children. The Frostig Developmental Test of Visual Perception (Frostig, 1961) measures eye-hand coordination, figure-ground, form constancy, position in space, and spatial relations. These diagnostic tests of overall information processing, motor skills, and visual skills are joined by other devices measuring auditory, reading, handwriting, and arithmetic skills.

The diagnosis of learning disabilities has not led directly to remediation, as some apparently believed it would. Much of the diagnostic testing sought to uncover causes of LD. Cause-oriented approaches to identification and remediation are extremely costly, tend to deemphasize the role of the teacher, depend heavily on the school psychologist, and tend not to lead toward practical programs of instruction. Clements (1966) pointed out in his analysis of the LD research that specific sense-related skills deficits represent a narrow view of behaviors associated with LD. He cited in order the ten most common characteristics of LD as found in that literature:

1. Hyperactivity
2. Perceptual-motor impairments
3. Emotional lability
4. General orientation defects
5. Disorders of attention (for example, short attention spans, distractibility)
6. Impulsivity
7. Disorders of memory and thinking
8. Specific learning disabilities in reading, arithmetic, writing, and spelling

9. Disorders of speech and hearing
10. Equivocal neurological signs and electroencephalographic irregularities

It has been found that focusing on the salient *effects* of LD rather than mining for its causes is effective and efficient. By locating children with significant discrepancies between estimated intellectual/academic ability and actual school performance, then combining that information with structured teacher ratings and instructional assessment, teachers can identify LD children in terms that are instructionally relevant. Wyne and Stuck (1977) reported results from two engineered resource rooms in two elementary schools that used this simple and inexpensive identification procedure, then set out to increase on-task behavior. Highly significant increases in on-task behavior and reading and math achievement were observed and were sustained over an entire school year.

Hyperactivity It is not clear how LD and hyperactivity are related. It may be helpful to conceptualize these phenomena as two distinct but overlapping circles. Even though hyperactivity is by no means a universal attribute of LD children, it often appears as a concomitant of LD, particularly in young males. McIntosh and Dunn (1973) drew five generalizations from the hyperactivity literature:

1. Only about 20 percent of school children classified as brain-injured, or some such synonym, will display noticeable hyperactivity. Furthermore, capable persons across the full intellectual spectrum will demonstrate this same characteristic at times. Thus all hyperactive people are not brain-injured, just as all brain-injured people are not hyperactive.
2. Hyperactivity, while a somewhat persistent trait, usually fluctuates with the situation. A pupil may be far more hyperactive in the classroom than at home watching T.V. or asleep. And children tend to outgrow hyperactivity as they reach adolescence.
3. It is not just the amount but the timing and type of hyperactivity that lead the teacher to refer the pupil for classification as brain-injured, minimal brain dysfunction, or SLD.
4. The six behavioral characteristics most frequently attributed to hyperactive children are: (1) restlessness, (2) inattentiveness, (3) distractibility, (4) excitability, (5) management problem, and (6) lack of frustration tolerance.
5. In terms of schoolwork, hyperactive children tend to be erratic. Further, they often make reversal and mirroring errors in writing.

The most common treatment for this syndrome is amphetamine-type stimulant drugs. For reasons not clearly understood, amphetamines actually have a tranquilizing influence on hyperactivity. This reversal of the expected influence of a drug is called a paradoxical effect. The careless prescribing and monitoring of these drugs, however, can have a deleterious effect on a child. When the drugs cause chronic drowsiness they can impede learning as seriously as the hyperactivity itself. A growing number of psychologists and educators are finding that some hyperactive children can be taught to monitor and control their aberrant behavior through the application of behavior analysis techniques (Schroeder and Routh, 1976; Safer and Allen, 1976).

3. *Interventions.* With such a variety of identification, etiological, and definitional points of view, it is predictable that approaches to remediation of LD would also vary greatly. Some of the principal approaches are *perceptual-motor* (Cruickshank, 1961; Kephart, 1971; Barsch, 1967), *visual-perceptual* (Frostig, 1973), *linguistic-central processing* (Bateman, 1964; Kirk, 1971), and *neurological reorganization* (Delacato, 1966).

The ways in which schools have organized and administered their intervention efforts show much less variance than the approaches. Prior to the development of the LD category, public school pupils labeled as brain-injured, neurologically handicapped, perceptually impaired, and the like were sometimes placed in classes for the educable mentally retarded. In some states (for example, California), parents of such children organized and successfully lobbied for special classes for neurologically handicapped children. By 1970, the many grassroots parent groups had combined their energies into the Association for Children with Learning Disabilities (ACLD), a powerful action group. Also, by 1970, special educators had come to realize the educational futility of the neurologically oriented search for LD causes. The value of the self-contained special class had also been seriously questioned. The influence of all of these streams of activity and knowledge not only created the LD category, but also gave the resource teacher concept a boost. Consequently, the two main plans for delivering services to LD pupils are the *resource room plan* and the *helping or consulting teacher plan.*

The resource room plan implies a physical place where special instructional materials and individualization are available. The resource room concept can be adapted to a variety of conditions. A risk in any of these is that they will simply be seen as the old special class with a new name. If resource teachers and classroom teachers do not find ways to combine and share their resources and responsibilities, that risk can easily become a reality.

The consulting teacher plan also permits LD children to remain in the regular classroom. In this case, the teacher comes to the child. This plan has been particularly suited to the open classroom or pod arrangement, where large groups of pupils and a team of teachers work together. Space permitting, the consulting teacher can more easily blend special education efforts with the ongoing regular program. Cooperation and communication between the classroom teacher and the consulting teacher are more easily assured under this plan.

Speech, Vision, and Hearing Impairments

Speech Impairments Table 5.1 shows that the number of children estimated to have speech handicaps represents the largest single group of exceptional children. Impaired speech ranges from minor and temporary articulation errors to serious, long-term, and organically related defects. Speech is the tool function of language. The production of oral language involves the ability to produce and articulate sounds, combine sounds into words, and organize words into meaningful units.

1. *Definitions and Descriptions.* Two definitions may be useful. The most widely quoted description of impaired speech is by Van Riper (1972): "Speech is defective when it deviates so far from the speech of other people that it calls attention to itself, interferes with communication, or causes the possessor to be maladjusted." Hull and Hull (1973) suggest a practical alternative description: "A speech deviation may be considered a disability when there is an interference in the production of audible utterances of such proportion that it does not serve satisfactorily as the basic tool for oral expression" (p. 308).

2. *Identification and Classification.* Speech disorders may be categorized into a number of classes:

Articulation Disorders. Speech sounds are omitted, distorted, or replaced with a substitute sound, generally the mispronunciation of sounds and words.

Voice Disorders. The pitch, quality, or loudness of voice is affected. Throat infections, chronic irritation, nasal and sinus problems, and misuse are causal factors commonly associated with voice disorders.

Stuttering. Frequent and severe interruptions in the normal flow of speech. This speech disorder has received more study than any other. Much controversy surrounds the theories of causation of stuttering.

Speech disabilities are also related to other handicapping conditions. The *hearing-impaired* child often shows misarticulation of speech sounds. About half of all children with *cerebral palsy* have impaired speech. Cerebral palsied children have language disabilities related to central nervous system damage, lack of control over the abdominal muscles that push air out, and great difficulty in effectively manipulating the tongue, lips, and facial muscles to articulate speech. A *cleft (split or opening) in the lip or palate* is a relatively common congenital defect in children that interferes with a normal flow of air, resulting in hypernasality and misarticulation. Even after successful surgery, therapy is required to help these children produce correct speech.

Three steps to identifying children with impaired speech are commonly taken. Teacher observation and referral, speech screening, and formal assessment, usually with a test for articulation, can be carried out in most school settings with a minimum of cost and staff time.

3. *Causes.* As with most other disorders, the critical distinction is between organic and functional causes. Many organic causative factors can be treated

surgically, some quite simply. Where no organic basis for a speech disability is found or suspected, the influence of cultural and ethnic differences, bilingualism, immaturity, emotional problems, and learned defective speech patterns need to be examined.

4. *Intervention.* Speech clinicians in the schools report that 75 to 85 percent of their cases have articulation disorders. Even though it is true that the majority of articulatory problems in young children disappear with maturation, the clinician is left with the problem of predicting which children will develop normal speech without correction and which require attention as early as possible.

Hull and Hull (1973) outline three major areas of intervention for the speech clinician:

1. To act as a resource person by providing consultant services to the classroom teacher and other staff members in regard to the improvement of communication skills in the classroom
2. To provide direct services for students with speech disabilities
3. To serve as a program administrator working with the school administrator in planning and operating the speech correction program

Most speech correction is provided in individual sessions, though small groups may often work together. The clinician usually serves more than one school on an itinerant basis. For too long, speech correction has been isolated from the child's regular program of instruction and from parents. The classroom teacher and the parents need to be involved in seeing that skills learned in therapy carry over and generalize to the child's total life space.

Visual Impairments Visual impairments are usually dichotomized into *blindness* and *partial sightedness.* People are often surprised to learn that many *legally blind* children can see. Even so, when so little residual vision remains that braille must be used to read, the loss becomes educationally significant.

1. *Definitions. Educationally,* blind children are those who principally read braille, and partially sighted children are those who principally read large print materials or magnified print.

Legally, blind children are those who have central visual acuity (sharpness or clearness of vision) of 20/200 or less in the better eye with corrective lenses or those whose peripheral visual field permits an angle of distance no greater than 20 degrees. The legal definition of partial sightedness applies to children who have central visual acuity between 20/200 and 20/70 in the better eye with corrective lenses. These legal definitions are important as eligibility criteria for services from public-support agencies, but have no practical value for the educator.

Identification Severe visual limitations are usually identified during infancy or early childhood. For mild to moderate vision problems, there is no substitute for the observant parent and classroom teacher. Comprehensive vision screening is still not available in many school systems throughout the United States.

The National Society for the Prevention of Blindness asks parents and teachers to be aware of ten symptoms associated with visual impairment:

1. Attempting to brush away blurs, rubbing eyes excessively, frowning
2. Shutting or covering one eye, tilting head, or thrusting it forward when looking at near or distant objects
3. Difficulty in reading or in other work requiring close use of eyes
4. Blinking more than usual, crying often, irritability when doing close work
5. Stumbling or tripping over small objects
6. Holding books or small objects close to eyes
7. Inability to participate in games requiring distance vision
8. Excessive sensitivity to light
9. Red-rimmed, encrusted, or swollen eyelids; recurring sties; inflamed or watery eyes; crossed eyes
10. Complaints of not seeing well; of dizziness, headaches, or nausea following close eye work; of blurred or double vision

3. *Causes.* Approximately half of the visual defects found in partially sighted children are due to *errors in refraction:* that is, the way light is focused on the retina. Farsightedness, nearsightedness, and astigmatism result from light-refraction errors. Nearly another 40 percent of vision deficits are the result of *structural and muscular defects* (for example, cataracts, albinism, strabismus or crosseye). The remaining 10 to 12 percent of eye defects are caused by injury and disease.

The largest single causative category in blindness is *prenatal causes:* optic nerve atrophy, congenital cataract, infectious diseases, and the like. Postnatal causes of blindness include glaucoma, injury, and diabetes.

4. *Intervention.* Most mildly visually limited children remain in regular classrooms and usually require little if any special attention. Children with moderate visual disabilities may be served by the itinerant teacher or the resource room plan. Where special print or special visual assistance is required for close academic work (such as reading and writing), the resource room can serve that function. The same child is usually able to remain for all other activities with his age-mates in the regular classroom.

Blind children are most often served in the special residential or boarding school. These schools offer a complete academic and social program. In addition, blind children receive mobility and orientation training to aid in adaptation to the physical environment and, it is hoped, to promote an appropriate degree of independent functioning.

Hearing Impairments Hearing impairments are classified into two categories: *hard of hearing* (or partially hearing) and *deafness.* The critical distinction between the two categories is based on the extent to which impaired hearing affects normal language acquisition and development.

1. *Definition. Deaf:* those whose hearing loss is so severe at birth and in the prelanguage period (before two or three years of age) that it precludes the normal development of spoken language.

Hard of Hearing: those whose hearing loss in the prelanguage period or later is not of sufficient severity to preclude the development of some degree of spoken language and those who have normal hearing in the prelanguage period but acquire hearing loss later (after McConnell, 1973).

Prevalence figures for educationally significant hearing loss in the school population differ, depending on the operational definition and testing methods employed by the researcher. It is, however, consistently reported that mild hearing losses are not usually detected by parents and teachers.

2. *Identification.* There are two dimensions of sound which must be measured in order to identify hearing impairment: *intensity,* or loudness, and *frequency,* or pitch. The scientific measurement of hearing requires the use of an *audiometer* and the services of an *audiologist* who is professionally trained and certified. The audiologist can determine the nature and extent of hearing impairment. It is important, for example, to determine if the child had impaired reception of sound waves conducted by air or by bone and to find out if the hearing loss is related to the loudness or the pitch (high or low frequency) of sounds.

Preschool and school group audiometric screening can be carried out simply and inexpensively. Kirk (1972) suggests that group screening for hearing impairment should be repeated periodically. Once children are identified, further testing and, if necessary, treatment by an *otologist* (medical doctor specializing in disorders of the ear) can be obtained.

3. *Causes.* Etiological factors associated with impaired hearing are usually grouped under two headings: *endogenous* or inherited causes, and *exogenous* or disease- and trauma-related causes. Impairment in hearing may occur before, during, or after birth. Gallaudet College in Washington, D.C. (the only known college in the world designed exclusively for the higher education of the deaf), does a periodic national demographic survey of hearing impairment. Table 5.3 shows the number of students enrolled in United States special education programs for the hearing-impaired according to probable cause of hearing loss (Gallaudet College, 1973).

4. *Intervention.* Most children with known mild hearing losses remain in the regular classroom and are not seriously limited academically. Where services are available, these children often work individually and in small groups with an itinerant resource teacher. Itinerant resource teachers for the hearing-impaired assist the regular teacher by providing instruction for these children in reading, language, and speech. In addition, the itinerant teacher may assist hearing-impaired children in the proper use of a hearing aid and amplified sound systems

TABLE 5.3. Students enrolled in participating special educational programs for the hearing-impaired by probable cause of hearing loss, U.S. 1970-71 school year

Probable Cause of Hearing Loss	Number
Causes of hearing loss with onset at birth	
Maternal rubella	6,077
Trauma at birth	916
Trauma to mother	253
Medication during pregnancy	271
Prematurity	2,207
Rh incompatibility	1,402
Complications of pregnancy	994
Hereditary	3,073
Other causes	844
Causes of hearing loss with onset after birth	
Meningitis	2,017
Mumps	351
Measles	1,114
Otitis media	927
Trauma	420
Fever	628
Other causes	2,000

and instruct in speech reading (attending to lip and facial cues) to supplement the residual hearing.

Deaf children receive their education in residential schools, special day schools, and day classes. Nearly 70 percent of all deaf children attend residential schools largely because of the unavailability of day schools and day classes in their own communities. Special day schools are most common in large cities, where the concentration of population provides a sufficient number of deaf children to warrant such a school. The potential value of day classes is the opportunity for deaf and normally hearing children to interact. Even though day classes are self-contained, the fact that they are usually located in a public school for normally hearing children can drastically reduce isolation and adjustment problems sometimes experienced by residential school pupils.

The curriculum in school programs for the deaf does not differ appreciably from that of the normally hearing pupil. More emphasis is placed on communication, socialization, and vocational skills. The long-standing argument among deaf educators is not over curriculum content, but method of teaching. The *oral-aural approach* (amplified sound-speech and lip reading) versus the *manual approach* (sign language-finger spelling) has proliferated an either-or dichotomy that makes little sense. The use of one or a combination of both methods of communication should be based upon the needs and capabilities of the deaf pupil. An approach called *total communication,* which employs any and all means of communicating for the deaf child, is being used increasingly.

The move toward earlier identification and intervention that has come to characterize the education of many other types of handicapping conditions is also popular among educators of the deaf. The sudden sharp increase in hearing impairments resulting from the nationwide rubella (German measles) epidemics of 1963–1965 (see Table 5.3) brought about the interest in preschool programs for deaf-blind children. Many states made special provisions in their public school laws by lowering to zero the age at which children may begin receiving tax-supported educational services.

Giftedness

The historical tradition of education in the United States is founded solidly on the concept of educating all children. Aside from employment, one of the reasons for emigrating from Europe to the United States was the opportunity for gaining an education. Many European countries provided education beyond about fourth grade only to children of the upper classes. Even though the selection of European students for secondary schools was not based on their academic performance, many modern American educators and parents still react sharply to the semblance of "élitism" in identifying academically gifted and talented pupils.

It was repeatedly pointed out early in this century (Terman, 1925; Hollingworth, 1942; Pressey, 1955) that the relevant and proper education of gifted pupils was being ignored. Briefly, during the Sputnik era in the 1950s, national attention turned toward producing outstanding scientists, but no comprehensive effort has ever been made equitably and realistically to provide differential educational opportunity to the gifted and talented. The United States Commissioner of Education pointed out several years ago (Marland, 1972) in a special report to Congress that gifted and talented pupils were still being poorly served by our educational system. Whatever personal loss accrues to each gifted pupil as a result of inadequate education seems to be a serious national waste of intellectual and artistic talent.

1. *Definitions and Descriptions.* There has never been a shortage of definitions of giftedness. Some definitions are very narrow, focusing strictly upon IQ scores or already expressed talent in one or more specific areas. Others have tried to encompass superior mental abilities, talent, superior academic achievement, and creativity. Kirk (1972), perhaps out of frustration with this definitional morass, described giftedness as "superior ability to deal with facts, ideas, or relationships" (p. 109).

Martinson (1973) described giftedness as:

Students with superior cognitive abilities include approximately the top 3 percent of the general school population in measured general intelligence and/or in creative abilities or other talents that promise to make lasting contributions of merit to society. These students are so able that they require special provisions if appropriate educational opportunities are to be provided for them.

2. *Identification.* Because of the wide variety of definitions and the even wider variety in school programs for the gifted, identification procedures also vary. In general, there are six procedures which are most commonly used in some combination: individual intelligence tests; teacher observations and ratings; group intelligence tests; achievement tests; tests of creativity; and previous accomplishments such as school grades.

Marland's (1972) report showed that teacher ratings and group tests (achievement and mental ability) were by far the most commonly used screening and identification methods. Gallagher (1975) suggests that teacher ratings alone represent a most inadequate screening method because many gifted pupils are overlooked. Used in combination with grades and group test scores, for example, teacher ratings can be valuable to the identification process. It is probably best to think of identification in two phases, *screening* and *identification*. Despite the expense and the controversy surrounding their use, the administration of individual intelligence tests should be given serious consideration in the final step of identification.

3. *Causes.* Since we cannot agree on what giftedness is, it may not be accurate to speak of its "causes." Most of the research literature, beginning with the Terman studies in 1925 and continuing through Gallagher's (1975) critical review, provides ex-post-facto and correlative data rather than established causative factors of giftedness. Examples of some of the factors that correlate highly with giftedness are:

1. Early encouragement from parents (Pressey, 1960)
2. More boys than girls; disproportionate number of children from Jewish and native-born parents (Terman and Oden, 1947)
3. Higher-socioeconomic-level families (Gallagher, 1959);
4. Superior early skill and interest in reading (Martinson, 1961);
5. Healthier, longer life spans, and physically skilled (Terman, 1925; Martinson, 1961);
6. Rich vocabularies, good sense of humor, relate well with peers and adults, socially popular (Dunlop, 1967).

These correlative data are generally based on definitions of giftedness which heavily emphasize measured intelligence. It is undeniable that our traditional concepts of giftedness have placed children with socioeconomic, cultural, minority-group, and value-system differences at a disadvantage. The use of group tests and of intelligence tests has received more than its due share of blame for this discriminatory exclusion. Ausubel (1965) has suggested that the proper attack should come not on the intelligence test, but on its improper use and on the sociocultural and environmental problems that spawn intellectual deprivation. After viewing the scarce and questionable nature of the research on giftedness and minority-culture children, Gallagher (1975) suggests a total-push strategy that includes expanding our narrow concept of giftedness, liberalizing and improving measures, intensive analysis of the school curriculum, and providing trained teachers and counselors.

4. *Intervention.* The three most commonly used school intervention plans for the gifted are acceleration, enrichment, and special classes. *Acceleration* shortens time spent in school by having the child skip an elementary grade or semester, early admission to kindergarten or first grade, early admission to college, and by telescoping grades through self-pacing in a nongraded program or by simply covering the regular curriculum more rapidly than normal. The research on acceleration is inconclusive, but the most common concern is that accelerated children and youth will suffer personal and social adjustment problems. Persons already biased either for or against can find research studies that support their particular view. Longitudinal data on the effects of acceleration are badly needed.

Enrichment takes many forms, but essentially it provides special experiences and activities above and beyond those available in the regular curriculum. Gifted pupils may receive special enrichment in the regular class from an itinerant resource teacher or they may leave the regular classroom and receive enrichment in a resource room from the special teacher. It is not uncommon to find enrichment for more able pupils being provided by the regular classroom teacher. Many schools that do have formal resources for the gifted attempt to serve the special qualities and needs of these pupils through ability grouping. Experts and researchers in the field (for example, Kirk, 1972; Gallagher, 1975) are critical of substituting ability grouping for well-planned, professionally implemented programs of enrichment for the gifted.

Special classes and *special schools* are seldom found in today's school systems. The small body of research available does not support the efficacy of these arrangements. Administratively and politically, they have tended to be difficult to justify. The bulk of the recent state and federal efforts in behalf of special education for the gifted clearly favors delivering the resources to the pupil, not vice versa.

Dunn (1973), Gallagher (1975), and Martinson (1973) predict a brighter future for the education of gifted pupils. Recent federal support for developing model teacher-training programs for the gifted bodes well, for example. The increasing militance of parent groups is likely to result in more and better resources as well.

THE CONSULTANT AND THE EXCEPTIONAL PUPIL

This concluding section sets out some of the implications of the trends and issues that are at work changing the form and substance of special education. A number of these trends were alluded to in earlier sections of the chapter. What follows is an attempt to blend the information base about exceptional children that comprises most of the chapter with a word about the needs and trends in special education. It is hoped that a kind of synopsis will emerge that has the consultant as its primary frame of reference.

Labeling and Categorization

The move away from medically oriented diagnosis of exceptional children using psychological and clinical instruments is well along (Hobbs, 1975). These practices are being replaced with criterion-reference measures, skill-related checklists, task analysis, and pupil-observation techniques, to name a few. Testing for the purpose of labeling and placing children is beginning to give way to testing for direct instructional purposes. Where labels must be used for purposes of administration, they are being used to designate skill-related or treatment-related disabilities.

In those cases (and there are still far too many such) where consulting professionals are expected to administer tests, there are important implications to be derived from the changes occurring in labeling and placement. First, classroom teachers and special education teachers who refer pupils for individual testing need help in finding more appropriate ways to approach the students' learning barriers. Whenever the consultant is able to meet with a referring teacher about some of the specific identification procedures described earlier in this chapter, doing so is preferable to simply refusing to test children. A referral from a teacher should be viewed as a request for assistance for the pupil *and* the teacher.

If the consultant is not sufficiently prepared to suggest appropriate alternatives to traditional psychometrics, outside resources should be obtained. In-service training in the selection and use of instructionally oriented assessment and observation might be useful for regular teachers, resource teachers, and administrators.

Where individual psychological testing is absolutely required for state or federal reimbursement purposes, that testing should be viewed as an administrative and not an instructional activity. Teachers need to be helped to find realistic, useful alternatives to IQ scores or to Bender-Gestalt results, for example. Until such instructionally oriented procedures are developed, teachers and administrators will continue to request psychodiagnostic data.

The counselor, school psychologist, and consulting resource teacher are at the crossroads where teacher, child, parent, and the school curriculum meet. These professionals can do more than any other by consulting with administrators and teachers who maintain a narrow, traditional view of pupil assessment. By demonstrating how to use instructional tests in reading and math, the consultant can help teachers to understand the critical difference between testing for instructional purposes and testing for administrative purposes. Consultants should take the lead in helping to develop an efficient, effective pupil testing program that is complementary to their school's program of instruction.

Mainstreaming

Educators and parents are not sure whether they should be elated, concerned, or just puzzled about mainstreaming. What is mainstreaming? Where did it come from? Why is it here? Is mainstreaming an administrative-organizational arrangement? a strategy for normalizing education? a principle? a philosophy? The answer is *Yes.* Mainstreaming is all of these things and more. Therein lies the current confusion about what mainstreaming means. MacMillan (1977) has proposed one of the clearest definitions of mainstreaming to date:

> Therefore, it is proposed here that mainstreaming for children at risk of segregation must entail the following elements:
> 1. The children are educated with children in a regular class to the maximum degree possible in light of each child's characteristics.
> 2. Responsibility for the child's education is *shared* by general and special education personnel — both are accountable.
> 3. The children are no longer classified as handicapped [p. 449].

The consulting professional can be of major assistance to pupils, teachers, administrators, and parents who are involved in mainstreaming. There is much concern and some hostility among regular educators regarding mainstreaming. A number of teacher groups have already attempted to negotiate contracts that stipulate teachers' right to exclude disturbing children.

The consultant's skills are at a premium in the movement toward mainstreaming mildly handicapped pupils into the school's regular program of instruction and socialization. The finest resource teacher available and the most intensive pupil preparations possible for returning to the regular classroom are utterly wasted if human relations are overlooked (and they so often are). The counselor has an opportunity to be a prime mover in laying the groundwork of understanding and acceptance of these changes on the part of the instructional and administrative staff. Organizing group planning, training, and discussion sessions with regular teachers, resource teachers, and support personnel can help build the interpersonal bridges that will permit exceptional pupils to receive the best and most appropriate education from the regular program and the special or resource program. This dialogue should be established as early as possible before the perceived barriers become real barriers. Counselors are also in the best situation to consult with the parents of mainstreamed children when there is misunderstanding or undue sensitivity. Group and individual sessions with parents can provide them with opportunities to communicate their concerns and to share their feelings and views. These sessions can also be used to have teachers and support personnel explain and demonstrate intervention objectives and materials to parents.

Over the short term, two potential areas require strong leadership and sensitivity on the part of the consulting counselor: *communication* and *planning*. The success of mainstreaming depends on developing close communication and cooperation between the regular program and the resource program. The counselor is especially qualified to assist this effort by creating settings and situations that enable regular teachers and special teachers to share feelings and information openly, as well as to plan together. Already, many schools have begun mainstreaming; misunderstanding, jealousy, withdrawal, hostility, and so on, among teachers and administrators has begun its destructive work, too. The curricular, organizational, and instructional problems created by mainstreaming are solvable. The critical human relations problems hold the key to these new efforts. This is one of those situations in which the counselor can best help children by helping those who help the children.

Mainstreaming provides school psychologists with an unparalleled chance to do something they have been trying to do for at least ten years: change the perception of their role. The needs of regular and special teachers for instructionally relevant assessment and for assistance in dealing with deviant behavior enable school psychologists to serve a true consultative function.

Carrying out systematic observations of children referred for disturbing behavior, assisting classroom teachers with appropriate instructional assessment, serving as a liaison between mental health personnel, community agencies, and administrators: these are examples of consultative responsibilities within the school psychologist's domain. Psychological testing will continue to fall to the school psychologist, but testing need not and should not circumscribe the whole of school psychology. School psychologists can serve a most important consultation role by using their expertise to help insure that each exceptional pupil is receiving instruction in the least restrictive and most appropriate setting.

In their consultative work with parents of exceptional children, school psychology consultants have an opportunity to aid the instructional staff by interpreting evaluative data gathered on exceptional pupils. The psychologist can assist parents by referring or recommending appropriate public or private mental health or medical resources when needed. It does not seem unrealistic to suggest that mainstreaming enables school psychologists to expand and extend their consultative roles both within and outside the school setting.

The role of consultation is quite unfamiliar to special educators. Traditionally, special education meant instruction, supervision, and administration (coordination). The return of mildly handicapped pupils to the mainstream of the school calls upon the special education teacher (resource teacher) to redefine these traditional responsibilities.

The consulting resource teacher must now develop new skills and services such as those described below.

A key element in successful learning strategies for mainstreamed pupils is the *cooperative working arrangement* between regular classroom teachers, resource teachers, and supporting services.

The consulting resource teacher should play an important role in the *orientation* of regular classroom teachers to mainstreaming policies and procedures. These periodic sessions can also be used to share ideas, information, or techniques, or to carry out workshops on behavior management, task analysis, parent training, and so on. These meetings, in turn, provide an excellent opportunity for regular teachers and teachers of support subjects, such as art, music, reading, physical education, and so on, to explain the objectives and procedures in their programs of instruction.

Few activities provide such an outstanding opportunity to convince their fellow educators of the unique contributions of the consulting resource teacher as *demonstration teaching.* Working in the regular classroom, the consulting teacher can take large and small groups of students, blending in mainstreamed pupils. By demonstrating new and unfamiliar materials, the consulting resource teacher can show a variety of ways to integrate mainstreamed students into the instructional and social program of the class.

One of the most commonly mentioned complaints regular teachers have about mainstreaming is the difficulty of finding appropriate instructional materials. The consulting teacher can support regular teachers and their pupils by helping to *modify, adapt, or find relevant materials.*

Legislation and Litigation

It is absolutely essential that consulting professionals become familiar with Public Law 94-142. The basic provisions of P.L. 94-142 have obvious implications for all of the needs and trends discussed in the concluding section of the chapter: labeling and categorizing exceptional pupils, mainstreaming, right to a public education for moderately and severely handicapped students.

Be assured that counselors, psychologists, and resource teachers are all much affected by P.L. 94-142. Reread the provisions of the law discussed earlier in the chapter and contemplate for a moment their implications for consultation. Individually and cooperatively, consulting professionals will be deeply involved in the implementation of this watershed legislation.

The consulting counselor may need to become an advocate for children who are in danger of becoming mislabeled or improperly placed in the school. Keeping parents and teachers informed regarding reasons for testing and placement or re-placement is crucial to good programming as well as to meeting the constitutional rights of due process. Counseling parents of children whose handicaps are such that they have been excluded from school can assist both school officials and parents in many ways.

School psychologists must be careful that they do not violate the rights of handicapped students and their parents. In addition, they should be prepared to assist teachers and administrators in the proper procedures for initial screening and referral of pupils believed to be eligible for special services. The least restrictive alternative notion means that school psychologists will be needed to consult with teachers and parents in determining ways to evaluate the effectiveness of particular placements for exceptional pupils.

The consulting resource teacher will play a critical role in the establishment of individualized educational programs (IEP). For each pupil identified as exceptional, an IEP must be developed, implemented, monitored, and revised as appropriate. Consultation with regular teachers, administrators, support personnel, and parents will be required at each step in this process.

Programs for Moderately and Severely Handicapped

Largely because of parent action through the courts and, more recently, because of P.L. 94-142, schools are now required to assume educational responsibility for severely handicapped children. The forms that discharging this legal responsibility will take have not yet been articulated. In the interim, much needs to be done toward assisting educators and parents in understanding the difficulties in developing and implementing new programs and resources for which there are very few existing models. Once new resources for severely handicapped children have been developed, many of these pupils cannot be served within existing school facilities. They may receive educational services through special arrangement with existing agencies, through new community-based day school or sheltered workshop facilities, or by way of contracts with private and public care-giving agencies. All of this portends a striking increase in new types of consultation services. It seems likely that in smaller school units, consultants will be asked to provide advocacy, liaison, and communication among and between various agencies in behalf of the school, family, and pupil. Where educational services for the severely handicapped are able to be delivered within school facilities and on school campuses, consulting professionals can do much to help these programs, teachers, and pupils to become integrated into and accepted by the rest of the school.

Along with the emphasis on the right to education for moderately, severely, and profoundly handicapped, a *normalization philosophy* has evolved. This notion implies that equal education for these individuals should come under the umbrella of education. Given the court decisions already made, P.L. 94-142, and continuing parental pressure, the responsibility of the school for serving severely handicapped pupils seems assured. As the emphasis shifts from custodial care to education and training, a marked increase in the need for consultation will result. Three areas exemplify the types of consultation so badly needed in educating severely handicapped students.

1. Assessment. The standard diagnostic and assessment tools presently used with the mildly handicapped, such as readiness, achievement, and instructional tests, will be of little use to teachers of the severely handicapped. School psychologists should be available to consult with teachers and administrators in the area of assessment. Teachers must become aware of the psychological and medical information concerning infancy and early childhood development. Developmental instruments such as the *Bayley Infant Scales of Development* (1969) and the *Denver Developmental Screening Test* (1975) need to become familiar tools. Consultation is required in learning to administer and interpret adaptive behavior scales such as the *AAMD Adaptive Behavior Scale* (1969) and the *Cain-Levine Social Competency Scale* (1963).

2. Curriculum. The curricular needs of the severely handicapped are widely divergent from those of the mildly handicapped or normal child. In addition, very few teachers of the moderately, severely, and profoundly handicapped are trained for their responsibilities. The need for consulting resource teachers is extremely critical in the area of curriculum development, implementation, and evaluation. Severely handicapped students need direct consultation to help coordinate the activities of the several disciplines and agencies that serve them and their families. The consulting resource teacher can conduct or arrange for in-service workshops, procure materials, help arrange for special space or furniture adaptations, assist in procuring prosthetic aids, coordinate referrals for medical, dental, and therapy services, carry out demonstration lessons, and coordinate training program plans.

3. Parent Involvement. All consulting professionals must be alert to the special family problems created by the presence of a severely handicapped child. Psychologists and consulting teachers should devise strong communication links between the school and the home. Consultation provided to parents of severely handicapped pupils by the school psychologist and consulting resource teacher may include: (a) explaining the purposes of testing and observation; (b) keeping parents up-to-date on progress as well as problems; (c) training parents to deal with undesirable behaviors, to reinforce skills and behaviors being taught at schools, and to use and care for prosthetic devices properly; (d) serving as a source of information about resources such as respite care, recreation, parent groups, legal assistance, health care, and volunteer services.

The counselor should be able to consult with parents in the following ways: (a) forming parent discussion groups to help share and manage the tension, anxiety, frustration, and guilt that attends families of severely handicapped children; (b) providing individual and group opportunities for the siblings of moderately and severely handicapped children to interact, and to share feelings and experiences; (c) explaining student abilities to help parents overcome the problems of under- or overprotection and inappropriate expectations — either too high or too low; (d) putting parents in touch with the appropriate professional in the school when school-related questions or problems arise.

Be reminded that this chapter contains only a sampler of information, trends, and implications of today's special education for the consultant. The reader should have gained the impression that a whole set of challenges and opportunities awaits the consulting professional. True, these challenges demand changes in professional training, roles, and in the nature of the client population. Some, perhaps many, consultants will continue to seek the security of traditional roles. Others will see these opportunities for increasing the life chances of exceptional children as a way to break out of imprisoning traditional roles and to extend the benefits as well as the horizons of consulting excellence.

REFERENCES

Abeson, A., and J. Zettel. "The End of the Quiet Revolution: The Education for All Handicapped Children Act of 1975," *Exceptional Children,* 44 (1977): 114-128.

Ausubel, D. P. "The Influence of Experience on the Development of Intelligence." In *Productive Thinking in Education,* ed. M. Aschner and C. Bish. Washington, D.C.: National Education Association, 1965.

Balow, B. "Teachers for the Handicapped," *Compact,* 5 (1971): 4, 43-46.

Barsch, R. *Achieving Perceptual-Motor Efficiency.* Seattle: Special Child Publications, 1967.

Bayley, N. *Infant Scales of Psychomotor and Mental Development.* New York: Psychological Corporation, 1969.

Bricker, W. A., and D. D. Bricker. "A Program of Language Training for the Severely Language Handicapped Child," *Exceptional Children,* 37 (1970): 101-111.

Cain, L. F., and S. Levine. *A Study of the Effects of Community and Institutional School Classes for Trainable Mentally Retarded Children.* San Francisco: San Francisco State College, 1961.

Cantor, G. N., and E. L. Girardeau. "Rhythmic Discrimination Ability in Mongoloid and Normal Children," *American Journal of Mental Deficiency,* 64 (1960): 621-625.

Clements, S. D. *Minimal Brain Dysfunction in Children.* NINOS Monograph No. 3. Public Health Service Bulletin No. 1415. Washington, D.C.: U.S. Department of Health, Education and Welfare, 1966.

Cruickshank, W., F. Bentzen, F. Ratzeburg, and M. Tannitauser. *A Teaching Method for Brain-injured and Hyperactive Children*. Syracuse: Syracuse University Press, 1961.

Delacato, C. *Neurological Organization and Reading*. Springfield: Charles C. Thomas, 1966.

DiNola, A., B. Kaminsky, and A. Sternfield. *TMR Performance Profile for the Severely and Moderately Retarded*. Ridgefield: Reporting Service for Exceptional Children, 1963.

Doll, E. A. *Vineland Social Maturity Scale*. Circle Pines: American Guidance Services, 1965.

Dunn, L. M. "Special Education for the Mildly Retarded: Is Much of It Justifiable?" *Exceptional Children*, 35 (1968): 5–24.

Dunn, L. M., ed. *Exceptional Children in the Schools*, 2nd ed. New York: Holt, Rinehart & Winston, 1973.

Frankenburg, W., and J. Dodds. *The Denver Developmental Screening Test – Revised*. Denver: Ladoca, 1975.

Frostig, M. *Frostig Developmental Test of Visual Perception*. Chicago: Follett Publishing Co., 1961.

Frostig, M., and P. Maslow. *Learning Problems in the Classroom: Prevention and Remediation*. New York: Grune and Stratton, Inc., 1973.

Gallagher, J. J. "The Future Special Education System." In *The Missouri Conference on the Categorical/Non-categorical Issue in Special Education*, ed. E. Meyen. Columbia: University of Missouri Press, 1971.

———. *Teaching the Gifted Child*, 2nd ed. Boston: Allyn and Bacon, 1975.

Glavin, J. P., and H. C. Quay. "Behavior Disorders," *Review of Educational Research*, 9 (1969): 83–92.

Grossman, H. J. *Manual on Terminology and Classification*. Washington, D.C.: American Association on Mental Deficiency, 1973.

Haring, N. "Social and Emotional Behavior Disorders." In *Behavior of Exceptional Children*, ed. N. Haring. Columbus: Charles E. Merrill Publishing Co., 1974.

Heber, R. *A Manual on Terminology and Classification in Mental Retardation*, 2nd ed. Monograph Supplement of the *American Journal of Mental Deficiency*, 1961.

Hobbs, N. "Helping Disturbed Children: Psychological and Ecological Strategies." In *Educating Emotionally Disturbed Children*, ed. H. Dupont. New York: Holt, Rinehart & Winston, 1969.

Hobbs, N., ed. *The Futures of Children: Categories, Labels and Their Consequences*, vols. I and II. San Francisco: Jossey-Bass, 1975.

Hollingworth, L. *Children above 180 IQ*. New York: Harcourt, Brace, and World, Inc., 1942.

Hull, F. M., and M. E. Hull. "Children with Oral Communication Disabilities." In *Exceptional Children in the Schools*, 2nd ed., ed. L. M. Dunn. New York: Holt, Rinehart & Winston, 1973.

Kephart, N. *The Slow Learner in the Classroom*. Columbus: Charles E. Merrill Publishing Co., 1971.

Kirk, S. A. *Educating Exceptional Children,* 2nd ed. Boston: Houghton Mifflin, 1972.

Kirk, S. A., and B. Bateman. "Diagnosis and Remediation of Learning Disabilities," *Exceptional Children,* 29 (1962): 72.

Kirk, S., and W. Kirk. *Psycholinguistic Learning Disabilities and Remediation.* Urbana: University of Illinois Press, 1971.

Kirk, S. A., J. J. McCarthy, and W. D. Kirk. *The Illinois Test of Psycholinguistic Abilities,* rev. ed. Urbana: University of Illinois Press, 1968.

MacMillan, D. L. *Mental Retardation in School and Society.* Boston: Little, Brown and Company, 1977.

Marland, S. P. *Education of the Gifted and Talented.* Washington, D.C.: U.S. Office of Education, 1972.

Martin, E. W. *Programs of the Bureau of Education for the Handicapped: U.S. Office of Education. Programs for the Handicapped.* Washington, D.C.: U.S. Department of Health, Education and Welfare, 1970.

Martinson, R. A. *Educational Programs for Gifted Pupils.* Sacramento: California Department of Education, 1961.

_____. "Children with Superior Cognitive Abilities." In *Exceptional Children in the Schools,* 2nd ed., ed. L. M. Dunn. New York: Holt, Rinehart & Winston, 1973.

Masland, R. L. "Mental Retardation." In *Birth Defects,* ed. M. Fishbein. Philadelphia: J. B. Lippincott, 1963.

McConnell, F. "Children with Hearing Disabilities." In *Exceptional Children in the Schools,* 2nd ed., ed. L. M. Dunn. New York: Holt, Rinehart & Winston, 1973.

McIntosh, D. K., and L. M. Dunn. "Children with Major Specific Learning Disabilities." In *Exceptional Children in the Schools,* 2nd ed., ed. L. M. Dunn. New York: Holt, Rinehart & Winston, 1973.

Mercer, J. R. *Labeling the Mentally Retarded.* Berkeley: University of California Press, 1973.

Mumpower, D. L. "Sex Ratios Found in Various Types of Preferred Exceptional Children," *Exceptional Children,* 36 (1970): 621–622.

National Advisory Committee on Handicapped Children. *Special Education for Handicapped Children, First Annual Report.* Washington, D.C.: Department of Health, Education and Welfare, Office of Education, 1968.

Nihira, K., R. Foster, M. Shellhaas, and H. Leland. *AAMD Adaptive Behavior Scale,* Revised. Washington, D.C.: American Association on Mental Deficiency, 1974.

O'Leary, K., and S. O'Leary. *Classroom Management: The Successful Use of Behavior Modification.* New York: Pergamon Press, 1972.

Penrose, L. S. *The Biology of Mental Defect.* New York: Grune and Stratton, 1963.

Peterson, D. L. "Educable Mentally Retarded." In *Behavior of Exceptional Children,* ed. N. G. Haring. Columbus: Charles E. Merrill Publishing Co., 1974.

Polani, P. E. "Chromosome Aberrations and Birth Defects." In *Birth Defects,* ed. M. Fishbein. Philadelphia: J. B. Lippincott, 1963.

Pressey, S. L. "Concerning the Nature and Nurture of Genius," *Scientific Monthly,* 31 (1955): 123–129.

Roach, E. G., and N. C. Kephart. *Purdue Perceptual Motor Survey.* Columbus: Charles E. Merrill Publishing Co., 1966.

Quay, H. C. "The Facets of Educational Exceptionality: A Conceptual Framework for Assessment, Grouping, and Instruction," *Exceptional Children,* 35 (1968): 25–32.

_____. "Dimensions of Problem Behavior and Educational Programming." In *Children against Schools,* ed. P. Graubard. Chicago: Follett Publishing Co., 1969.

Rhodes, W. C. "The Disturbing Child: A Problem of Ecological Management," *Exceptional Children,* 33 (1967): 449–455.

_____. "A Community Participation Analysis of Emotional Disturbance," *Exceptional Children,* 36 (1970): 309–316.

Rhodes, W. C., and M. L. Tracy. *A Study of Child Variance,* Vols. 1 and 2. Ann Arbor: Institute for the Study of Mental Retardation and Related Disabilities, The University of Michigan, 1972.

Safer, D. J., and R. P. Allen. *Hyperactive Children.* Baltimore: University Park Press, 1976.

Schroeder, C., and D. Routh. "The Use of Operant Conditioning to Determine the Vote of Suppression of Hyperactive Behavior in Older vs. Younger Hyperactive Children." (Unpublished Manuscript.) Chapel Hill; Division for Disorders of Development and Learning, University of North Carolina, 1976.

Schultz, E. W., A. Hirshoren, A. Manton, and R. Henderson. "Special Education for the Emotionally Disturbed," *Exceptional Children,* 38 (1971): 313–320.

Soule, D. *Behavior Maturity Check List.* Goldsboro: O'Berry Center, 1973.

Strauss, A., and L. Lehtinen. *Psychopathology of the Brain-injured Child.* New York: Grune and Stratton, Inc., 1947.

Terman, L. M., B. Baldwin, and E. Bronson. *Mental and Physical Traits of a Thousand Gifted Children. Genetic Studies of Genius,* Vol. 1. Stanford: Stanford University Press, 1925.

Terman, L. M., and M. Oden. *The Gifted Child Grows Up.* Stanford: Stanford University Press, 1947.

Torres, S. *A Primer on Individualized Education Programs for Handicapped Children.* Reston, Virginia: The Foundation for Exceptional Children, 1977.

Van Riper, C. *Speech Correction: Principles and Methods,* 5th ed. Englewood Cliffs: Prentice-Hall, 1972.

United States Office of Education. *Estimated Number of Handicapped Children in the United States, 1971–72.* Washington, D.C.: U.S. Office of Education, 1971.

Walker, H. M. *Walker Problem Behavior Identification Checklist.* Los Angeles: Western Psychological Services, 1970.

Walker, H. M., and H. Hops. "Increasing Academic Achievement by Reinforcing Direct Academic Performance and/or Facilitative Nonacademic Responses," *Journal of Educational Psychology,* 68 (1976): 218–225.

Weinstein, L. "Project Re-Ed Schools for Emotionally Disturbed Children: Effectiveness as Viewed by Referring Agencies, Parents, and Teachers," *Exceptional Children,* 35 (1969): 703–711.

Weintraub, F. "Understanding the Individualized Education Program," *Amicus,* March (1977): 23–27.

Wiegerink, R., and R. Simeonson. "Public Schools." In *Mental Retardation and Developmental Difficulties,* Vol. VII, ed. J. Wortis. New York: Brunner-Mazel, Inc., 1975.

Woody, R. H. *Behavioral Problem Children in the Schools.* New York: Appleton-Century-Crofts, 1969.

Wyne, M. D., and P. O'Connor. *Exceptional Children: A Developmental View.* Lexington, Mass.: D. C. Heath and Co., 1979.

Wyne, M. D., and P. Skjei. "The Counselor and Exceptional Pupils: A Critical Review," *Personnel and Guidance Journal,* 48 (1970): 828–835.

Wyne, M. D., and G. B. Stuck. *Rocky Mount (N.C.) City Schools, ESEA Title III, Final Evaluation Report.* Raleigh: State Department of Public Instruction, Division of Development, 1977.

CHAPTER SIX Curriculum Consultation

Jack E. Blackburn
W. Conrad Powell

This chapter addresses problems and processes of curriculum and instruction development. The act of curriculum development involves many processes, including the responsibility of determining curriculum design. A curriculum design includes courses and content to be taught, organization of staff, and organization of time (scheduling).

A curriculum consultant facilitates the selection and development of a curriculum design or designs for a school program. The design takes on meaning when the curriculum components of the design are related to groups of students and to individual students. The importance of relating the curriculum design to students is based upon the following beliefs and assumptions:

1. People learn at different rates and in different ways.
2. Individuals are cherished for their uniqueness as well as for their similarities to other individuals.
3. Schools are human inventions created to nourish individual differences and similarities and to assist students in their affective, cognitive, and psychomotor growth.

4. Curriculum and instruction are the school environment's primary means of providing opportunities for student growth.
5. A student's school experiences become more individualized and meaningful when the school environment offers a wide variety of curriculum and instruction alternatives.
6. Alternatives in curriculum and instruction must be related to the students being served and to the competencies of teachers and other education personnel.
7. Success experiences foster other success experiences; curriculum and instruction should be designed and implemented in such a way that each student has a good chance of being successful each day.

This chapter attempts to provide the curriculum consultant with a basic understanding of the nature of curriculum and the processes of curriculum consultation. The chapter includes discussions of curriculum definition, a conceptual model for curriculum, and the roles of the curriculum consultant.

DEFINING CURRICULUM AND INSTRUCTION

Curriculum and instruction practices should result from reasoned planning. Such planning is usually guided by the consideration of several kinds of questions and concepts. Curriculum thinkers pose both similar and different questions for curriculum conceptualization. These thinkers also have varying perceptions regarding how such questions should be answered.

Table 6.1 identifies conflicting conceptions of the definitions and sources of curriculum based upon the beliefs of twelve recognized curriculum authorities.

An analysis of the definition statements indicates a wide range of viewpoints about the nature and scope of curriculum. Some theorists would have us believe that everything a student experiences in school is a part of the curriculum. Other theorists believe that curriculum considerations are highly specific and must be contained in written documents and plans.

Curriculum and Instruction Definitions Used in This Chapter

"Curriculum and instruction" as used here encompasses many of the beliefs of the theorists cited in Table 6.1. Some of our definitions are similar to and build upon the curriculum and instruction considerations of others.

TABLE 6.1. Selected conceptions of curriculum definitions and sources

Curriculum Authority	Curriculum Definition	Curriculum Sources
Beauchamp	". . . a curriculum is a document containing an organized set of decisions about what shall be taught in a school, or group of schools" (1961, p. 175).	Educational foundations, community characteristics, personalities of persons involved, curriculum experience, the subject matter from disciplines and subjects, and social and cultural values (1968, pp. 113–114).
Bobbitt	"Curriculum is the entire range of experiences, both undirected and directed, concerned in unfolding the abilities of the individual" (1918, p. 43).	Activities of adult life (1924, p. 8), practical experience (1924, p. 34), contemporary society (1924, p. 35), standards set by community (1924, p. 37), and individual learner (1924, p. 42).
Caswell	". . . the school curriculum is held to be composed of all the experiences children have under the guidance of the teachers" (1935, p. 69).	Psychology, philosophy, sociology, and subject matter fields (1935, p. 69).
Goodlad	"A curriculum consists of all those learnings intended for a student or group of students" (1963, p. 25).	Society, learners, subject matter, values (1966, p. 65), subject specialists (1966, p. 68), and conventional wisdom or popular beliefs, customs, et cetera (1966, p. 68).
Hass	"The curriculum is all of the experiences that individual learners have in a program of education whose purpose is to achieve broad goals and related specific objectives, which is planned in terms of a framework of theory and research or past and present professional practice" (1977, p. 5).	"The four bases are social forces, human development, the nature of learning, and the nature of knowledge" (1977, p. 6).
Herrick	"Experiences children have in school: direction, balance emphasis. These experiences	Our society, its institutions, and social processes (1965, p. 4), man's categorized and

TABLE 6.1 (continued)

Curriculum Authority	Curriculum Definition	Curriculum Sources
	also have a subject matter and a process" (1965, p. 28).	preserved knowledge and subject fields (1965, p. 4), the individual to be educated, his nature, needs, and developmental patterns (1965, p. 4), and value referents (1965, p. 10).
Johnson	"[A] curriculum is a structured series of intended learning outcomes" (1967, p. 130).	"1. The needs and interests of the learners, 2. the values and problems of the society and 3. the disciplines or organized subject matter . . . may . . . impose criteria for the selection of curriculum items, but . . . the source of curriculum . . . is the total available culture" (1967, p. 132).
Metcalf	"We shall define curriculum not as 'all the experiences a child or youth has in school' but traditionally as 'the formal course work taken by students' " (1970, p. 359).	"We suggest that the schools incorporate in their curriculum a study of an important social movement, rejection by youth, and that this study emphasize examining, testing, and appraising the major beliefs caught up in this movement" (1970, p. 360).
Saylor	". . . a plan for providing sets of learning opportunities to achieve broad goals and related specific objectives for an identifiable population served by a single school center" (1974, p. 6).	1. Students to be educated, 2. society which provides and operates schools, 3. accumulated knowledge available and feasible for educating students (1974, p. 103).
Smith	"A sequence of potential experiences . . . set up in the school for the purposes of disciplining children and youth in group ways of thinking and acting" (1950, p. 4).	"The curriculum is always, in every society, a reflection of what the people think, feel, believe, and do" (1950, p. 4).

TABLE 6.1 (continued)

Curriculum Authority	Curriculum Definition	Curriculum Sources
Taba	"A curriculum is a plan for learning" (1962, p. 11).	1. Analyses of society and culture (p. 10), 2. studies of the learner and the learning process (p. 10), and 3. analyses of "the nature of knowledge and the specific characteristics and unique contributions of the disciplines from which the content of curriculum is derived" (p. 11). These should "be sifted through certain value criteria . . ." (1962, p. 11).
Tyler	"A curriculum is an educational program" (1967, p. 4).	1. Learners (1950 A, p. 4), 2. contemporary life outside school (1950 A, p. 11), 3. subject specialists (1950 A, p. 16), 4. psychology of learning (1950 A, p. 24), and 5. philosophy (1950 A, p. 22).

The ideas and practices presented in this chapter are based upon the following definitions:

Curriculum consists of all the planned educational activities within the school environment. It is primarily concerned with how the environment is organized, what activities and content are offered to students, and what learning resources are available.

Curriculum development is the process for determining overall school goals, the selection of the appropriate curriculum design or designs for the achievement of these goals, and the development of specific instructional designs to carry out and assess the goals. Development is continuous, and it embodies the concepts of both formative and summative evaluation. Curriculum development takes place during the initial preparation and during revision of a school's curriculum.

Curriculum theory is a set of beliefs that forms the basis for all curriculum decisions. Beliefs are derived from an examination of sources of curriculum, including the learner and learning theory, society, and the disciplines and organization of knowledge.

Curriculum design is derived from a curriculum theory or theories. Designs include specifications of how content and learning experiences will be organized and delivered to students. Such specifications are related to scope and sequence of learning, time and scheduling considerations, teacher organization for instruction, resources needed for instruction, and the location of the instructional setting.

Instructional design is a plan for a specific area of learning or educational activity within the curriculum environment. The plan lists what students are to learn, proposed ways of learning, and means of assessing learning. The instructional design is developed prior to instruction and provides direction and suggested resources for instructional activities. The various instructional designs within a school, taken together, help to make up the school curriculum. Instructional designs might also be referred to as curriculum plans.

Instruction encompasses the interactions and transactions that occur between students and teachers as well as between students and peers, students and community members, and students and other learning resources. It is the implementation of the instructional design.

Individualized curriculum is based upon an instructional design. It occurs in one or a combination of the following ways:

1. a predetermined instructional design developed either commercially or by a local staff, and students matched to the plan based upon their abilities, interests, and learning styles;
2. teacher(s) and student(s) jointly develop an instructional design for an individual student or group of students;
3. students, with teacher guidance, develop their own educational objectives and activities.

Individualized instruction consists of all those activities and processes involved in the actual implementation of the individualized instructional design. Specifically, it means providing for students content and processes at the appropriate times, either through teacher prescription or student choice. Individualized instruction does not necessarily mean that students work alone all the time, nor does it mean that the teacher works with only one student at a time. It can occur when one student works alone or with one student or a group of students. It usually includes some combination of all of these.

A CONCEPTUAL MODEL FOR CURRICULUM AND INSTRUCTION DEVELOPMENT

The proposed model in Figure 6.1 assumes (1) a total school faculty working together to offer the best possible curriculum for its students; and (2) the necessity for someone knowledgeable in the steps of the model to be available

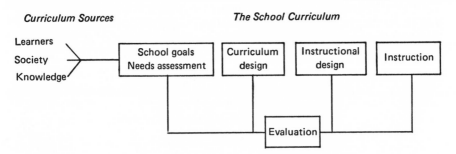

FIGURE 6.1. A conceptual model for curriculum and instruction development

for facilitating the process: that is, the curriculum consultant. The following discussion focuses upon the *content* of the model. The roles of the consultant in the process will be presented at the end of this chapter.

Although the discussion will emphasize total faculty involvement, it should be apparent that the process, with some modifications, can be used with specific departments or grade levels, or individual teachers.

The model suggests that a faculty begins the process of curriculum development by examining beliefs and arriving at mutually agreed upon decisions about (1) the needs of its students, (2) the present and future needs of society, both in terms of the immediate community and the larger society, and (3) the essential knowledge, processes, and skills to be learned, and optimum ways of organizing those for learning.

On the basis of these decisions, the faculty then decides on school goals and conducts a needs assessment to give added direction to the development of the remainder of the process. Once goals for the school are established, the success of the program relies upon the development of appropriate curriculum designs and plans, the implementation of the plans through instructional procedures, and regular evaluation and revision as required.

This process is depicted graphically in Figure 6.1. The development of a model such as this one is both risky and difficult, in the sense that the model cannot convey to the reader all the intricacies and interactions that should, can, and do happen in curriculum and instruction development. Although the component parts appear in a linear pattern, we recognize that all the events suggested by the components will not necessarily occur in the sequence as illustrated.

The following discussion elaborates upon the component parts of the model.

Sources of Curriculum

Curriculum development is a decision-making process. Whoever makes the decisions, whether one person (an administrator, a department head, a teacher) or, preferably, a broad group of people (professionals, lay persons, students), some referrents, some sets of personal and educational beliefs, are used as criteria for choice. Too often, criteria or beliefs are implicit, ill-defined, and inconsistent or contradictory.

Thus one of the first steps in the curriculum development process is to establish a base for decision making, a set of internally consistent beliefs that can be referred to for direction through the remainder of the process. Three distinct areas, or sources, are useful for examination in order to establish such a base: the needs of learners, the needs of society, and the nature and organization of knowledge.*

Needs of learners as a curriculum source is primarily concerned with stages of human growth and development and with ways in which people learn. Questions that might be considered in deriving a set of beliefs are:

1. How should differences and similarities in human growth and development of students be accommodated in schools?
2. What is the importance of the intellectual development of students, and what role should the school assume for this development?
3. What are the stages of development of students — intellectual, physical, and emotional? How can schools best accommodate growth through these stages?
4. How can accommodations be made for variations in learning styles of students?
5. Which learning theories are most effective for accomplishing particular educational aims?
6. What role does the school play in fostering student interests and attitudes and in clarifying students' values?
7. How can the school respond to the student's perceptions of his personal future: for example, career choice, further education, leisure time, parent, individual life-style?

Needs of society as a curriculum source is concerned with the relationship between the school and the society that supports it. Questions for consideration include:

1. How do you decide what to teach as society changes (for example, metric system, women's liberation)? Where should such "new" content be included in the curriculum?
2. What parts of the cultural heritage should be included in the curriculum?

---

*Generally, curriculum theorists agree upon these three sources of curriculum, though some include additional sources.

3. Should schools try to change the society which supports them? If so, in what direction? Who should decide?
4. Will (and should) any government allow one of its institutions to change the status quo of the society?
5. How can schools prepare students for the future, for an unforeseeable society in which changes in job requirements and choices; in mores, customs, and values; in mobility and relationships; indeed in every part of life, have become the only constant?

Organized knowledge as a curriculum source is concerned with:

1. What knowledge is important enough to be included in the curriculum?
2. How can changes in knowledge (and obsolescence) be reflected in the curriculum efficiently and with minimum lag time?
3. How can knowledge best be organized for teaching and learning: for example, chronologically or logically, around certain important concepts and generalizations within a discrete discipline, or with little regard for disciplines or chronology but using student interests or problem areas for organizing?
4. How important are the processes by which certain types of knowledge are discovered? Should these processes be part of the curriculum?

Overall Goals of the School and Needs Assessment

Goals are broad statements of intent. Overall school goals should be derived directly from faculty beliefs and decisions relative to sources of the curriculum. They should be stated in terms of student outcomes (for example, the student will practice good health habits) rather than in terms of what teachers will do or the school will offer. This set of goals is important, since they should provide direction for all curriculum and instruction decisions that follow.

Needs Assessment Too often curriculum development activities occur on the basis of whim, intuition, or expedience rather than on the basis of specific, documented needs; for example, faculty members in a given school might be concerned about growing discipline problems and urge passage of tougher rules and regulations without examining the reasons for the discipline problems. In such a case the proposed remedy might be concerned only with an indicator of the problem (student behavior) rather than with the problem itself, which might be any number of things, such as lack of student involvement in setting behavior standards, or an inappropriate curriculum.

Another type of needs assessment might focus on the discrepancy between school goals and actual curriculum and instruction practices. For example, an overall school goal might be related to the development of communications skills. An assessment could be made to determine the discrepancy between the students' actual skills and the desired skills, and curriculum and instruction practices could be based upon assessment findings. Or a faculty might have a goal related to the development of positive student self-concepts. An analysis could be done to determine the number and appropriateness of instructional activities designed to improve self-concept, and additions or changes be made based upon the analysis.

A needs assessment is designed to pinpoint problems and analyze the discrepancy between an existing state and a preferred state (goal), between "what is" and "what is desired." Ralph Tyler (1950) expressed this idea in relation to learners a generation ago:

> Studies of the learner suggest educational objectives only when the information about the learner is compared with some desirable standards, some conception of acceptable norms, so that the difference between the present condition of the learner and the acceptable norm can be identified. This difference or gap is what is generally referred to as a need.

Steps in the needs assessment process include: (1) determining the area to be assessed and types of appropriate data to be collected (for example, in the area of discipline, one type of datum to be analyzed might be the number of office referrals for disciplinary reasons); (2) collection of data (including finding and/or constructing instruments when appropriate); (3) analysis of data; (4) discrepancy analysis; (5) stating and assigning priorities to statements of needs, based on the discrepancy analysis (for example, there might be need for a reading program capable of significantly reducing the number of students who are reading below grade placement, a need to include in the instructional program more activities and materials designed to improve student self-concepts).

Possible Areas of Assessment   In conducting a needs assessment that will give direction to curriculum development processes, it is important to examine data from a number of areas and from a wide variety of people (for example, parents, students, teachers, administrators). Following is a list (Powell, 1975) of possible types of data which might be collected.

Absenteeism. Look at the average daily attendance report and calculate what percentage of students is absent on an average day. Is it too high? Is it higher for boys than for girls? Is absenteeism a problem with older students or younger students? Is there anything the school could do about it? Is it a serious problem? (If attendance already averages over 90 percent, for example, it will be hard to show much change.)

For final evaluation of your "increase attendance" project, again calculate the percentage of students absent from school on an average day. Or if your goal was to increase attendance among a certain group of students, then look for improvement in that group.

Grades. Count the number of A, B, C, D, and F semester grades given to students. What percentage of the grades are D or F? Are too many being given at certain grade levels, in certain classes, or at certain reading ability levels? Should steps be taken to make the curriculum more appropriate for these students?

Suspensions. Count the number of students suspended during the semester, and the days they lost from school because of suspension. Using the data on the nine-week suspension reports, set up categories for pinpointing *why* students were suspended. Count the number of suspensions in each category. Are too many of the students being suspended in certain categories, or at one grade level, or are suspensions higher at certain times of the year? If so, what could be done about it?

Discipline Referrals. Count the number of discipline slips written on students during the semester, or during a nine-week period. Set up categories from information on discipline slips pinpointing why students were referred (for example, fighting, rudeness, tardiness). Are there too many discipline slips at one grade level, from a few sources, at certain times, or for certain reasons? What patterns do you see, and what could be done about them?

Broken Windows and Vandalism. Is a record kept of how many broken windows have to be replaced per year in the school? How about dollar estimates of damage due to vandalism? These figures can provide a useful index to student morale and attitude toward school. (Allowances should be made for special factors: for example, new construction usually tempts vandalism.) If extensive changes are made in school curriculum, and other evidence points to increased student satisfaction or a better student-teacher relationship, then a record of decreased window breakage and vandalism can be persuasive indicators of changes in student behavior.

Teacher Turnover. Count the number of teachers who left the school during or at the end of last year and had to be replaced. What was the percentage of staff turnover? Was there normal attrition, or was the number too high? If teachers left through job dissatisfaction, is there any way to find out what they were dissatisfied with? Could the school do anything about it?

Curriculum Choice. Count the number of different courses being offered to students in each subject area. Consider each grade level and each curriculum area. How much real choice do students have in course selection? Should the curriculum be more diversified? How could the number of different courses offered to students be increased?

Student Vocational Plans. How many students in your school are able to outline definite vocational or further educational plans by the first semester of their senior year? Could you set up a routine way of counting them? Are many students worried or apathetic about career plans? If so, what could the school do to help them with these decisions?

Student Involvement. Count the total number of students involved in all extracurricular activities. Calculate the average number of activities per student by dividing this number by student enrollment. Is lack of participation in activities a problem in the school? If so, is there anything the school could do about it?

Student Leadership. Count the number of seats in student government to be filled by student vote. Then count the number of students running for these seats. How many candidates are there for how many seats? How many candidates are there for how many positions on the school newspaper staff, the cheerleader squad, a talent contest? What do these figures tell you about student leadership and its development? Do the same students seem to take leadership positions most of the time? If so, could your school plan more ways to encourage student participation in these activities, or diversify the types of activities offered? If you don't know how students feel about participating in activities, could you ask the student government to design a student poll to find out?

Achievement Scores. Count the number of students in your school whose standardized reading or math scores fall below the fiftieth percentile. Are there too many of them? What kinds of strategies could the school use to improve students' skills?

Select a random sample of about 10 percent of your students, or at least 100 students. Make a list of their names and standardized reading and math scores. How many of them fall below the tenth percentile? Between the tenth and nineteenth percentile? Between the twentieth and twenty-ninth? . . . and so on up to the ninety-ninth percentile. After plans to improve students' skills have been in operation for a full year, look at the same students' new scores. Again count the number that fall below the tenth percentile. On the whole, did scores change more among low- or high-scoring students, or among average students? Can you tell which groups did or did not benefit from the first year of innovations?

If you are quite serious about evaluating your school program by using scores on a standardized achievement test, start with the youngest grade in your school this year. Make sure these students are given a standardized test this year, and that the same test is used next year. (If the CTBS eighth-grade test is used this year, then the CTBS ninth-grade test should be used next year, and so on.) Your plan might be to have the same students tested every year with the same type of test, from the time they enter your school until they graduate. (Discard all scores of students who leave before graduation.) This will tell you how this group of students changed as they went through your school. Ideally, each grade should be tested every year, as improvement is likely to occur only in small increments over a period of years.

To be on the safe side, get some advice from a testing or evaluation consultant before you start your innovations. With achievement tests, baseline measures are essential.

Discrepancy Analysis If needs assessment data are to be helpful in curriculum development they must be analyzed in terms of a preferred or ideal state. The data will provide a picture of the present state, or *what is*. Staff beliefs and school goals will provide the preferred state, or *what is desired*. An analysis of the discrepancy between the two provides direction for the curriculum development process. When placed in priority order, the discrepancies further provide a sequence of activities for the process.

The results of a discrepancy analysis might be presented in a form such as the following (Winecoff and Powell, 1975):

What Is (data)	What Is Desired (beliefs, goals)	Discrepancy (needs)	Rank Order of Needs

Curriculum Design

The school curriculum is based upon the overall goals of a school, and it is exemplified through the selection and implementation of a curriculum design or designs consistent with the overall school goals. This suggests that a school curriculum might accommodate more than one design. In reality, probably all school curricula are made up of several designs. The inclusion of alternative designs within a total curriculum is consistent with the contemporary emphasis upon individual student growth and the cultural diversity of student populations. According to Taba (1962):

> Curriculum design is a statement which identifies the elements of the curriculum, states what their relationships are to each other, and indicates the principles of organization and the requirements of that organization for the administrative conditions under which it is to operate. A design ... needs to be supported with and to make explicit a curriculum theory

which establishes the sources to consider and the principles to apply. Both are needed in making consistent decisions about the curriculum.

The curriculum design that has been prevalent since the time when people became conscious of curriculum has been the *separate subjects* design. This mode of organizing curriculum is still in practice in many schools today, especially at the secondary school level. Such a design is organized to stress and present subjects such as mathematics, physical education, communication, art, homemaking, and so forth as separate, discrete subjects.

Various attempts have been made to correlate, merge, interrelate, or combine subjects in designs that attempt to eliminate the concept of subject matter as separate and discrete. Such designs focus upon relationships in and among subject areas and are referred to as *broad field* designs. For example, subject matter from geography, history, economics, and political science has been combined and called social studies. Or some curriculum designers have chosen to combine the content from English and social studies to help students see relationships such as the influence of an historical setting upon literature. Another example of this type of design is the combination of all subject areas offered in an elementary school to bear upon one topic. The American Indian might be the topic. All other subject areas are studied in relation to the American Indian.

Bold designs have been offered that begin with problems and interests that students express as being important to them. Traditional subject matter is studied only in relation to interests and concerns expressed by students. Typically this design is referred to as *core curriculum.*

In the 1950s and 1960s the *structure of the disciplines* design emerged. The concern of this design was to identify key ideas or major concepts of disciplines, such as history, English, botany, and economics, and to arrange the concepts in such a manner that they could be taught effectively at various grade levels. In a structure of the disciplines design, subject matter is selected only to elaborate upon concepts and generalizations which form the structure of the disciplines. Another essential aspect of such a design is to help students approach a given discipline in much the same way as a "scholar" in the discipline would approach his work. These students learn how to "discover" knowledge in a given discipline. BSCS Biology and CHEM Study Chemistry are examples of this particular design.

The late 1960s and the 1970s witnessed a trend toward *humanistic curriculum* designs. The humanistic design is represented by such practices as "open classrooms," "student-centered programs," "community-experience-based curriculum," "the new humanities," and "storefront schools." The humanistic approach reflects the concern that discipline-centered and subject-centered curriculums can and often do become dehumanizing. This is to say that the major emphasis of the subject and discipline designs is not with human beings, but with the content to be taught by teachers and learned by students.

Reflecting some contemporary educators', politicians', and parents' heightened concern for improved educational practice, the *performance* or *competency-based* design is characterized by specific performance objectives, specific sequential learning activities, and criterion-referenced tests to measure achievement of objectives. This approach can be used in every subject matter area, but it is particularly suited to the skills and specialized-training areas such as the language arts and to vocational and technical subjects.

A seventh view of curriculum design emphasizes *cognitive processes:*

> This approach to curriculum is primarily concerned with the requirement of intellectual operations. It refers only rarely to curriculum content, focusing, instead, on the how rather than the what of education. Aiming to develop a sort of technology of the mind, it sees the central problem of curriculum as that of sharpening the intellectual processes and developing a set of cognitive skills that can be applied to learning virtually anything [Eisner and Vallance, 1974].

Several educators have attempted to categorize curriculum design types. For example, one might categorize curriculum designs according to discipline types or interdisciplinary types. Subject matter and structure of the discipline designs would fall under the discipline types. Core curriculum and the new humanistic centered designs would fit into the interdisciplinary types.

Others might analyze curriculum designs according to cognitive and affective emphases. Cognitive designs begin with predetermined material such as disciplines to be learned by students (subject matter and concepts from the organized disciplines of knowledge). In contrast, affective designs have as their starting points the concerns, feelings, values, and interests of students as human beings.

Instructional Design

The term *instructional design* refers to intentions of what students will learn, proposed ways of learning, and means of assessing learning. Instructional designs are developed prior to instruction and provide direction and suggested resources for instructional activity. While curriculum design refers to the overall school organization, instructional designs are developed for specific classes, students, or courses. Activities involved in instructional design include selection of content, sequencing of the content in the order in which it will be taught, specification of instructional objectives, and development of preassessment procedures, learning alternatives and resources, and postassessment procedures for each objective. Table 6.2 illustrates the relationship between instructional design, which precedes instruction, and actual instructional activity.

The next section of this chapter elaborates upon a concept of instructional design.

TABLE 6.2. Steps in implementing instructional designs

Educational Goals of the School

Instructional Design (provides direction for planned educational activities)	Instructional Processes (implement instructional design)			
	Preassessment (diagnosis): determines what student knows in relation to objectives student interests, background, experience student learning styles	Prescription: selection and choice of learning alternatives for students to engage in, based upon informal/formal assessment	Learning Alternatives: student engages in alternative instructional modes, e.g., contracts learning packages learning centers independent study which contain specific activities, using self-paced materials role playing group work lectures, speeches trips projects simulations peer teaching textbooks	Postassessment (student evaluation): determines student achievement in relation to objectives student reactions to and attitudes toward the instructional processes
Selection of content Sequencing content Specifying objectives Designing preassessment Designing learning alternatives Designing postassessment				

Selection of Content   Curriculum development must start with general goals and move toward more specific plans for various curriculum and subject areas, grade levels, and distinct groups of students. As a curriculum is planned for specified groups and individual students, certain themes, topics, concepts, skills, interests, problems, and processes will be identified for those students to inquire about, discover, study, learn, and enjoy. This process results in a clear specification of the content of a curriculum area. It occurs before instruction takes place, sometimes far in advance (for example, in a summer curriculum planning workshop for teachers) and sometimes in a classroom, with students, immediately preceding instruction.

There are numerous sources for deriving the content to be taught. Appropriateness of any of these sources depends upon school goals, staff attitudes regarding student involvement in curriculum planning, and the specific content area. Some sources for determining content are located outside the school environment. They include curriculum guides developed by state departments, universities, or district-wide committees, commercially prepared curriculum materials, and textbooks, which traditionally have been the primary sources of content to be taught. Within the school environment a teacher or teachers might assess the learning needs of the student body and community expectations for the school and select content designed to meet those needs and expectations. Selection might be done by the staff or it might be done by students and staff planning together.

Course Sequence   After the desired content is identified, it is necessary in some areas of instruction to arrange the content in the sequential order in which it is to be learned. This is more likely to be true in skill areas such as reading, mathematics, industrial arts, typing, home economics, physical education, and certain parts of science courses than in humanities, language arts, and social sciences. In the latter category, students might determine their own individual sequence, but in a science course, for example, a student probably should demonstrate proficiency in measurement before conducting laboratory experiments with chemicals.

Instructional Objectives   Objectives are a part of the curriculum design; more than any other part of the design they provide direction for educational intentions and instructional activities. As an integral part of the curriculum, objectives provide guidelines for making decisions about the selection of student activities: that is, they provide a basis on which to assess students and to suggest appropriate prescriptions, learning alternatives, assignments, or other educational activities.

Objectives, as a part of instructional designs

reflect the desired intentions and outcomes of a school's faculty and students;

are based upon the beliefs and values a school faculty holds regarding students, the society and the world in which we live, the nature and sources of subject matter, how human beings learn, and other areas that affect curriculum and instruction decisions;

can be developed and written by teachers and teachers and students, or they can be secured from objective banks;

should be based upon a humanistic approach: that is, objectives should reflect what is important for and needed by a particular student or group of students and should be written to include opportunities for growth in the affective, cognitive, and psychomotor areas of learning;

can be designed and arranged so that students can choose from alternative objectives;

provide direction for instructional activities. Deciding on appropriate materials, resources, and learning alternatives for students becomes an easier task if the question "Will it help to achieve the objectives?" is asked about each possibility;

communicate to students what is expected of them, thus eliminating an element of game-playing from the instructional process. No longer do students have to decide what to study by guessing what is expected of them, and no longer do they have to wonder what is really important in a subject or instructional sequence;

help teachers set levels of classroom performance, based on student abilities, ages, and content or subject areas, and then hold themselves accountable for those standards. Specifying instructional objectives provides a basis for a teacher to analyze continually both the curriculum plan and instructional processes and make revisions accordingly. Without specific intent or direction, it is difficult to determine which instructional processes and materials are helping students achieve and which are not;

help teachers to reflect on the worth and feasibility of content to be taught and the appropriateness of instructional processes for teaching that content;

improve procedures for assessing student growth. In a well-written instructional objective, assessment criteria and form are either stated or clearly implied; thus assessment procedures flow directly from instructional processes;

provide motivation. Many students work much better when there are clear objectives with an end in sight. The feeling of accomplishment that accompanies the completion of objectives is often enough motivation to cause a student to pursue other objectives or move on to other activities;

help manage student progress in an individualized classroom. Simple individualized progress charts can be constructed to show quickly the objective on which a given student is working. Such charts are particularly helpful in grouping for instruction because the teacher can readily determine which students are working on the same objectives.

Types of Instructional Objectives. Instructional objectives are typically written to represent three domains of learning:

1. The *cognitive* domain consists of behaviors and processes related to intellectual growth. The behaviors range from simple recall of information to more abstract and complex problem solving. When designing instruction it is important to insure that objectives are developed for all levels of cognitive processes.
2. The *affective* domain categorizes the more personal dimensions of human growth, such as values, attitudes, feelings, interests, and appreciations. Affective behaviors range from compliance with rules or expectations to the development of a personal value system.
3. The *psychomotor* domain refers to physical behaviors and skills: for example, typing, running, sewing, hitting a baseball, talking, and handwriting. Psychomotor learning might be reflected in improved speed, coordination, strength, and consistency.

The identification of the three learning domains is a convenient way of organizing objectives and learning experiences for planning, analysis, and evaluation. Such classification does not mean that an individual's learning occurs in only one domain at a time; nor does it mean that the domains do not interact with and depend upon each other. Rather, learning almost never occurs in only one domain, even though the primary objective for a learning experience might be either cognitive, affective, or psychomotor.

For example, when engaged in learning experiences based upon objectives related to the presidency and impeachment, the student extends intellectual processes and gains cognitive knowledge; clarifies and expresses values, beliefs, and feelings about impeachment; and develops psychomotor skills by writing, talking, illustrating, or dramatizing knowledge and feelings related to the presidency and impeachment.

Similarly, when a student is called upon to create a product using an art form, his values and interests are called into play, his knowledge of a subject is needed, and his psychomotor skills are required to create the artistic product.

Even though each of the domains interacts with and depends on the others, there is value in gaining knowledge about each domain and identifying objectives representative of the domains. Such activities facilitate and encourage a conscious effort to include growth in all domains.

Component Parts of Instructional Objectives. Correctly stated objectives that provide direction for instructional processes:

1. *Specify observable behaviors* (for example, the student lists, performs, chooses, completes, sings, creates, draws).
2. *Specify the conditions under which the behavior will be observed* (for example, in not more than five minutes, in a simulated recital, upon completion of this contract, when given mood music and asked to write, when given a graph to plot, after viewing a favorite television show).
3. *Specify performance level, standards, or evaluation criteria* (for example, the student writes a grammatically correct paragraph, chooses classical over popular music at least half the time, answers seven questions correctly, creates a script and makes a movie according to criteria developed in class, identifies all locations given on a map, demonstrates two out of three swimming strokes, takes apart and puts back together a small engine in the time allotted).

Instructional objectives provide direction for all remaining parts of the instructional design.

Learning Alternatives and Resources

Learning alternatives and resources are the proposed educational activities and materials from which students and teachers choose in order to achieve instructional objectives or accomplish educational plans. Alternatives help to promote the learning of concepts, themes, topics, and skills and to clarify values, interests, attitudes, and personal goals. More specifically, learning alternatives are : statements that suggest purposeful educational activity for students. These statements include proposals of what a student is to do, how he is to do it, and what can be done with results or products. Alternatives are usually written prior to instruction, as part of the instructional design, and selection of specific activities for students from the alternatives follows, based upon preassessment of particular students and/or student choice.

An instructional design must include a variety of learning alternatives to facilitate student growth. It should provide for differences in preferred learning styles, in backgrounds, and in student interests. Well-defined, varied, and multiple learning alternatives suitable for specific groups of students are major determinants of a successful classroom instructional program. All too often teachers and students create or select alternatives that have not been well planned. It seems important that some general criteria be established for recommending or selecting alternatives. Even though the selection will depend upon the purposes to be served, some general criteria apply to the creation and selection of alternatives, regardless of purposes.

Six criteria are suggested for designing learning alternatives:

1. Are the alternatives designed for individuals with varying interests, learning styles, and levels of ability?
2. Are the learning alternatives likely to help students accomplish the objectives for which they are designed?
3. Are the alternatives explained fully and concretely enough so that they can be used by students?
4. Are there alternatives available for small group activity as well as individual activity?
5. Do the alternatives provide for the continuation and reinforcement of desired basic skills?
6. Do the alternatives include all essential information for the student, including:
   a. *what to do* (read, construct, write, draw, dramatize, listen, view);
   b. *where to find information and what media to use* (read three books in the classroom library, construct a model of a stage, write his or her feelings about ecology, draw a scale model of the United Nations, dramatize scenes from a favorite story or play, view the film on how to play basketball);
   c. *what to do with any products or results from the alternative* (place the student's chart on the classroom bulletin board, prepare and present a puppet show to the class depicting his or her findings, display his or her model in the school library).

Summary Statements about Learning Alternatives

1. Learning alternatives are created to promote purposeful educational activity for students as they enjoy and learn more about a concept, theme, topic, or skill.
2. Many alternatives are needed for students and teachers to choose from in order to maximize individualization.
3. Both teachers and students can create learning alternatives. Teachers develop alternatives as a part of an instructional design and also develop alternatives as needed during instruction. Students create alternatives in planning and learning situations.
4. Alternative statements should be fully developed and should enable the individual student to know the intent of and the procedures for completion of the alternative.
5. Alternatives can be created and developed for all ages and levels of ability. Students of some ages and ability levels will require careful explanation of the requirements and intent of the alternative.
6. Learning alternatives are designed to accommodate curriculum intentions and will reflect affective, cognitive, and psychomotor areas of learning.

Pre- and Postassessment

Pre- and postassessment are the parts of instructional design that determine student knowledge, skills, needs, interests, values, learning styles, progress, achievement, and performance. Preassessment facilitates the development and revision of curriculum plans for students, and postassessment enables a student and teacher to determine progress and whether or not objectives have been attained.

There are two major categories of preassessments. First there is a general pre-assessment, which usually occurs near the beginning of the school year. The purposes are to determine a student's overall knowledge of and attitude toward a subject area; to assess student interests, goals, and learning styles; and to determine student proficiency in any prerequisite skills needed for successful completion of an area of study: for example, reading level, safety rules for laboratory or shop work.

Second is a more specific assessment which is usually done before the introduction of a new unit or topic of study. Specific preassessment is designed to determine what a student already knows in relation to the objectives of a curriculum plan and to select and/or develop objectives and learning alternatives from curriculum plans for individual students or groups of students.

Postassessment occurs after instruction and is designed to determine the student's achievement of an objective or set of objectives; to enable the student and teacher to select other learning alternatives to help the student achieve objectives not yet attained; and to inform interested parties of a student's growth and progress.

Assessment Procedures. The following suggested procedures can be used in both pre- and postassessment activities. Determination of how to use the means will depend upon teacher/student purposes. For example, standardized test results can be used to determine what a student already knows (preassessment) or to determine what a student has achieved following instruction; role playing can provide information about student attitudes and knowledge, which can be either for prescription (preassessment) or for determining progress (postassessment).

1. Standardized tests
2. Teacher-made diagnostic tests (pre- and postassessment)
3. Observation of student behavior
4. Anecdotal records
5. Sociograms
6. Role playing
7. Model building
8. Demonstration of skill or performance

9. Values-clarification activities
10. Self-assessment forms
11. Group work assessment forms
12. Essays and creative writing
13. Conducting experiments
14. Personal journals

Implementing Instructional Designs through Instructional Processes

Instructional processes are the educational activities involved in implementing the instructional design in actual classroom environments. These processes and educational activities encompass the interactions and transactions that occur between and among the students and the teacher(s), students and peers, students and community persons, students and other educational personnel, and students and media and materials. Instructional processes include activities related to preassessment, prescription, engaging in learning alternatives, and postassessment.

The primary mechanism for going from the instructional design (intent) to instructional processes (student experiences) is known as prescription — the process of choosing, selecting, or assigning objectives and learning alternatives to students. Prescription is based upon the preassessment of students.

Prescription is intended to make possible the best relationship between an individual student and an instructional design. The act of prescribing involves choosing and creating appropriate activities from learning alternatives for students. The teacher prescribes for individual students, and for groups of students when there is a common need. Some individualized approaches provide for student self-prescription. Prescription can occur during individual or small group conferences. It might also be done through the use of classroom management activities such as prescription sheets and records, student folders, assignment boards' and students' classroom study and activity schedules.

The prescribing of learning alternatives is the heart of the instructional process. Students have either assessed themselves or have been assessed, instructional objectives to be accomplished have been identified, and selections have been made from learning alternatives. Now the student begins the pursuit of learning, understanding, and appreciating a concept, theme, topic, skill or other personal interests. Students will read, draw, write, discuss, construct, report, interview, figure, experiment, plan, dramatize, and listen. They will also use contracts, learning packages, media, peer teaching, learning centers, independent study, textbooks, self-paced materials, role playing, group work, trips, projects, and simulations. The success of any curriculum development process is directly dependent upon the appropriateness of the prescriptions for individual students.

Evaluation of the Curriculum and Instructional Processes

Evaluation is distinguished from assessment in that it focuses on the curriculum and instruction program, while assessment focuses on student performance. Evaluation procedures should be designed to determine the overall effectiveness of curriculum plans and their implementation through instructional activities. More specifically, curriculum evaluation is concerned with such questions as:

1. Is there congruence between curriculum plans and school goals?
2. Do instructional designs communicate intent? Are they specific? Do they have the necessary components?
3. Are they internally consistent (that is, do objectives flow from goals; do resources and planned activities relate to objectives)?
4. Do curriculum plans (either commercial or staff-developed) conform to design specifications, that is, do they do what is expected/needed?

Evaluation of instruction focuses on areas such as:

1. Congruence between instructional activities and the instructional design;
2. Appropriateness of instructional activities and resources for specified students and teachers;
3. Conformity to design specification, that is, does instruction accomplish objectives?
4. Feasibility of implementation: for example, are specified resources readily available?

Table 6.3 illustrates the concepts of curriculum and instruction evaluation as used here.

ROLES OF THE CONSULTANT

The curriculum consultant is primarily one who helps others (school staff) specify what they would like to accomplish, determine the most feasible means for accomplishing their desired outcomes, and determine implementation procedures and procedures for evaluating and revising programs and curricular plans.

More specifically, the consultant provides leadership in the following areas.

1. *Assessing.* What is the present situation? What do faculty, students, and the community desire, both in terms of programs and student outcomes? What teacher skills and other resources are available?

Finding answers to these and related questions often involves helping a staff identify beliefs from curriculum sources (learners, society, knowledge), specify goals based on those beliefs, and analyze the existing curriculum in relation to those goals. It also means providing expertise in helping assess students' strengths and weaknesses, through means ranging from standardized tests to informal observations.

2. *Planning.* Once goals have been established and discrepancies between what exists and what is desired are identified, then specific planning is called for. Do new materials need to be developed and/or bought? Is in-service training required? If so, who will do it? Who will be involved? Where and when will it occur? Ideally the consultant only helps with the planning process, as opposed to doing the actual planning, since there is a greater likelihood of someone (for example, a member of the faculty) carrying out his or her own plans than of carrying out those developed by someone else. In addition, the more specific the plans are, the better chance that they will be completed. Thus, for any needed activity, it is usually helpful to have a staff specify precisely *what* is to be done, *who* is to be responsible, and *when* the activity must be completed.

3. *Coordinating and Communicating.* The process of curriculum development requires a great deal of coordination with various people and agencies. If parents and students are to be involved in the planning process, then meetings must be planned and scheduled. Often it is desirable to involve the state department of education, and necessary to inform and/or involve the school district's central office staff and the school board. Universities often have resources available, but their utilization must be coordinated with other agencies and people and must be consistent with school needs.

If parents and other community members are not to be involved in the process of curriculum development, then effort must be made to communicate as fully as possible the nature of and rationale for any contemplated changes. Many excellent educational innovations have been killed because the community was not adequately informed of them, and therefore would not support them.

4. *Implementing.* Once curriculum plans have been made, careful attention must be paid to the steps required for successful implementation. Has thorough orientation for all persons involved occurred? Are all necessary materials available? Have time, space, staff, and other requirements been met? Is the procedure for implementation orderly and systematic? Is it gradual enough to prevent overwhelming any persons involved? Have all training requirements been met (that is, can the staff do what is expected of them in new programs)?

The curriculum consultant usually is not involved directly in the implementation stage; classroom teachers usually have most of the responsibility for implementation. Nonetheless, making sure that adequate preparation has been made is a vital function, and one that logically falls on the consultant. Often it is helpful, and possible, to get a staff to chart the steps necessary for successful implementation (for example, order materials, schedule workshops, hold open house to inform parents) and to check those off as they are completed.

TABLE 6.3. Steps in evaluating curriculum and instruction

Purpose	Suggested Procedures	When Implemented
To determine if school goals are consistent with the educational beliefs of parents, students, and staff	Questionnaire to each group for rank-ordering sets of beliefs	Yearly
	Meetings of representatives of each group to analyze and revise school goals	Self-study period for accreditation
	Accreditation and self-study reports	
To determine if school goals, instructional designs, and school organization (for example, scheduling, grouping), are consistent.	Principal and faculty curriculum committee analyze program, recommend needed changes, and work with staff on implementation	Ongoing
To determine if instructional designs meet needs and expectations	Examine achievement test scores	Yearly
	Develop system, including target dates and persons responsible, for monitoring implementation steps: for example, are materials ordered on time? Has necessary staff training occurred? Are facilities ready?	Continual monitoring
	Follow-up studies of students: for example, do they have job skills? Do they succeed in college? Do they participate in democratic processes?	Ongoing
	Examine records: for example, are there fewer dropouts? Is there a reduction in vandalism? Is there a reduction in absenteeism?	Ongoing

To determine if instruction is appropriate and accomplishes objectives	Examine learning alternatives to determine if they are clear, varied, consistent with intent of objective(s)	As developed
	Observe students to determine which alternatives are chosen, which are of no interest	Ongoing
	Administer questionnaire (oral or written) to students to determine feelings about instructional processes, materials, and learning alternatives.	At the end of units of work
	Record percent of students able to accomplish objectives	Ongoing

5. *Analyzing.* Once the process of implementation has begun it is important to help a staff observe and analyze that process. Did all major activities occur on schedule? Was anything forgotten? Do new materials conform to specification (for example, appropriate reading level)? The primary role of the consultant as analyst is that of helping a staff look out for possible trouble spots and having, or quickly preparing, contingency plans for any problems. Often problem areas can be corrected quickly if observed, analyzed, and treated when they first occur.

A second major function of the consultant as analyst is helping teachers analyze classroom procedures. If a trusting relationship has been established between the consultant and the teacher, the consultant might be asked to come and observe a new activity or instructional process in order to provide an objective reaction.

6. *Evaluating.* The consultant should help a staff look at two functions of evaluation: process and final product. Are activities occurring on schedule? Are they accomplishing what they were designed to accomplish? Do interim achievement (and other) checks suggest that final objectives are likely to be met? What revisions in the plans need to be made? Then, did the staff reach the "what is desired" state? Much of the evaluation activity at this stage will be to repeat the collection and analysis of data from the needs assessment step. For example, if needs assessment data showed that 10 percent of the students in a school dropped out annually, and the faculty felt that no more than 2 percent should drop out, then dropout figures would be examined again at the end of the program to see if the desired state had been reached (interim, or process, checks might be made also to see if progress is being made).

Helping a staff decide on needed evaluation data and means for collecting those data (appropriate tests, records, inventories, surveys) is an important consultative function. Once data are collected and analyzed, the consultant's role, in a sense, goes back to the beginning of the process; that is, of helping a staff make needed curriculum revisions. Thus evaluative data serve two functions: a check on program effectiveness and a guide for further curriculum development activity.

REFERENCES

Beauchamp, G. A. *Curriculum Theory.* Wilmette: The Kagg Press, 1961.
_____. *Curriculum Theory,* 2nd ed. Wilmette: The Kagg Press, 1968.
Bloom, B. S., ed. *Taxonomy of Educational Objectives. The Classification of Educational Goals. Handbook I: Cognitive Domain.* New York: David McKay Company, 1956.
Bobbitt, F. *The Curriculum.* Boston: Houghton Mifflin, 1918.
_____. *How to Make a Curriculum.* Boston: Houghton Mifflin, 1924.

Caswell, H. L., and D. S. Campbell. *Curriculum Development.* New York: American Book, 1935.

Eisner, E. W., and E. Vallance, eds. *Conflicting Conceptions of Curriculum.* Berkeley: McCutchan Publishing Corp., 1974.

Goodlad, J. I. *Planning and Organizing for Teaching.* Washington, D.C.: National Education Association of the United States, 1963.

Goodlad, J. I., R. Von Stoephasius, and M. F. Klein. *The Changing School Curriculum.* New York: The Fund for the Advancement of Education, 1966.

Hass, G. *Curriculum Planning,* 2nd ed. Boston: Allyn and Bacon, Inc., 1977.

Herrick, V. A. *Strategies of Curriculum Development.* Ed. J. B. McDonald, D. W. Anderson, and F. B. May. Columbus: Charles E. Merrill Publishing Co., 1965.

Johnson, M., Jr. "Definitions and Models in Curriculum Theory," *Educational Theory,* 17 (1967): 127–140.

Krathwohl, D. R., B. S. Bloom, and B. B. Masia. *Taxonomy of Educational Objectives. The Classification of Educational Goals. Handbook II: Affective Domain.* New York: David McKay Company, 1964.

Metcalf, L. E., and M. P. Hunt. "Relevance and the Curriculum," *Phi Delta Kappan,* 51 (1970): 358–361.

Powell, W. C. *Changing Schools: A Model for Statewide Change in Public Education.* Columbia: The University of South Carolina, 1975.

Saylor, J. G., and W. M. Alexander. *Planning Curriculum for Schools.* New York: Holt, Rinehart & Winston, 1974.

Smith, B. O., W. O. Stanley, and J. H. Shores. *Fundamentals of Curriculum Development.* Yonkers-on-Hudson: World Book Co., 1950.

Taba, H. *Curriculum Development: Theory and Practice.* New York: Harcourt, Brace, & World, 1962.

Tyler, R. W. *Basic Principles of Curriculum and Instruction.* Chicago: University of Chicago Press, 1950.

Tyler, R. W., R. Gagne, and M. Scriven. *Perspectives of Curriculum Evaluation.* Chicago: Rand McNally & Co., 1967.

Winecoff, H. L., and W. C. Powell. *Focus: Seven Steps to Community Involvement in Educational Problem-Solving.* Midland: Pendell Publishing, 1975.

CHAPTER SEVEN Consulting with Students

This chapter will be a rather brief journey into what is a relatively uncharted area: student consultation. To be sure, consultants are increasingly aware that students can be helpful in their efforts to facilitate the development of other students. However, most of the writing to date has focused upon preparing students to act in a peer-counseling role. Kern and Kirby (1971) reported that children who had been involved in groups involving counselors on the one hand and peer helpers on the other were perceived as making gains, as indicated by teacher ratings on the Walker Problem Identification Checklist. It is important that the children in the peer helper group made greater gains than those in the groups led by counselors. In an earlier study Vriend (1969) reported that high-performing inner-city adolescents assisted low-performing adolescents to increase classroom skills, raise academic achievement, and raise their career aspirations through peer-counseling activities. Mosher and Sprinthall (1971) also indicated that peer counseling had helped students to grow psychologically through group activities, although neither these authors nor Vriend compared peer counseling to counselor-led activities. Schmitt and Furniss (1975), in a study similar in some respects to those reported by Mosher and Sprinthall and Vriend, reported that high-school-age counselors made a significant and positive impact upon teacher ratings of the misbehavior of children.

In two slightly different types of studies Briskin and Anderson (1973) reported two successful case studies where students had been used as contingency managers, and Leibowitz and Rhoads (1974) found that adolescents could be trained to make empathic responses. They concluded that adolescents may be potentially helpful in the counseling relationship.

Varenhorst (1974, p. 272) has outlined a program for training peer counselors. Her recommendation follows:

I. Communications skills (4 weeks)
   A. Verbal one-to-one conversation
   B. Behavioral communication (groups of three)
   C. Communication with small groups of peers who are strangers
II. Decision making applied to working on common problems (4 weeks)
   A. Family difficulties
   B. Peer relationships
   C. School problems (being a new student, cliques, and so on)
   D. Health (drugs, physical handicaps, and so on)
III. Ethics and strategies of counseling (4 weeks)
   A. What is counseling?
   B. Potential resources for peer counselors
   C. Limitations and potentials of peer counselors' role
   D. Getting started, confidentiality, and records

Frank, Ferdinand, and Bailey (1975) have also written regarding the training of peer group counselors, but were somewhat less explicit than Varenhorst. However, they cite one reference, *Peer Counseling Handbook,* edited by G. W. Kranzow (1973), which may be of use to consultants moving into this area.

Finally, Brown (1974), writing about the impact of a broader group on helpers, paraprofessionals, reported that the evidence generally supports using them. However, he enumerated a number of concerns about using any type of helper who is less than fully qualified. One of these, which would be of little concern when considering using students in a helping role, is a concern about power struggles that might result between the two groups: professionals and paraprofessionals. Perhaps a more serious concern has to do with the harm that might result from the use of minimally prepared, unsophisticated helpers, whether they be used as counselors or consultants. Brown (1974) goes on to indicate that the evidence is sufficient to indicate that while this should be a concern, the data would tend to minimize it.

The reader may at this point be wondering why the emphasis upon peer counseling and the rise of paraprofessionals in a chapter designed to focus on consultation. As was stated at the outset, consulting with students is a relatively unexplored area and thus little literature has been developed in this area. The purposes of the foregoing have been (1) to show that consultants are interested in expanding their services through the use of students, (2) to provide some empirical basis for the use of students, and (3) to present some of the issues that have arisen regarding the rise of nonprofessionals in helping roles.

THE STUDENT AS CONSULTEE

Consulting with students is conducted for the same purpose as is parent or teacher consultation: that is, to enable students to facilitate the personal growth and development of other students. The process may be initiated by either the consultant or the student and follows the same steps. These steps, which have been listed earlier, are relationship, information taking and diagnosis, goal setting, selecting strategies, and evaluation. The outcomes of the process are expected to be an improvement in the functioning of the target student and an ability on the part of the student to assist other students with similar problems in the future.

Student consultation can be conducted either individually or in groups. These types of consultation procedure have much the same advantages and disadvantages as those listed for teachers, with one major difference. The school environment provides a number of intact groups, such as clubs or even entire classes, that can be involved in the consultation relationship. Let us look at some of the approaches that might be used with these larger groups.

Class Conferences

Techniques for assisting entire classes to facilitate the personal growth of students in that class have been described earlier by Glasser (1969) and Brown (1970). Approaches designed specifically to facilitate psychological growth are generally classified under the "catchall" rubric of psychological education, however. In these meetings the consultant meets with a class, helps them identify specific problems, helps them to understand the nature of the problems by learning psychological principles, assists the class to set goals, and then assists the class members to evaluate the outcomes of their efforts. Let us look step-by-step at the class conference.

First Conference The format of the first class conference will vary according to the age of the participants. With younger children it is suggested that the conference begin with a milling exercise such as that described by Zide (1973). This essentially involves instructing pupils to behave as they would normally in free play. Usually students are inhibited during the first few minutes of this activity, particularly if the teacher is present. However, once they see that they are going to be allowed freedom, they display a variety of behaviors. These behaviors, both positive and negative, can then be used as the basis for discussing behavior in general.

With students above fourth grade, and particularly those in junior high and high school, it is better to open the conference with a brief presentation of your intent. The following is an example of an introductory statement which I have used.

> My purpose here today is to discuss with you the way we get along together in our classrooms and outside in the school and in our community. This is the beginning of what I hope will be a series of sessions where we work together to improve all of our behavior, not because we behave badly but because we can all act better than we do. Let's start by looking at the positive or good things that people do.

The last statement about looking for the positive things that people do is the beginning of building a list of both positive and negative behaviors that occur not only inside but also outside the classroom. With younger children, the consultant should write behaviors on the board as they are listed, but with older students, a volunteer from the class may be used for this purpose.

Once student ideas about positive and negative behavior have been exhausted, the consultant should pose the question about why individuals behave as they do. Doing so usually results in a wide range of answers, some somewhat sophisticated and some rather naive. Again, these explanations should be recorded.

Another question that may be posed at this point is "What do you do when you do not like the way that they behave?" Answers usually range from hitting or punching to ignoring completely. The range of the answers will be related to the age of the students involved in the class conference.

A question should now be asked regarding how students try to influence or change the functioning of other students. One way of stating this question is to pose a hypothetical question such as "Suppose there was a student with whom you were friendly who needed to change some aspect of his or her behavior? How would you accomplish this task?" Another way to deal with this is to ask students how they would attempt to provide the best possible classroom atmosphere.

The purpose of these early exercises and questions is twofold. First, it is necessary to develop an atmosphere of open communication. In order to accomplish this, the consultant should involve all students and make certain that all responses are valued. This can be done by simply restating each answer and by making sure that it is recorded. Second, it is important that students begin to think about human functioning and how they can facilitate positive growth. Although it is suggested here that the initial focus be on classroom behavior because concrete examples can be easily listed, sets of questions and areas of functioning could be used.

One precaution that should be taken in the early stages of the classroom conference is to ask pupils to focus on behavior and not on specific individuals. This is particularly true when negative behavior is being discussed. If some students are mentioned as having these traits, they may be hurt and thus alienated by the process. This is, of course, the opposite of the hoped-for outcome.

The first session should be ended by inquiring whether or not students would like to learn why people behave as they do and would perhaps like to explore strategies for facilitating behavior change. If their answer is affirmative, a second session should be scheduled approximately one week later. If a second session is scheduled the students should be asked to monitor their own methods of trying to influence the behavior of others. They may wish to take notes both about their approaches and the results of their efforts.

Second Conference The second session should begin with a review of the first meeting and by having students discuss their observations. At this point the consultant should introduce his or her own explanation of behavior change. This explanation, like that given to parents or teachers, should be made in the simplest possible terms. The author has found that first grade students can understand the principles of behavioral psychology. Other consultants have reported to me that young students can grasp the concepts of Adlerian psychology, Transactional Analysis, particularly when the terms used in *T.A. for Kids* (Freed, 1971) were employed, and others. When children experience difficulty in understanding theoretical concepts it usually is because the concepts are presented as abstract ideas rather than as simple principles. Oddly enough, graduate students have the same problems with their professors.

Once the theory, or part of a theory, has been presented, the students should then begin to analyze classroom behaviors, using the principles which they have learned. The question "Why do students disrupt the classroom?" can now be addressed in more specific terms. At this point the students should be assigned to analyze at least one behavioral transaction, using the concepts which they have learned, before the next conference.

Third Conference This session is really an extension of the second session in that additional theoretical concepts may be introduced and there is a continuation of the effort to analyze classroom behavior by using the concepts that have been introduced. However, there is one important difference, and that is that students are asked if they wish to work on influencing or changing their classroom situation. If the answer is positive, goal setting should be done at this point. It has been suggested in an earlier paper (1975) that while these goals may be quite diverse it is perhaps better to select positive areas and promote these rather than to focus on correcting negative behavior. This is done so that the efforts of the class can be focused upon the entire group rather than on a few students who are discipline problems. However, if it is the consensus of the class that negative behavior should receive attention, goals should be set in this area.

The next step is to specify what specific behaviors will be the target of class action. Let us assume for the sake of this discussion that the class decides to focus upon bettering race relations in the classroom. The class must then decide what behaviors are to be encouraged and discouraged and then how to utilize the principles that they have to attain the goals that they have established. The class might decide, for example, to encourage:

1. More conversation
2. Integrated work groups
3. Cooperative homework
4. Positive comments

and discourage:

1. Name-calling
2. Fighting or bickering
3. Racially tinted words and phrases

After goals are established, the class should be involved in determining the incidence of these behaviors. Various students or subgroups could be made responsible for counting the behaviors and preparing a report for the next session.

Fourth Conference This session would be dedicated to selecting strategies to accomplish the goals that have been established. These would, of course, be related to the theoretical model. Students who had conducted preliminary evaluation procedures would be asked to continue work on a periodic basis.

Fifth Conference This session would typically be scheduled for the purpose of conducting a formal and informal evaluation of the progress being made toward the goals that had been established. The formal evaluation would relate to the counting process that had been established. The informal evaluation would involve the reports of students regarding the interracial relationships in the classroom. If the process has been successful, the class may wish to return to goal setting and tackle other types of classroom problems or to promote positive behaviors. However, if the attempt has not been successful, a step-by-step analysis of the process should be conducted until the reason for the failure is uncovered. This deficiency should then be remedied and the process reinstituted.

Finally, classroom conferences should continue until the students are familiar with the principles and can apply them independently of the consultant. Realistically speaking, this process may take a period of months.

Consulting with School Clubs

Most school clubs are formed for the specific purpose of promoting some facet of school life. Clubs may promote scholarship, citizenship, moral development, the utilization of leisure time, vocational interests, and so on. Since the purposes of these organizations are already set, the consultant's role usually is to help members fulfill the goals of their club's charter.

Many of us have experienced the frustration generated whenever club members are trying to develop worthwhile projects. The result of these efforts are often superficial efforts such as "A Pick Up and Clean Up Day," a citizenship contest, or an essay contest. Similarly, academically oriented clubs may try to encourage scholarship by giving awards to the outstanding senior. Although these may all be desirable activities, they certainly are not efforts that have a positive impact upon the bulk of the student body. Let us consider some of the interventions that a consultant might attempt with various clubs, interventions that would potentially be beneficial to large numbers of students.

Academically oriented clubs might wish to develop and, perhaps, be personally involved in a cross-grade tutoring program that would involve more capable students in instructional and/or tutorial roles with less able students. This type of program could also be used as a same-grade enrichment procedure, where students with high degrees of academic skill in a given area would help other students develop their knowledge level beyond whatever the instructional staff might be able to do.

It also seems that students in academic clubs might be the ones best suited to developing programs in study skills and conducting those programs once they are developed. Bandura (1969, 1971) has made an impressive case for the importance of modeling in the learning process. Certainly these students could serve in the capacity of models for other students. One possibility is that students might wish to develop a series of videotapes that could be shown by teachers to illustrate how successful students approach the problem of studying.

Student government is typically an impotent organization that is viewed by many students as having little importance. However, the purpose of student government is supposedly to give students a voice in the decision-making process and to foster self-discipline. Although it is true that teachers and administrators often manipulate this organization so that it will cause as little difficulty as possible, the decision-making and self-discipline goals are worthy ones and should be pursued. There are a number of approaches that could be used to help students achieve these purposes.

In our society we are increasingly aware of the rights of individuals. The consultant might wish to help student government design programs to inform students of their rights, such as those granted by the Family Privacy Act of 1974, which enables the families of students to have access to school records. Once the individual reaches age eighteen, that right passes to the student. Recent Supreme Court Rulings have also set forth student rights regarding expulsion and the administration of corporal punishment. Essentially these pronouncements guarantee students the right of due process.

The recommendation that counselors help students become aware of their rights is not new. In 1971 Kinsey outlined a model Bill of Rights for students. In her article she listed the following rights, which are guaranteed by the Constitution.

FIRST AMENDMENT RIGHTS
1. The right to free speech, including the wearing of symbolic expressions such as armbands
2. The right to freedom of press
3. The right to refuse to participate in ceremonies such as salute to the flag
4. The right to free assembly. This includes the right to form political and social organizations.
5. The right to be protected from the establishment of religious practices in a school

FOURTH AMENDMENT RIGHTS
1. Protection against unreasonable practices such as search of personal property
2. The right to privacy regarding school records

FOURTEENTH AMENDMENT RIGHTS
1. The right to be made aware of laws and their enforcement procedures
2. The right to due process

Kinsey (1971, p. 54) spells this out as follows:

The right to written nature of the charges before a hearing
The right to a hearing before suspension, expulsion, or transfer
The right to a lawyer
The right to an impartial hearing examiner
The right to due process within the hearing . . .
The right to a translator when necessary
The right to a written transcript of the hearing
The right to be told the results of a hearing within a few days
The right of effective appeal
The right to a mistrial if any of the above rights have been abrogated

OTHER RIGHTS

1. The right to free education for all, including pregnant, handicapped, and other students.

Most of the rights enumerated by Kinsey have been strengthened by either court cases or additional legislation since she listed them.

Perhaps even more important than helping students become aware of their rights would be the design of programs that would help students to assert these rights within the school. Morgan and Wicas (1972) reported that a majority of the principals, teachers, and counselors whom they surveyed agreed that students were entitled to due process, increased involvement in governance, and freedom of speech. However, for two reasons this does not mean that movements to increase student involvement in these areas would be met with widespread approval. First, the study was conducted using educators from Massachusetts, Connecticut, and Rhode Island, an area of the country that may not be representative. Second, as Morgan and Wicas (1972) pointed out, principals tended to be considerably more conservative than teachers and counselors on these issues. This is perhaps so because they perceive the granting of students' rights as an erosion of their traditional powers. Unfortunately, principals may be in a position to delay change effectively in this area.

Nevertheless, the fact that there may be opposition to change should not deter the consultant from functioning in this area. The consultant may help students develop programs ranging from assertiveness training, as delineated in Albert and Emmons (1974), to bringing in specialists to help student groups learn collective bargaining strategies. These types of program can give student government purpose and meaning, can foster the goals of education, and are possible through the consultation relationship.

Athletic Teams and Clubs

Recently a consultant whom the senior author was supervising was approached by a coach to gain help with conflicts that he felt were hampering the performance of his football team. He related that he had tried every strategy that he knew, including pep talks, suspension of individual members for what he considered to be selfish play, and conferences with parents of the boys involved. Consequently, this individual became a human relations consultant to the football team. The approach he utilized was very similar to the one spelled out by Main and Roark (1975), which is a consensus approach to conflict resolution.

The assumptions underlying the consensus conflict-resolution approach are (1) that the basis of the conflict is misperception or miscommunication, (2) that the best means of reducing conflict is through face-to-face contact, and (3) that the individuals involved in the conflict must not be placed in a win-lose situation (Main and Roark, 1975). The steps in the approach are as follows:

1. Operationally describe the conflict situation so that all parties agree that the description is accurate.
2. Elicit the feelings of the individuals involved, so that all understand the emotion involved.
3. Describe the situation as it should be.
4. Determine the necessary changes and areas where individuals are willing to change.
5. Set up a plan of action to attain the desired situation.

In exploring the situation that existed on the football team, it was discovered that the coach had switched a back to the position of linebacker and replaced him with a popular student. The boy who had been switched felt that the reason had been to give the popular student a more glamorous position, not because of his ability but because of his popularity. Once the objective data were presented to the cliques that had supported the protagonists, both agreed to work toward a common goal: playing better football. The consultant had facilitated this goal through his efforts.

Athletic clubs are developed for reasons that, while complimentary to the overall goal of the athletic program, are also more diverse and far ranging. Improved sportsmanship, physical fitness, and citizenship are common objectives of these clubs. Because of the status many members of these clubs enjoy, they are often in a position to influence other members of the student body, although, like members of other clubs, they are often at a loss as to how this can be accomplished. Two types of program in which these groups can be involved will be discussed here.

First, members of the athletic club might become involved in a drug abuse prevention program. Those readers who have watched National Football League football will undoubtedly remember a series of videotape clips developed to combat drug abuse, highlighting certain stars of the NFL. While this is commendable, it seems doubtful that this was a very productive effort. Warner (1973) summarized the literature on drug abuse and identified two factors that seem contributary in this area. These were student boredom and peer influence. Warner went on to recommend that drug abuse focus on these two elements. He also made it clear that any drug abuse program should focus on more than just providing information, since there is little support that these activities have any meaningful impact. On the other hand, programs that have focused on the clarification of values and attitudinal development seem to have been more effective in the prevention of drug abuse (Brayer, 1970; Warner, 1973).

Hurst (1971) and Aubrey (1971) have both enumerated the effective ingredient of a good drug abuse program. Their ideas and the recommendations made by Warner (1973) can provide the framework for a successful drug abuse program, particularly when the program is carefully planned with an influential student group. Let us now look at an outline for this type of program.

Step 1. Enlist the support of the athletic club or some other appropriate organization.

Step 2. Form an advisory committee made up of students, parents, teachers, administrators, and counselors. This group should assume the responsibility of liaison and communication with the various groups in the school.

Step 3. Select students who are to be peer group leaders. Hurst (1971) suggests that these leaders should have the following characteristics:

(a)   The ability to relate to other students
(b)   Commitment
(c)   Maturity
(d)   Training

Step 4. Train the group leaders in communication skills, information about drugs, and values clarification techniques. See Simon, Howe, and Kirschenbaum (1972).

Step 5. Identify outside resources such as physicians and law enforcement officials who can be available to give specific input or to help drug users.

Step 6. Organize groups. This step should include scheduling meetings with group leaders so that ongoing consultation can occur regarding group leadership skills and attitudinal development.

Step 7. Evaluate and recycle if necessary. It should be pointed out that process evaluation should occur on an ongoing basis.

A second activity in which an athletic club could engage is either the development of or assistance with an intramural sports program. This could contribute to the drug abuse prevention program by reducing student boredom, a factor in drug abuse (Warner, 1973). It is suggested that this type of activity could be initiated by the consultant, interested parents in the community, members of the coaching staff, and other interested parties. It would contribute not only to the drug abuse prevention program but to the physical fitness of the student body. Perhaps the main ingredient in this type of program would be that it provided a broad enough range of activities to attract a large segment of the student body. In order to ascertain the nature of the students' interests, a simple survey could be conducted as the first step in such a venture.

Vocationally Oriented Clubs

Most high schools and some junior high schools have clubs that are vocationally oriented. These include Future Teachers of America, Future Farmers, Future Nurses, Future Homemakers, and mathematics clubs. The members of these clubs comprise a rich resource for facilitating the career development of all students. It is up to the consultant to tap this resource.

Gysbers and Moore (1975) have suggested that in order to facilitate life career development, consultants must help students to develop self-knowledge and interpersonal skills, career planning and self-placement competencies, the ability to relate curricular offerings to the world of work, and a broad understanding of one's place and all facets of one's existence. This recommendation corresponds quite closely to those made earlier by Evans, Hoyt, and Mangum (1973), Gibson (1972), and Herr (1972), to mention but a few. Gysbers and Moore go on to delineate three areas of responsibilities, which they term *curriculum-based, on-call guidance,* and *individual facilitation.* They suggest that the curriculum-based responsibilities be fulfilled directly by the consultant through classroom activities, small groups, individual contact, or teacher consultation. Similarly, Gysbers and Moore expect the consultant to assume the primary responsibility for individual facilitation and on-call guidance activities.

Miller and Benjamin (1975) recommend that a four-step process be followed in the career development program. These steps are needs assessment, developing goals and objectives, selection of strategies, and evaluation. Noeth, Roth, and Prediger (1975) conducted a study of approximately 32,000 students in grades 8, 9, and 11. They explored the extent to which students had participated in career planning activities and exploring occupational experiences. They also developed a scale to ascertain students' career planning knowledge and asked students what these perceived needs were. The conclusion of the authors follows:

> By and large guidance programs appear to be falling short of student's needs, even in those areas involving the more commonplace career guidance activities long advocated in counselor education programs and textbooks [p. 217].

The survey by Noeth, Roth, and Prediger (1975) may very well serve as the prototype for a local needs assessment. Students can obviously provide leadership in the development and conduct of such a survey, just as they can in the strategies that might be selected to deal with the needs that are identified. Miller and Benjamin (1975) recommend that Achievement Motivation Training, assessment techniques, career learning centers, curricular experiences, decision-making training, and media and values clarification are all useful strategies for facilitating career development. Let us look at how students might be helpful in a number of these strategies.

Achievement Motivation Training (Alschuler, 1973) is a four-stage process: teaching students the characteristics of high achievers, teaching approaches that may lead to high achievement, assisting students to set both short-term and long-term goals, and providing a supportive climate to help students attain the goals that they have set for themselves. McMullen (1973) breaks these four stages down into six steps. The first of these is attending, getting the students' attention. McMullen suggests that one way to do this is to indicate that the students will gain insight into why people behave as they do. Second, students are involved in role playing or game experiences where they will experience the

". . . behavior, thinking and feeling which is associated with achievement motivation" (p. 644). These experiences could involve such activities as having students estimate how close they would come to completing a task for which they all had equal ability. Then the leader should process what they said, what they thought, and how they felt.

Third, according to McMullen, students should begin to learn a vocabulary that will enable them to conceptualize the thoughts, feelings, and behavior of achievement. Words and phrases such as *risk taking, fear of failure, confidence,* and *personal limitations* would be included here. This exercise would be followed by having the students relate the vocabulary they have used to their own lives. This is step four. In the fifth step, students are asked to apply the information they have gained and establish goals and may enter into a contract to work toward these goals. Sixth and finally, the instructor fades the contract and withdraws from the situation. This step McMullen labels *internalizing.*

At the outset of this chapter, a research study by Vriend (1969) was reported, which demonstrated that high-performing students can assist low-performing students to increase their achievement. While it is not necessarily true that this finding would generalize to all settings, it does seem likely that students can successfully lead achievement motivation sessions.

Students can also learn to establish learning centers that feature careers, assist in decision-making training, and sponsor and present media programs. It also seems likely that older students could become successfully involved in values clarification programs for younger students. Simon (1973) outlined some of these exercises. A book coauthored by Simon, *Values Clarification: A Practical Handbook of Strategies,* has already been cited as a useful resource in this area. Another useful series of books, *Structure and Experiences for Human Relations Training* (University Associates, Box 615, Iowa City, Iowa 52240), may also be helpful in structuring a values clarification program.

It should perhaps be stressed again at this point that student activities grow out of a comprehensive plan for fostering career development and that they should be carefully coordinated. However, it is not difficult to see how enriched a program of this type would be if only one hundred students could be involved.

Other Student Activities

We hope that it has become clear that through the consultation function students can be involved in myriads of activities that are now either being neglected or are being attended to superficially. Only two more will be listed at this point, and these only briefly. Both of these ideas have been borrowed from college programs. One involves a crisis center and the other academic advising. (For details on college procedures see McCarthy and Berman, 1971, and Upcraft, 1971).

Counselors have long complained about the burdensome chore involved in scheduling activities. They have often overlooked what can be a vast resource: the students in the upper grade levels. Peer advising makes a great deal of sense when one considers that students have more knowledge about instructors, building layout, and a number of other factors simply because they have experienced them, usually very recently. To be sure, peer advisors would need to make referrals whenever counseling was called for or whenever major problems arose. Such contingencies could be built into the training program, however.

Hotlines or crisis centers have become commonplace in most communities. Drug problems, mental health disorders, runaways, and a variety of other problems present in our society have given rise to these. High school students, perhaps in cooperation with various other community agencies, can be involved in these programs and by doing so can provide an extension of the school's mental health program into after-school hours.

SELECTING CONSULTEES

The only real literature that is available to us in approaching the issue of selecting consultees is that from peer counseling. Frank, Ferdinand, and Bailey (1975), in a study reported earlier, used a variety of methods to select the peer counselors utilized in their research. They first used sociometric data, but found that the students selected in this way did not meet the other criteria that they had established. They ultimately used a rigorous interview procedure to determine attitudes toward peers and toward school and authority figures as well as to discern whether or not students were empathic, genuine and flexible and had a strong sense of personal identity. They also tried to determine if students had matured to the point where they could accept supervision. Leibowitz and Rhoads (1974) relied upon interviewing, role playing, and teacher recommendations as the basis for their selection of adolescent peer counselors. These researchers seemed to be asking the same questions that must be asked by the consultant in selecting consultees. Let us look at some of these now.

Will the student serve as a model? The research literature shows us that students are more apt to be influenced by individuals of relatively high status than by those with lower status (Bandura, 1969). Since our intent is to influence certain types of behaviors and foster the development of certain types of attitudes, it would seem wise to select those students who would be most helpful in accomplishing these goals. High sociometric status is one indicator of social value in the school. So are teacher recommendations and a student's holding various types of elective office. These indices, used collectively, should be helpful in selecting consultees.

Can the student relate to other students? It is possible to achieve sociometric status because of one's achievements in the academic area or in other activities such as sports. In short, it is possible to have high status without having good human relations skills, skills that are mandatory in carrying out many of the activities which have been enumerated throughout this chapter. Teacher ratings may be helpful in determining which students relate well to others, but at times these ratings are biased by how a particular student relates to teachers themselves. Therefore, it seems that an interview strategy coupled with role playing may be the best way to determine which students have these skills.

Is the student relatively free from psychological impairments? It has become standard fare in the psychological literature to recommend that trainees be selected who are free from psychological problems. This same recommendation seems to be appropriate for selecting consultees.

Is the student committed to helping other students? There is no foolproof way to determine whether or not a particular student wants to be helpful to others. Perhaps the best way to predict this is to look at those activities in which the student has been engaged in the past. Two questions need to be answered during this perusal. First, has the student persevered, has he or she seen the project through? Second, what is the nature of the student's role in various projects? Specifically, was it a helping role? Utilizing these types of data is in keeping with an old adage, "the best predictor of future behavior is past performance."

Can the student become involved without endangering his or her own education? Students, like adults, tend to overcommit themselves from time to time. In selecting consultees, the consultant should be as concerned about the potential welfare of a consultee as he or she is about the remainder of the student body. If it is apparent that the student cannot spare the time required to work in a project, that student should be bypassed.

PREPARING THE SCHOOL

What has been proposed thus far has tremendous implications for the school if implemented in its totality. Please keep in mind that the programs that have been suggested are only portions of what could be done to increase the potential impact of student involvement. Earlier, it was suggested that the principal might resist the types of activity recommended here. Resistance may arise from teachers and parents also if a certain amount of preparatory work is not conducted.

Perhaps the first step in the preparation process is to have the faculty accept the idea of the school as a therapeutic community. Alfred Adler advocated this concept throughout his life, and Karl Menninger instituted the idea in his Kansas clinic, which was designed to treat the mentally ill. Certain correctional institutions, such as the Kennedy Youth Center in Morgantown, West Virginia, have also adopted this concept. In simple terms, a therapeutic community is one in which all persons who are involved in that institution contribute to efforts that will stimulate psychological growth. In a prison this would involve the warden, the guards, and the inmates. In a school the principal, teachers, counselors, students, psychologists, and custodial staff make up the "residents" of the community. When a school staff accepts the philosophy that they should be facilitative rather than debilitative, a high degree of student involvement will be accepted.

Second, open lines of communication should be established among teachers, consultants, and administrators so that all parties are kept abreast of activities. The author has often suggested that consultants meet with their principal at least once per week in order to keep him or her informed about their program. It is also wise to circulate a one-page newsletter to faculty members and a similar note to parents so that they are kept well informed.

Third, initial consultation efforts aimed at students should probably have limited goals and, if possible, be directly supportive of already existing school activities. Cross-grade tutoring programs would certainly fall into this category, and so would many of the career development activities described earlier. This strategy serves two purposes: first, it allows faculty and staff to become accustomed to student activity in various facets of school life; second, it provides students an opportunity where they can involve themselves in various activities in a responsible manner. It is surprising how many persons involved in education think of students as immature and irresponsible.

Fourth, those activities that may cause resistance should be planned carefully. If students wish to have more input in establishing school rules, they should provide a carefully devised rationale as well as a carefully considered plan to monitor the program that they are proposing. If it is carefully conceived, a plan cannot be rejected because it is immature, a common ground for denying the value of students' efforts.

Sixth, a careful plan for evaluation of the overall program must be prepared. If a consultant is to devote time to consulting with students, there must be a justification for doing so. A plan for evaluation can provide the objective data needed to develop a rationale for student consultation.

DEALING WITH RACIAL DISCRIMINATION: A CASE STUDY

Background Donna, a black sixth grader, came to the counselor's office to discuss a problem that she and the other black students were experiencing with one of the white aides. According to Donna's report, the aide took the white students' side in arguments, enforced rules more vigorously when black students were involved, and failed to provide the same assistance to black students that was provided to white students in academic areas. It was decided that a number of the other students should be involved in the next meeting.

Session One Eight students, four black and four white, were invited to attend a consultation session on human relations. Donna opened the session with essentially the same complaint that she had provided in the background session with the counselor. All students agreed with the situation that she described, but one of the black students added that he felt that the teacher supported the aide in her discriminatory behavior. He also believed that some of the white students took advantage of the situation by starting trouble whenever the aide was watching because they knew that they would be protected. After other students gave their opinions, the students were asked to describe explicitly the situation that existed in the classroom at the present time. Then the students were asked to describe the situation as they would like it to be. Their two statements follow:

As It Is. Black students are treated badly. Aide picks on them by blaming them for things they do not do and making things rougher by being stricter about rules.

As They Would Like It to Be. All treated fairly, particularly by aide. Students will treat each other fairly, too.

The students were then asked to consider alternatives to establishing a more egalitarian attitude in the aide and in some of the other students. The first session ended at this point.

Second Session The second session began by having students list alternative ways of attaining the goal that they had established. The alternatives listed were as follows.

WITH AIDE
1. Go to the teacher (because she is the aide's boss) and get her to help.
2. Have white students go to aide and complain about the situation.
3. Bring the principal in if 1 and 2 do not work.

WITH STUDENTS
1. Complain to teacher about activities of the students.
2. Have groups of black and white students talk to white students involved in starting problems.
3. Ignore the white students involved and get other students with similar views to do the same.

Since the first alternatives for dealing with the aide and the students involved the teacher, role-playing activities were conducted to prepare four students to talk to the teacher. The session ended after these activities.

Third Session The committee reported that the teacher had rejected suggestions that the aide be asked to be more fair in dealing with all students. The teacher also rejected the idea that students were engaging in discriminatory activities against other students. Two subcommittees were then formed, one to approach the aide and one to approach some of the students. Both were involved in role-playing activities to prepare them to discuss the problem with the aide and the students.

Fourth Session The groups that had contacted the aide said that she had rejected their suggestions that she was discriminating against black students. She had also told them that she did not appreciate their causing trouble with the teacher. The students indicated that they should have contacted the aide before going to the teacher.

The group that had contacted the students reported that many of the students had agreed to refrain from their activities *if* the black students would stop complaining about them.

The group then decided that the principal should be involved in the situation.

Fifth Session The eight students, the counselor, and the principal met to consider the situation. The principal reported that some parents had complained about the situation that existed in the classroom. He indicated that he was preparing to take steps to remedy the situation. One step was to request that the counselor conduct some classroom activities designed to improve racial relations. He also indicated that the aide was to be transferred to a clerical post, a step that was taken two weeks later.

The students were asked to evaluate the oucome of their activities. They indicated that in the future they would first contact the persons involved and not try to go to their superiors until that had failed. However, they believed that the overall impact was in the desirable direction. They added that they believed that they need more skill and practice in approaching people with their complaints. The counselor agreed to include this in the classroom guidance activities.

SUMMARY

This chapter has been a journey into a rarely discussed area: consulting with students. While the rationale for consulting with students is much the same as that for training peer counselors – that is, to increase the efficiency of the pupil services program – the potential rewards seem far greater.

Two types of consultation procedure have been emphasized. The first is procedures dealing with entire classrooms. The purpose of that activity is to help students in the individual classes produce a climate more conducive to personal development. Second, working with school clubs has been stressed because these are intact groups with stated goals and purposes. It has been recommended that the counselors help develop activities commensurate with their goals.

Finally, in presenting the idea of selection of consultees and the steps for implementing a student consultation program, perhaps the most important idea was that student consultation is a move toward establishing a therapeutic community in the school.

REFERENCES

Alberti, R. E., and M. L. Emmons. *Your Perfect Right: A Guide to Assertive Behavior,* 2nd ed. San Luis Obispo: Impact, 1974.

Alschuler, A. *Developing Achievement Motivation in Adolescents: Education for Human Growth.* Englewood Cliffs: Educational Technology Publications, 1973.

Aubrey, R. F. "School-Community Drug Prevention Programs," *Personnel and Guidance Journal,* 50 (1971): 17–24.

Bandura, A. *Principles of Behavior Modification.* New York: Holt, Rinehart & Winston, Inc., 1969.

_____. *Social Learning Theory.* Morristown: General Learning Press, 1971.

Brayer, H. O. "The Coronado Drug Abuse Prevention Project." Coronado: Title III Program, Coronado Unified School District, July, 1970 (mimeographed).

Briskin, A. S., and D. M. Anderson. "Students as Contingency Managers," *Elementary School Guidance and Counseling,* 7 (1973): 262–268.

Brown, D. *Changing Students' Behavior: A New Approach to Discipline.* Dubuque: Wm. C. Brown, 1970.

_____. "Social Modeling and Psychological Education." Unpublished paper, Chapel Hill, N.C., 1975 (mimeographed).

Brown, W. F. "Effectiveness of Paraprofessionals: The Evidence," *Personnel and Guidance Journal,* 53 (1974): 257–263.

Evans, R. N., K. B. Hoyt, and G. L. Mangum. *Career Education in the Middle/ Junior and High School.* Salt Lake City: Olympus, 1973.

Frank, M., B. Ferdinand, and W. Bailey. "Peer Group Counseling: A Challenge to Grow," *The School Counselor,* 22 (1975): 267–274.

Freed, A. M. *T. A. for Kids.* Los Angeles: Price-Sloan-Stern, Publishers, 1971.

Gibson, R. L. *Career Development in the Elementary School.* Columbus: Charles Merrill, 1972.

Glasser, W. *Schools without Failure.* New York: Harper & Row, Publishers, 1969.

Gysbers, N. C., and E. J. Moore. "Beyond Career Development – Life Career Development." *Personnel and Guidance Journal,* 53 (1975): 647–652.

Herr, E. L. "Unifying an Entire System of Education around a Career Development Theme." In *Career Education: Prospective and Promise,* ed. K. Goldhammer and R. Taylor. Columbus: Charles Merrill, 1972, pp. 63–104.

Hurst, F. W. "A University Drug Education Project," *Personnel and Guidance Journal,* 50 (1971): 11–16.

Kern, R., and J. H. Kirby. "Utilizing Peer Helper Influence in Group Counseling," *Elementary School Guidance and Counseling,* 6 (1971): 70–75.

Kinsey, L. "Student Right: A Program for Counselors," *Personnel and Guidance Journal,* 50 (1971): 52–57.

Kranzow, G. W., ed. *Title III ESEA Peer Counseling Handbook.* Gurnee: Special Education District of Lake County, 1973.

Leibowitz, Z., and D. J. Rhoads. "Adolescent Peer Counseling," *The School Counselor,* 21 (1974): 280–283.

McCarthy, B. W., and A. L. Berman. "A Student-operated Crisis Center," *Personnel and Guidance Journal,* 49 (1971): 523–528.

McMullen, R. S. "The Achievement Motivation Workshop," *Personnel and Guidance Journal,* 51 (1973): 642–645.

Main, A. P., and A. E. Roark. "A Consensus Method to Reduce Conflict," *Personnel and Guidance Journal,* 53 (1975): 754–759.

Miller, J. W., and L. Benjamin. "New Career Development Strategies: Methods and Resources," *Personnel and Guidance Journal,* 53 (1975): 694–697.

Morgan, L. B., and E. A. Wicas. "The Short, Unhappy Life of Student Dissent," *Personnel and Guidance Journal,* 51 (1972): 33–38.

Mosher, R., and N. Sprinthall. "Psychological Education: A Means to Promote Personal Development during Adolescence," *Counseling Psychologist,* 2 (1971): 3.

Noeth, R. J., J. D. Roth, and D. J. Prediger. "Student Career Development: Where Do We Stand?" *Vocational Guidance Quarterly,* 23 (1975): 210–218.

Schmidt, L. C., and L. E. Furniss. "An Elementary Adjunct: High School Helpers," *Personnel and Guidance Journal,* 53 (1975): 778–781.

Simon, S. B. "Values Clarification: A Tool for Counselors," *Personnel and Guidance Journal,* 51 (1973): 614–618.

Simon, S. B., L. Howe, and H. Kirschenbaum. *Values Clarification: A Practical Handbook of Strategies for Teachers and Students.* New York: Hart, 1972.

Upcraft, M. L. "Undergraduate Students as Academic Advisors," *Personnel and Guidance Journal,* 49 (1971): 827–831.

Varenhorst, B. B. "Training Adolescents as Peer Counselors," *Personnel and Guidance Journal,* 53 (1974): 271–275.

Vriend, T. "High-performing Inner City Adolescents Assist Low-performing Peers in Counseling Groups," *Personnel and Guidance Journal,* 47 (1969): 897–904.

Warner, R. W., Jr. "Preventing Drug Abuse: Where Are We Now?" *Personnel and Guidance Journal,* 51 (1973): 523–529.

Zide, M. M. "Group Dynamics Techniques," *Personnel and Guidance Journal,* 51 (1973): 620–622.

CHAPTER EIGHT Parental Consultation and Education

INTRODUCTION

Some confusion seems to exist in the current literature regarding the nature of three processes: parent counseling, parent consultation, and parent education. Articles such as Shaw's (1969), which was supposedly a report concerning the feasibility of parental group counseling, but described the facilitator's role as one of consultant, has contributed to this confusion. So has the stand taken by Dinkmeyer and Carlson (1973), in that they seemed to equate the three processes. They asserted that the aim of work with parents, regardless of label, is to provide direct assistance to parents and indirect aid to students. Tavormina (1974) further clouded this already murky issue by reviewing the literature regarding various interventions with parents and titling the article "Basic Models of Parent Counseling."

Tavormina seemed in his review to agree with Dinkmeyer and Carlson when he pointed out that the goals of parent education and parent counseling (and I presume consultation) are the same. Citing Auerbach (1968), he listed these goals as familiarizing parents with the concepts of child growth and development; helping parents clarify family roles; and increasing parental understanding of home life so that better management decisions can be made.

While the goals of parental counseling, consultation and education may be similar, it seems that each has some salient features that characterize it and these have been blurred. An attempt will be made to clarify differences among these approaches at this point.

Parent Education

Parent education can be distinguished from either parent counseling or parent consultation on both the content and process level. The content of parent education groups is primarily subject matter that has been identified by the leader or adopted by the group. This material ranges from books such as *Parent Effectiveness Training* (Gordon, 1970) to mimeographed material developed for the course by the group leader. The process of these groups is primarily pedagogical or leader-centered in nature. In some community college courses on parenting, the instructor utilizes a strict lecture-discussion method much as one would in the teaching of history or chemistry. In other parent education groups, participant discussion is the primary approach. This discussion focuses upon certain topics, which are often listed on a syllabus of some type. To be sure, participants are encouraged to apply the principles that they are learning to their own family situations, and thus the discussions are made personal. The anticipated outcome of parent education is that parents will learn to use in their own families the principles that they have learned.

To summarize, parent education is a systematic approach to learning principles that typically are discussed in books or other materials. It is primarily a didactic process, which typically is operated using traditional pedagogical procedures.

Parent Counseling

Counseling is a process in which clients are engaged for their own benefit. While third parties such as children may benefit, it is the clients who hope to be the primary beneficiaries of the service. In this context, then, parents would be involved in the counseling process whenever they are experiencing personal adjustment problems that are at the root of the family difficulty. Parents have often been found to be at the root of school phobia, for example (Lazarus, Davison, and Polefka, 1965). Alcoholic parents also are the basis of family problems, as are other parents with various other types of problem. Parent counseling is a more in-depth process than parent education and has as its goals the amelioration of certain problems that the parents are experiencing that are negatively influencing their functioning and that of other family members.

Parent counseling as described here is most often conducted either in community mental health centers or in private practice. It is rarely practiced in school settings.

Parental Consultation

Parental consultation can be depicted in much the same manner as teacher consultation in that it follows the same process and has as its goal providing assistance to children rather than parents. However, some specific features of parental consultation will be delineated in order to distinguish it further from both parent counseling and parent education. First, parent consultation may be initiated by either the parent or a member of the school staff. In either case, parent-school contact grows out of a concern for the child's functioning. Because of this fact, the primary focus from the outset is upon the student.

Second, in parent consultation educational approaches such as assigned readings, films and filmstrips, or direct teaching are adjunct to the process, not its essence. As is the case with all consultation, the acquisition of knowledge and skills is an important goal, but this occurs as a result of the process, not because a course syllabus dictates a certain lesson.

Third, it is assumed that parents who are involved in this process are psychologically healthy and have a genuine desire to cope with their child in a more meaningful manner. When it becomes clear that parents are in fact in need of direct counseling or therapy because of difficulties they are experiencing, the consultant must decide whether or not to continue with the consultation sessions. If the sessions are continued, parental counseling may also well become an adjunct to consultation.

Fourth, parental consultation is often conducted in concert with teacher consultation in order to insure that both of these important influences in the student's life are working toward similar goals and employing similar techniques. It is not uncommon for teachers, parents, and the consultant to meet in a single consultation session, thus increasing the efficiency of the consulting procedure.

Fifth, the process and techniques employed in parental consultation are similar to those employed in teacher consultation and will not be discussed here.

Finally a presentation of some similarities and differences among parental counseling, consultation and education can be seen in Table 8.1.

THE RATIONALE FOR PARENT CONSULTATION

At least four arguments favoring parental consultation can be developed. These are that parental consultation enables the school to establish a liaison with parents which will result in greater support for education; will increase the effectiveness of pupil services programs; is needed because of the plight of the

TABLE 8.1. Counseling, parent consultation, and parent education compared

	Counseling	*Consultation*	*Education*
Relationship	Important	Important	Less important
Use of materials	Little	Adjunct	Core
Individual or group	Both	Both	Usually group
Primary focus	Parent	Parent/child	Parent/child
Modality	Affective	Cognitive/ affective	Cognitive
Content	Personal	Personal	Books, films, handouts
Number of sessions	Varies — may be long-term	Varies — often short term	Set number
Psychological state of parent(s)	Assumed poor	Assumed good	Assumed good

family in our society; and will enhance students' academic functioning. Gaining parental support for education is extremely important.

In the first paragraph of her article Evans (1973) speaks to the concerns which parents have about our educational institutions:

> As schools have grown larger and more complex, school-community relations have tended to deteriorate. Parents talk about the disappearance of the personal element. They are confused about whom to contact in order to discuss the particular needs of their child. In fact, they appear fearful that the schools are no longer interested in the individual student and that one pupil's concerns may seem trivial to this impersonal bureaucracy [p. 729].

The chasm that has developed between our schools and the home can be narrowed through parental consultation. Not only do parents have an opportunity to meet face-to-face with one or more members of the school staff, but the consultation session itself is an expression of the school's concern for the unique problems of their child.

There is a growing concern about the effectiveness of various pupil services programs. Through parental consultation we have an opportunity to increase our effectiveness by involving the family. O'Dell (1974) cites "... the growing trend toward working in the natural environment ..." (p. 419) as a part of his article. Certainly school psychologists, counselors, and special educators have often been frustrated by their attempts to make effective interventions because they seemed to be blocked at every turn by the family. Through parental consultation those barriers can often be removed.

We must look at the situation of the American family if we are to become fully aware of the need for parental consultation. Although precise statistics regarding the nature of the family are difficult to obtain, it now appears that there are 4.2* million children being reared by single parents. This number is the result of a 30-to-35-percent divorce rate, death, and, increasingly, the decision of women experiencing extramarital pregnancies to remain unmarried. According to a 1973 article in *Newsweek* magazine, the single parent is most likely to be divorced or separated, female, white, and to have an income of less than half of the national average. As Brandwein et al. (1974) point out, the head of a single-parent family can be successful, but the task is a more difficult one.

In two-parent families the problems are also great. The mobility of the American family, the increase in the number of working mothers (females now make up over 40 percent of the work force),† the influence of mass media upon children, and similar factors have thrown the family into chaos. This situation has prompted Margaret Mead (1970) to suggest that we are in need of new approaches to family living. What is also needed is greater assistance to parents in helping them to cope with the day-to-day problems of family living, to assist them to develop a family environment that will nurture the child during his or her developmental years and that will assist parents in their efforts to maximize their child's educational experiences.

Finally there is a growing unrest about the inability of schools to develop basic skills. This has resulted in a "back to basics" move in many school districts. Other districts have developed alternative schools, which stress traditional approaches to education and do away with the so-called frills. Regardless of the approach, school districts are responding to parental demands that their children be able to read, compute, and write logically.

What is ironic about parental unhappiness about the educational enterprise is that parents are a part of the problem. Family background, perhaps more than any other factor, accounts for school achievement.†† This fact dictates that educators involve parents in the educational process. It has been demonstrated that parents can be valuable assistants to developing academic skills such as reading. Through consultation and education, this valuable resource can be tapped.

PARENTAL CONSULTATION

Parental consultation can be done either individually or in groups. The arguments for and against both approaches are similar to those already discussed in

---

*See *Statistical Abstracts of the United States,* 1971.

†*President's Manpower Report,* 1975.

††Some estimates are that family background accounts for 50 percent of the variance in school achievement.

Chapter Four regarding teacher consultation and will not be repeated. The steps in group and individual parental consultation are very much the same for both, however, and will be presented.

Step 1. Relationship

There are a number of special considerations involved in the process of establishing a consulting relationship with parents (Brown and Brown, 1975 A, B).

First, many parents are unaccustomed to dealing with any school staff members unless their child is in some type of difficulty. As a result, a concerted effort must be made to allay parental fears. It is suggested that ambiguity be eliminated by addressing this problem directly. Simply assure parents that their child is not in difficulty and indicate that the purpose of the session is to help the student. Statements such as those that follow can be used for this purpose: "I'm sure you must be wondering why I have asked you to come in today. Well, let me assure you that John is not in any trouble here at school. My concern is to enlist your support in helping your son to function better. My feeling is that if the teachers, parents, and counselors work together, every student will benefit." Or "John has been experiencing some difficulties in mathematics. My purpose here is to enlist your support to help us in our efforts to help him overcome this difficulty."

Second, a concern that deserves attention is the discomfort which many parents feel when they come to school. This discomfort may be particularly acute among parents who have had unfortunate experiences in school or those who are unable to dress according to standards that they deem appropriate. It is up to the consultant to provide a comfortable setting and an atmosphere where these fears can be overcome quickly. In order to do this, the consultant should be ready to receive parents whenever they arrive. In some instances, the consultant should be prepared to go to the home to conduct the session.

Third, parents may also be concerned that they will be blamed for the student's difficulties (Brown and Brown, 1975 A, B) and thus be defensive. This may be particularly true of parents who have taken their children to mental health clinics for help and found that they themselves were the ones being treated. In order to avoid raising this fear and the defensiveness that it engenders, it is often wise to focus almost entirely upon the children involved.

Fourth, relationship in parental consulting is established in much the same way as are all other counseling and consulting relationships. Open communication and mutual trust are essential ingredients.

Fifth, the consulting relationship with parents can be greatly facilitated by structuring the relationship as carefully as possible (Sonstegard, 1964). To a certain extent, statements assuring the parent that the student is not involved in a situation requiring disciplinary action are a part of the structuring process.

However, structuring must be carried much further. The first item to be determined is why the session is being conducted. If the consultant initiates the session, parents should know why the request was made. If the parents requested the session, they should be given an opportunity to give their reasons for their action. Once both parties understand fully why the session was initiated, structuring has begun.

When the rationale for the consulting session has been established, relationships need to be discussed as a part of building the structure of the consultation process. One idea that should be clarified from the outset is that if the outcome of this and future sessions is to be successful, parents must act. A statement such as "I believe that Johnny can be more effectively helped if we all work together" implies that action is to be taken by the parents as well as the consultant and others involved. This concept can be strengthened by being more explicit. The statement "We believe that Johnny will benefit more fully if actions taken here at school are accompanied by related actions at home" certainly is a stronger indicator that parental action is *expected.*

Structuring should also include an indication of the length of sessions and the approximate number of sessions required. While the length of a parental consultation session is usually about one hour, the number of sessions required may vary considerably. Although parental consultation is not a long-term process under most circumstances, it is perhaps wiser to leave the number of sessions somewhat vague. Again, structuring statements such as "It would seem desirable if we could meet for an hour every other week for a few weeks so that the situation can be cleared up" will suffice.

The idea of structuring for termination has been stressed throughout this book, and parental consultation should be no exception. It should be made quite clear to the parents that they are expected to gain the skills needed to deal with the situation at hand, and once this occurs the process will be terminated. Statements such as "I feel confident that you will have the situation in hand in a very short period of time" communicates to parents the hope that the consultant will not have to be available on an indefinite basis.

Finally, the structuring process should involve establishing role relationships. This is accomplished more through actions than words, but the consultant's role typically consists of helping the parent assess the situation and develop strategies to deal with it. The parent's role is to make observations of the behavior in the home situation, report these interactions accurately, implement strategies, and evaluate the outcomes (Brown and Brown, 1975 A, B).

Step 2. Information Taking and Diagnosis

The type of information sought and the diagnosis of the problem will depend largely upon the theoretical basis of the consultant. Let us look briefly at three

approaches to this step. Sonstegard (1964, pp. 74–75), a noted Adlerian psychologist, suggested that the following outline be used when interviewing parents.

I. Under what conditions did the complaint or problem arise?
   A. At what age?
   B. What has been its duration?
II. What is the child's relationship to siblings?
   A. Position in sibling sequence
      1. Distribution of males and females?
      2. How are siblings different?
      3. How are siblings similar?
   B. With whom is the child compared?
      1. Whom is the child most like?
      2. Whom is the child least like?
   C. Nature and extent of
      1. Conflicts?
      2. Rivalry?
      3. Competition? (Explain.)
      4. Submission?
      5. Rebellion?
         a. Active?
         b. Passive?
III. Environmental Influences
   A. Relatives
      1. Grandparents
      2. Other relatives
   B. Other people living in the house
   C. Neighbors
IV. What are you doing about the problem?
   A. Relate in detail the interactions.
   B. Clarify if necessary: "What do you mean by that?"
V. In what other ways does the child stand out?
   A. Conditions under which he functions adequately?
   B. In what way is he successful?
VI. What is the nature of the daily routine?
   A. How does the child get up in the morning?
      1. Who awakens him?
      2. Is he called more than once?
      3. What about dressing?
      4. What about breakfast?
   C. Describe the lunch hour, the dinner (each mealtime).
   D. How does the child get off to bed? At what time?

VII. What happens when the family goes out together?
    A. Preparation for going out and special efforts.
    B. What happens when away?
VIII. How are the child's social relationships?
    A. Ability to make friends with others
       1. Neighborhood children
       2. Adults
       3. Children at school
    B. Does he have pets and does he take care of them?
    C. Attitude toward school
       1. Schoolwork
       2. Relationships with teachers
       3. How does he deal with people in authority?
    D. What impressions has he gained from the family situation?
       1. Has there been any tragedy in the family?
       2. Who is boss?
       3. What methods of discipline have been used?
       4. What kind of punishment?
       5. What kind of supervision?
IX. What does the child think about his future?
    A. What does he want to be when he grows up?
    B. What is the occupation of other members of the family?
X. Does the child have nightmares, bad dreams?

This is, of course, a lengthy and detailed interview schedule, and Sonstegard cautions against rigid adherence to it. However, the format is established so that the consultant can determine the development of social interest in the child, the means by which the family affords the child an opportunity to feel a part of the family, and, indirectly, to infer the life-style of the child or children in the family. Specifically, the consultant is interested in the useless behavior employed by the child to gain belongingness.

The focus of the behavioral consultant would be upon the interactions of the children, the children and parents, and the children and other significant peers and adults. Because of this focus Sonstegard's interview schedule could be adapted quite nicely to ascertain behaviors which are being reinforced and the means by which they are reinforced, the nature of the behavior being modeled by the parents and significant others, and the maladaptive behavior that has developed as a result.

Let us assume, for example, that the presenting problem was that the child consistently failed to complete seat work. During the course of the interview the parent related that the child seems unable to complete household chores, demands a great deal of help when doing homework, and generally is unable to take care of himself. An Adlerian consultant might conclude that the child was attempting to get attention by playing helpless. A behavioral consultant might conclude that the parent is unwittingly reinforcing maladaptive behavior. The interventions will be somewhat different, but the information is valuable to both.

It should be noted at this point that the diagnosis is a working hypothesis about the nature of the problem and may have to be altered or changed completely as more data become available.

To this point the focus of data collection has been upon the parents. The children are an additional source of data about the family and can, when interviewed separately, tend to confirm or disconfirm parent observations. It is suggested that whenever possible children's perceptions of the situation be obtained as a means of increasing the reliability of the information used in the diagnostic process.

Some behavioral consultants establish elaborate data collection procedures by asking parents and children to monitor their own and each other's behavior. While this has the obvious advantage of adding precision to the observations and providing means for evaluating the progress of the consultation sessions, these procedures also tend to help parents to understand more fully the nature of the problem. One parent of a particularly dilatory child found that she reminded the child over a hundred times per day to perform various activities. It was unnecessary for the consultant to point out that she was reinforcing the behaviors that she hoped to eliminate.

Charting and record keeping such as those required by many behaviorists can also have a negative impact upon the outcomes of consultation because the time required becomes a chore. If charts and observations are to be required, the charts should be furnished, behaviors to be monitored clearly defined, and observation procedures modeled and rehearsed.

As perhaps the reader has discerned, there are not clear-cut guidelines for collecting diagnostic information. Situational variables such as the availability of the children and time restrictions plus personal preferences should ultimately determine the consultant's approach.

Step 3. Stating a Hypothesis

Once the consultant has developed what seems to be a clear picture of the family situation, a statement should be made that as succinctly as possible presents these ideas to the parents. This statement should be made tentatively so that parents will feel free to take issue with the hypothesis. The following are a few examples of statements which illustrate the concept of the hypothesis. "It seems to me that what is happening is that the children are receiving attention for the negative things they do and not the positive things." (Parents are reinforcing negative behavior.) "Could it be that communication is pretty much one way, that you are not hearing what the children are trying to say or even that they don't have an opportunity to express their feelings?" (There is poor communication in the family.) "The children seem to have the family in an uproar. They seem to be constantly competing for your attention." (Sibling rivalry exists which manifests itself in various power struggles.)

Once the tentative hypothesis has been stated, the consultant may need to clarify the rationale upon which it is based. However, if it is made in simple enough terms and captures the essence of the family problem, this will not be the case. It is of utmost importance that this hypothesis be accepted by the family members, since it serves as the basis for the action to be taken. One danger is that parents will seem to agree with the consultant but still will retain their own ideas. The author recalls observing a demonstration family consultation session where the parents were seemingly in full accord with the consultant's diagnosis. They participated in a session where goals were established and action steps elaborated. However, once the parents were in the hallway the father said to the mother, "He really didn't get it. You have to hit Harold to keep him in line. He'd drive us all crazy if we didn't beat him once in a while." The implications of these statements are simply that the consultant should not conclude too quickly that agreement about the nature of the problem has been quickly reached.

Step 4. Explaining the Principle

Once the nature of the family problem has been agreed upon between the consultant and the parents, an explanation of the psychological principles utilized by the consultant seems necessary so that effective communication can take place (Brown and Brown, 1975 B). It should be noted that there would not be unanimous agreement on this point among all family consultants. Rudolf Dreikurs and Manford Sonstegard have asserted that parents and others should first learn techniques unencumbered by the theory upon which they are based.* After experiencing success with a technique, a parent or other individual will be more willing to learn the underlying principles. It should also be indicated that both Dreikurs and Sonstegard have been leaders in establishing in the United States parent education centers, which sponsored programs to teach parents principles of Adlerian psychology.

To reiterate, parents need to know some of the basic premises underlying any techniques that might be utilized in the consultation process. In addition to facilitating the communication process, an explanation of theoretical concepts seems necessary so that parents can understand the nature of their own problems, and begin to function independently of the consultant.

---

*These assertations were made during speeches and presentations made at West Virginia University, Morgantown, between 1968 and 1971.

Explanations of theoretical propositions should always be made as simply as possible without losing the essence of the concepts involved. Brown and Brown (1975 B) point out that positive reinforcement could be explained "... as an event which increases the probability of a behavior occurring in the future" (p. 7). They go on to recommend that common-sense examples of positive reinforcement are more readily understood by parents. Similarly, communication can be explained in terms of senders, receivers, channels of communication, nonverbal communication, and verbal communication. It can also be explained by talking about hearing and understanding people, and again some common-sense examples of this process can greatly augment the explanation.

When Alfred Adler developed his personal explanation of human functioning, he avoided the esoteric terminology employed by other psychologists of his time such as Sigmund Freud. Presumably Adler did so because he placed a great deal of stress on working with lay persons and needed to communicate effectively with them. As a result, Adlerians use the term *useless behavior* instead of *maladaptive behavior, involved with* instead of *power struggles,* and other common-sense terms. This tactic should be emulated by other consultants.

The explanation of principles should not be pedantic, that is, using one-way communication. It should be conducted in a manner that allows parents to discuss the principles and give examples of ways in which they are used in their own family, or perhaps misused, as the case may be. Once it becomes apparent that parents have arrived at a high degree of understanding of the concepts to be utilized, it is time to proceed.

Step 5. Reexamining Family Patterns

Once the psychological principles to be employed are fully understood, the consultant and parent should review the existing family patterns. The consultant should encourage the parents to do this by asking them simply to explain what is occurring in their particular situation. The process can be facilitated by pointing to specific examples. The consultant might use some of the following leads. "You were telling me about the difficulties you were having with the siblings fighting and your role in these fights. How would you explain those now?"

"What types of behaviors are you reinforcing when you are attempting to get your children to complete their homework?"

"You were telling me that you had a lot of trouble getting your teenagers to understand the financial situation in your family. Can you analyze what is going on in that area?"

This step is in a sense a check on parental understanding of the principles to be utilized. However, the focus at this time should be upon those areas that seem to be of major concern to the family and in that sense is a prelude to good setting and selection of strategies.

Step 6. Establishing Goals and Selecting Strategies

The goals that are established in parental consultation should be those of the parents. The consultant may want to point out specific areas that seem to be of major concern, but the parent should ultimately select the area of greatest concern and establish goals for dealing with the problem. On the other hand, the consultant will probably play a major role in the process of selecting strategies to meet the goals that the parent has established.

From the outset the importance of operational goals has been stressed. The establishment of behavioral goals is particularly important in the consultation process so that the progress of the process can be monitored. Parents who come to the counselor often do so as a last resort. They often express the concern that they have tried everything they can think of and the hope that the counselor can be of assistance. Implicit in this statement is very often the expectation that the counselor may fail also. Because of this attitude, specific goals with techniques to monitor progress toward them are of great importance so that parents can get feedback regarding their efforts and counselors can ascertain the extent to which progress is being made.

Another important aspect of this process is that goals be somewhat limited, at least in the beginning. Parents who are having disagreements over rule setting, sibling fighting, getting children to complete homework, and allowances may want to attack all of these problems simultaneously. To do this would be tantamount to failure because a variety of complex strategies may be necessary and the monitoring of progress toward the goals in these various areas may act as a deterrent to action. It is also quite likely that if one or two of the problem areas are cleared up, these others will tend to get better. The following are goals that have been established in parental consultation:

Children will get themselves out of bed each day without being called by either parent; and

Children will get themselves dressed and ready for breakfast by 8:10 each morning without parental reminders; and

Children will collect their schoolbooks and be ready for the school bus when it arrives in the morning without parental prompting.

These goals were selected by a set of parents who obviously had as their greatest concern the early morning behavior of the children. They were stated as three independent goals because they involved three different behaviors and so that progress toward each target behavior could be more carefully measured. One aspect of the foregoing goals which in one sense is not necessary is the part that specifies that these behaviors are to occur in the absence of parental action. However, it was included to remind the parents that they were not to involve themselves with children in these various morning activities.

As has been pointed out throughout the book thus far and particularly in the chapter on teacher consultation, the strategies utilized in goal attainment will result largely from the theoretical bias of the consultant. Neo-client-centered consultants will train parents in communications procedures and problem-solving procedures, while behavioral counselors will involve parents in strategies using reinforcement and modeling procedures. Adlerian counselors will assist parents in developing procedures to make the child find his or her place in the family and to encourage useful behavior.

Step 7. Including the Child

If children have not been included in the consultation process, a plan should be developed to make them aware of the goals that have been established and to apprise them of the strategies to be employed. Again, this should not be a one-way process: that is, children should not simply be told what has happened. Their opinions about the goals and strategies should be solicited. It will often be the case that these will be altered because of this input. It is desirable for children to be included in the session where goals and strategies are developed, but if this is not possible, the counselor and the parents should develop a plan whereby the parents consult with the children in the home. Once the children are included, the parents should implement the strategies that have been devised.

Subsequent Sessions

The first consultation session that was outlined in the foregoing section typically lasts from one to one and one-half hours. At the end of this session, a second session should be scheduled. Consulting sessions with parents are typically scheduled one to two weeks apart, with the determining factor being the amount of time required to implement the strategies that have been developed. If sessions are scheduled two weeks apart, it is usually wise to telephone parents in order to determine progress that was made after one week had elapsed.

Subsequent consultation sessions should be opened with a review of the progress that has been made toward the goals that have been established. If goals have been attained, new goals can be established, and the session proceeds in much the same manner as the first session. However, if progress has either been slower than would be expected or is nonexistent, some troubleshooting must be conducted by the counselor with the purpose of determining the causes underlying the situation.

One of the first areas that should be examined in the troubleshooting process is the parents' level of understanding of the psychological principles and strategies. This can be accomplished by asking parents to relate what they did on a step-by-step basis. At times it is helpful to role-play the interactions that occurred in order to attain additional insight into the difficulty. It is not uncommon to find that parents continued to reinforce negative as well as positive behavior or that logical consequences were misused so that the child interpreted them as punishment. If the counselor ascertains that parents do not have a complete grasp of the psychological principles or the specific techniques, these should be carefully reviewed before any further action is initiated.

If the parents fully understood what actions were to be taken, the counselor should review the home situation. It is possible that some of the vital factors were overlooked in the first interview. For example, the influences of peers, relatives, and siblings upon the situation should receive special attention. So should factors such as parental disagreement about approaches to be utilized and the possibility of a family schedule that prohibits the systematic utilization of certain strategies such as a family meeting. Typically, whenever progress has not been made, the counselor has either failed to explain the approaches sufficiently or has overlooked key factors in the family. However, there is one other factor that may have contributed to this situation.

At the outset of this chapter it was pointed out that some parents are in need of counseling because their own behavior is the causal factor in the family difficulty. Levitt and Rubenstein (1957) and Bird (1964) have suggested that parents often distort advice that is preferred by members of the helping professions. This may be in part true because of the parents' own problems.

Parental resistance can stem from sources other than personal disorders. Approaches advocated by mental health specialists often run contrary to cultural ideas about child rearing. Ideas such as that children should be seen and not heard and that children should obey their authoritarian parents run deep in our culture and are constantly reinforced by the authoritarian nature of much of our societal structure. Democratic family structure and open communication are, of course, contradictory concepts to these traditional ideas and are thus either distorted or ignored by parents, in spite of the fact that they are experiencing difficulty in their relationships with their children.

Overcoming resistance resulting from personality disorders is difficult and has already been discussed. However, one technique that has proven to be of some use in overcoming parental resistance for other reasons is to ask parents what children are learning as a result of child-rearing techniques. The first step in this process is to ask parents what behaviors or values they are trying to teach their children. The typical answers are honesty, loyalty, cooperation, good citizenship, independence, and so on. Then parents are asked to relate what their children are learning as a result of parental treatment. The father who does not listen soon recognizes that one cannot teach cooperation without communication, just as the overly protective parent recognizes that sheltering children and making decisions for them results in dependence rather than independence.

Parents who expect their children to assume no responsibility in the home or who make excuses for them when they do not can hardly expect those children to become highly responsible citizens.

Termination

Termination of the parental consultation process should occur whenever the parents are able to understand their own problems and act on those insights. Termination may occur earlier if either or both parents are in need of some type of therapeutic assistance, with the result that the problem interferes with the consulting process. Early termination may also occur where parents hold values or beliefs that are contradictory to good mental health practice.

It is suggested that approximately one month after termination a postcard follow-up note be sent to parents in order to determine whether or not progress is being continued. This survey should also extend an opportunity for parents to reenter the consultation process if progress is not satisfactory. This serves both the purpose of providing some evaluation of the process and enabling parents who either terminated or were terminated earlier to avail themselves of the consultant's services.

GROUP PARENTAL CONSULTATION

Dinkmeyer (1973) has presented the idea of the "C" group, so labeled because it involves collaboration, consultation, and confrontation and because it clarifies belief systems, is made up of concerned and committed members, and is confidential. He goes on to enumerate the helping forces in the "C" group as acceptance, feedback, universalization or becoming aware that one's problems with children are not unique, altruism or stimulation through assisting others, and spectator therapy or the process of receiving help by observing others being helped.

Consultation groups, unlike the education group to be discussed in the next section, do not have an agenda. Typically, these groups are initiated by the consultant, usually through a mailed survey to parents. Dinkmeyer (1973) suggests that the groups be restricted to parents having children at a single grade level, that the groups meet for six to eight weeks, and that the meetings be approximately one and one-half hour in duration.

The initial letter that is sent to parents should begin the structuring of the consultation group. Essentially the group should be described as a place where parents share their concerns about their children and receive help with these concerns. This letter should also specify the time, place, and dates of the meetings to be held. One additional component should be included in the first letter:

the procedure for selecting participants. This is included because often more parents will volunteer for the group than can be accommodated initially. Therefore, the letter may need to contain dates for later sessions and a request that the parents list the dates in terms of priority.

The process of the consulting group is much the same as that described for the teacher group consultation. The first session should be devoted to getting comfortable, establishing relationships, and establishing roles. The consultant should lead the discussion, using the same procedures described for teacher consultation groups.

Subsequent sessions should focus on the general concerns of parents, with a gradual shift toward the particular concerns of individuals as the session progresses. Since a termination date has already been established, this is generally not an issue, although at times there will be some pressure brought to bear to continue the group. If this occurs, the counselor may encourage the group to continue independently or may meet with them, depending upon individual circumstances.

Parent groups, like other groups, allow counselors to use their time more effectively, and increase the resources available to the individuals in need of help. Parent groups may cause fewer scheduling problems than teacher groups, but someone must take the responsibility for arranging space and keeping members informed about the group. This should be one of the parents, particularly if the group meets outside the school for any reason. Finally, parental consulting groups, like teacher groups, do not lend themselves well to confidentiality. Dinkmeyer (1973) indicates that this is an important aspect of the consulting group, and it may be desirable to try to establish confidentiality as a norm. As a matter of practical significance, however, it is not likely that confidentiality will exist, and thus it may be wiser to acknowledge this from the outset.

PARENT EDUCATION

We hope that it was made clear at the outset of this chapter that parent education and parent consultation are dissimilar for a variety of reasons. However, parent education can serve as a useful adjunct to the parental consultation program because it provides an opportunity to teach psychological principles and techniques to a large number of parents. This in turn can enhance the consultation process whenever parents are involved. On the other hand, parental consultation can and often does lead parents to a point where they wish to have more knowledge about the principles of parenting. Therefore, parent education and parent consultation are viewed here as mutually supportive activities that contribute to one common goal: enabling parents to facilitate the development of their children.

A number of individuals have written in support of involvement of parents in educational programs. Luckey (1967) asserts that not only should parent education be a part of the school, but that parents are eager for these services. She believes that there are many areas such as sexual information, behavioral standards, and attitudinal development that parents are unable to deal with effectively, although they are essentially family matters. Parents can and should be helped with these and other concerns through parent education, according to Luckey. Banks and Brooks (1971) took a position similar to Luckey's and reported a program that involved more than 200 parents. Topics such as efficient use of time, understanding modern education, and career development were included in the program that they developed for parents. McWhirter and Cabanski (1972) reported that a program designed for parents with children with learning disabilities and emotional disorders was well received by parents and resulted in behavioral changes in children, according to teacher reports. Their educational program was designed to teach child development principles and behavior modification approaches.

At least two rather ambitious studies have been conducted to evaluate the outcomes of parent education. Larson (1972) investigated the impact of three approaches, Achievement Motivation Program (AMP), Parent Effectiveness Training (PET), and Discussion Encounter Group (DEG), upon family communication and other dependent measures. An analysis of logs kept by the parents showed that PET participants listed increased listening skills more often than did participants in other groups. PET participants also noted improvement in the area of problem solving and better communication skills with individuals other than children as positive outcomes. AMP participants most often cited that they had successfully met weekly goals that had been set in the group. They also indicated that family relationships had improved and that they had more positive mental attitudes. The logs completed by DEG participants were less revealing, but they listed more personal openness as the main positive outcome. Not unexpectedly, the foregoing results are directly related to the type of educational programs provided.

In a second, better controlled and more systematically analyzed study, Frazier and Matthes (1975) compared Adlerian and behavioral approaches to parent education. Their criterion instruments were parental responses to Attitude Toward the Freedom of Children Scale II (ATFC), Child-Rearing Practices Scale (CRPS), and Freeman Behavior Checklist. Frazier and Matthes reported that parents in the Adlerian group had less restrictive attitudes toward their children, as measured by the ATFC, than those in either the behavioral or control group and that there were no significant differences in perceptions of children in the experimental and control groups. Their third finding, the one dealing with child-rearing practices, indicated that parents did tend to adopt the procedures that were espoused in the two educational approaches, particularly in the Adlerian group. One finding reported by Frazier and Matthes, which cast a shadow of doubt on the findings, particularly those with regard to the two experimental groups, was that in leading the Adlerian group, facilitators were viewed as more encouraging than they were when they led behavioral groups. This suggests a bias on the part of the education group leader.

The evidence is not overwhelming, but it is generally positive with regard to parent education. This, coupled with the support of various professionals cited earlier, plus the day-to-day observations of consultants, certainly provides a sufficient rationale for parent education. Let us now turn briefly to examine three parent education approaches.

A COMMUNICATIONS APPROACH

Parent Effectiveness Training (Gordon, 1970) is by far the most popular communication approach to parent education, although a very useful format has been developed by Brownstone and Dye (1973). This approach attempts to teach parents communications skills, develop methods of conflict resolution, and help parents clarify their values, identify the ways in which values induce conflict, and teach parents ways of influencing the values of their children.

McWhirter and Kahn (1974) describe a communications approach to parent education based upon Gordon's (1970) ideas and to a certain extent those of Carkhuff (1972 A). They recommend a seven-session format, which is outlined here.

Session I. Course Introduction and Communications Patterns
    A. Get acquainted.
        a. Learn names.
        b. Have each discuss family situation.
    B. Introduce Course.
        a. Describe different types of parents.
        b. Have parents describe themselves.
    C. Introduce communications patterns.
        a. Emphasize acceptance.
        b. Describe role playing.
Session II. Communication with Children
    A. Introduce active listening.
Session III. Sharing Parental Problems with Children
    A. Discuss "owning" the problem (get parents to recognize when they have a problem).
    B. Use confrontation (Carkhuff).
Session IV. Conflict in Family Relationships
    A. Parents demonstrate present procedures used to deal with conflict.
    B. Discuss negative aspects of authoritarian role.

   C. Introduce "no-lose" approach to conflict resolution (see Chapter 11, Gordon, 1970).

Session V. Conflict Resolution

   A. Apply "no-lose" method. (The procedure is much the same as that described earlier in this book for problem solving.)

Section VI. Parental Values

   A. Help parents clarify values.

   B. Draw up lists of issues that do and do not involve parents' values.

   C. Discuss influencing values.

     a. Modeling

     b. Consulting

     c. Accepting

Session VII. Review and Evaluation

Throughout the foregoing and other approaches to parent education, parents are encouraged to utilize the techniques, which are discussed with their families, as a means of enhancing the learning process.

In summary, the communications approach to parent education is based upon the premises set forth in Chapter Two in the Neo-Client-Centered section. The basic concern, because of these premises, is to teach effective communication. Gordon (1970) and Carkhuff (1972 A, B) go beyond the basic communication idea and introduce methods of conflict resolution and problem-solving techniques that can be of great assistance to parents in coping more effectively with their children.

A BEHAVIORAL APPROACH

Behavioral approaches to parent education have become popular because of the availability of useful materials and because of the ability of parents to grasp quickly and implement the concepts of behaviorism. Patterson and Gullian's (1967) book *Living with Children* has been used extensively as a text in parent education classes. A newer book by Krumboltz and Krumboltz (1972) is also extremely useful for use with parents. Another particularly helpful set of materials has been developed by Edward B. Rettig (1973) and is titled *ABC's for Parents*. This set of materials contains nine lessons, which fully cover the principles of behavior modification. It is important that an inexpensive workbook is available for parents. A brief outline of the nine sessions recommended by Rettig follows.

Session I. Analyzing Behavior

   A. Introduce Behavior Modification.

   B. Pretest.

C. Identify behavior to be changed.

D. Establish goals.

Session II. Observing and Tracking Behavior

A. Operationalize target behaviors.

B. Explain systematic observation.

C. Explain charting behavior.

Session III. Developing an Intervention

A. Discuss reinforcement and punishment.

B. Explain negative reinforcement.

C. Explain extinction.

D. Tell how to select reinforcers.

E. Develop strategy.

Session IV. Strengthening and Maintaining Behavior

A. Focus on positive reinforcement and negative reinforcement; for example, how to select reinforcers.

B. Discuss principles involved in the utilization of reinforcers.

C. Suggest home token economy systems.

D. Explain self-reinforcement.

Session V. Weakening and Eliminating Behavior

A. Discuss the use of punishment.

B. Discuss extinction.

C. Explain counterconditioning and satiation.

Session VI. Modeling and Shaping

A. Discuss cues and their use.

   a. Physical cues

   b. Verbal cues

B. Discuss modeling and the development of behavior.

C. Explain shaping the use of approximations.

Session VII. Returning to Baseline

A. Parents return to old methods.

   a. Plot behavior as a result.

B. Review Principles.

Session VIII. Return to Intervention

A. Stretch the schedule of reinforcement.

B. Begin fading.

C. Continue to plot behavior.

Session IX. Looking to the Future

A. Anticipate problems ahead.

B. Design programs in advance.

C. Summarize principles.

A session-by-session evaluation is included in the program prepared by Rettig (1973). These evaluations can be very helpful in determining the progress being made in the workshop. As can be seen in the foregoing outline, an attempt is made to have parents thoroughly learn behavioral principles and to prepare them to use these principles after the educational sessions are completed. It is suggested here that the counselor be available to parents after the sessions end to help them with any problems which might arise.

ADLERIAN PARENT EDUCATION*

Adlerian counselors, like counselors with other theoretical orientations, attempt to teach parents to utilize the concepts of Adlerian theory in their child rearing. At times materials such as *Children the Challenge* (Dreikurs and Soltz 1964) are used as adjuncts to the educational program. Other Adlerians simply prepare handouts that deal with topics such as encouragement, natural and logical consequences, and other concepts that are stressed in the educational program. The following is an outline of a ten-session parent education program conducted by one Adlerian counselor. The sessions should last from one and one-half to two hours and should include ten to twenty parents, with the lower number being ideal.

Session I. Overview of Theory
  A. Introduce Adlerian model.
      1. Behavior purposive
      2. Behavior socially imbedded
      3. Family constellation: influence of ordinal position
      4. Cooperation a necessity of human survival: family as a social unit
      5. Understanding purpose of behavior accomplished by looking at behavior of others, not child
  B. Generate script of family problem.
      1. Problem written out in detail
  C. Develop strategy.
  D. Make assignment to deal with problem.
Session II. Review of Scripts and Outcome of Action Taken
  A. Understanding of purposiveness of behavior developed
  B. Parents helped to understand why they succeeded or failed
Sessions III and IV.
  A. Introduce Encouragement.
      1. Listening for purpose of communication: family council

*Appreciation is expressed to Dr. William H. McKelvie, Bowie State College, Bowie, Maryland, for supplying material for this section.

    2. Means of encouraging introduced
      a. Tailored to individual
      b. Physical contact
      c. Focus on positive
  B. Each session would end in assignments on listening and using encouragement.

Session V. Encouraging Responsibility
  A. What is responsibility? Why are people responsible?
  B. Social elements that encourage responsibility
  C. Some methods of encouraging responsibility
    1. Do not do things for children they can do for themselves.
    2. Allow children to assume tasks without intervention.
    3. Emphasize child's part in social structure (family conflict resolution).
  D. Logical and natural consequences
  E. Assignment: pick an area of responsibility to encourage.

Sessions VI–IX. Specific Problems Parents Are Encountering. Some typical ones are:
  A. Establishing rules (hours)
  B. Homework and school problems
  C. Getting children to do chores
  (In each instance script analysis is conducted, role playing is utilized and encouragement is stressed.)

Session X. Review and Evaluation
  A. Principles reviewed
  B. Parents assess their progress

In some ways the Adlerian approach described here approximates parent consultation because of the emphasis upon helping parents with their particular problems. In the other approaches, the focus upon problems is used more as a teaching mechanism. This component is retained in this approach, too.

Baruth and Jones (1975) present a slightly different format for Adlerian parent study groups. Their parent education groups meet for ten sessions and discuss the following topics:

1. Registration, Dreikurs, Mt. Pleasant tape. (Discusses democracy in the home.)
2. Encouragement
3. Mistaken goals
4. Consequences
5. Reward and punishment
6. Respect for order

7. Family council
8. Overprotection
9. Staying out of fights
10. Downgrading bad habits

In summary, parent education can be a useful means of helping parents deal more effectively with children. It can also facilitate the consultation process because parents who have completed parent education courses are more likely to understand the psychological principles which need to be employed.

CASE STUDIES

Two case studies will be presented at this time: first, one that involves both a parent and a teacher. This case is presented to show how parents can be used to facilitate the teacher consultation process. In the second situation, the consultation is conducted directly with the mother of a teenage boy. Both of these consultation cases were conducted by Adlerian consultants.

Case One: Teacher-Parent Consultation*

Background The fourteen-year-old black student had often been in trouble with his English teacher, who was also black. The student was well-behaved as long as the teacher was involved with him in some way, but as soon as she shifted her attention, the student would make a noise, drop a pencil, or engage in some other distracting act. The consultation session was precipitated when the boy called his teacher a racist during one of his classes with her. The teacher requested that the boy's father be present (his mother had died five years earlier).

Session One The first step was to establish ground rules. These were that (1) we were trying to understand the nature of the problem, (2) we were trying to determine how each party perceived the situation, and (3) no one would be considered right or wrong.

The student was asked to state his point of view first. He stated flatly that the teacher was unfair and that the white students got a better break than he did or any of the black kids did, for that matter.

The teacher, who had been involved in study groups, declared that the student was an attention-getter, referring to Dreikurs's Goal One. She went on to tell

---

*Appreciation is expressed to Dr. William H. McKelvie of Bowie State College, Bowie, Maryland, for supplying material for this section.

how the student constantly kept her involved; she defended her position. She stated that she cooperated when the students cooperated, which was an offhand way of saying that the student was uncooperative.

The father was obviously hostile by this point and made it clear that he felt that the school was racist in character. He said that he resented coming to school and missing work, although he had been told that we would meet at a time convenient to him. It became obvious that many of the father's views coincided with those of his son.

At this point I summarized the situation by stating as accurately as I could the situation as each seemed to perceive it. These summaries were:

Student: Didn't feel that he received deserved recognition. Also did not want to be bossed.

Teacher: Wanted control and was concerned about lack of cooperation. Didn't want to lose status.

Father: Felt that school is racially biased, doesn't really care about kids. Didn't want to give in to the institution.

I identified these perceptions and then summarized the issue as "Who is going to win?" All agreed that I had accurately restated their positions and agreed with the central issue. I then made the point that before we embarked upon a problem-solving process we must have commitment and cooperation. I specifically made the point that you cannot make someone do something that he or she does not want to, and so any of them could sabotage the process. All agreed that this was true and agreed to work toward a solution to the problem.

I then asked what we could do so that no one would lose. I put it in these terms:

1. How can the student get the recognition that he desires?
2. How can the teacher maintain her place in her own classroom?
3. How can the father *not* give in to a racist institution?

We then went on to answer these questions. The teacher suggested that she could give the student jobs and could try to emphasize his good points more. The student indicated that he felt that doing this would help and he would therefore try to keep from distracting the classroom. I suggested to the father that since the teacher was cooperating perhaps the best thing he could do was to allow the teacher and student to work it out, and he agreed.

I then raised the question about what would happen if the student did not live up to his agreement. It was suggested that the logical consequence of such action would be for the student to leave the room and not be able to return until further action was discussed. This was agreed to by all parties.

The final step in the session was to write up all agreements that had been made and to schedule a follow-up session for two weeks later.

Follow-up Session We reviewed the written agreements and all parties reported that the situation was much improved. The session was terminated in about thirty minutes.

Case Two: Parental Consultation

Background Ted, a fifteen-year-old high school sophomore, had been an excellent student before coming to high school. At that point he had stopped doing his work and was either out of school ill or left during the day much of the time. The principal suggested that a conference be held with the boy's mother, a divorcee.

Session One The session was initiated by explaining that school officials were greatly concerned about Ted's absences from school and that this was not a disciplinary session. The purpose of the session was outlined as trying to initiate a cooperative effort among the student, the parent, and the school to rekindle Ted's interest in school.

Ted sat silently while the mother related that she had tried just about everything that she could with Ted and welcomed any help. The tone of her conversation was one of exasperation aimed both at Ted and her ex-husband, who she felt had set a bad example for Ted. She also communicated that she had tried to be a good mother but had failed.

Ted, it was discovered, was the older of two children. His sister, who is three years younger, was, according to the mother, a model child.

We then looked at a typical day in the household. It became apparent that the mother was almost constantly involved with Ted and had been since he was quite young. This involvement ranged from getting him up in the morning and off to school to getting him to complete his chores. The situation in the morning was made more acute by the fact that the mother was also getting ready to go to work. One other problem mentioned was that Ted and the mother disagreed about his staying out at night. She wanted Ted to be in by 8:00 P.M., and he felt that he should stay out until 10. Ted was often in conflict with his younger sister also. The mother indicated that she felt that Ted usually started these fights and that she usually had to settle them by sending the children to bed.

Ted agreed that the situation in the home was pretty much as described except that he felt that his sister started the fights as often as he did. He also indicated that his mother tried to run his life by choosing his friends and his clothes and setting all the rules. He indicated that he did not have the same privileges as other boys his own age.

When asked about school Ted said that he had just lost interest in it. He said that the work was boring and that most of his friends were at another school as a result of a move that had occurred between junior and senior high school. He indicated that the students in this school were "stuck up."

One other point of conflict was uncovered at this point. Ted had a part-time job which paid rather well. His mother wanted him to save all of his money, but he wanted to buy clothes and records with it. The mother admitted that she could give Ted only a small allowance but felt he should save for his college education.

At this point I summarized the session from both the student's and the mother's point of view. The mother seemed to be indicating that her efforts to be a good mother were being undermined by Ted and that Ted was not really old enough to make independent decisions. Ted felt that the mother wasn't giving him the credit he deserved and was trying to control his life. The central issue seemed to be one of control. Both agreed that this accurately described their perceptions.

At this point the idea that the present situation needed changing was introduced and both agreed. The idea that some cooperative arrangement needed to be worked out was also agreed to. Two target areas were selected as being critical: rules regarding coming home at night and the utilization of money.

After some discussion it was tentatively agreed that Ted could stay out until 10 P.M. In return, he was to keep his mother informed regarding where he was going so that the mother would feel more comfortable.

After it was suggested that Ted needed to begin to accept responsibility for his own behavior, it was decided that he could spent some of his money as he wished and save some. In return, the mother would continue the small allowance that she was now providing.

Then the idea of providing encouragement to Ted and the sister was discussed. Some of the good points about each child were listed and the mother indicated that she would try to emphasize these more. It was also suggested that Ted and his sister should solve their own problems. The mother was skeptical about this idea but agreed to stay out of their arguments.

A follow-up session was scheduled for two weeks later, and it was requested that the sister be included.

Session Two The mother, Ted, and his sister arrived at the appointed time. All agreed that the home situation was somewhat better, although there were still problems. Ted was still having trouble getting up in the morning and was not completing his chores. A discussion of the family as a social unit that required a great amount of cooperation followed. Also the idea of natural and logical consequences was introduced.

It was decided that Ted would start accepting full responsibility for getting out of bed and getting off to school. It was stressed that the mother should not intervene in this process because in a sense she was expressing the idea that Ted couldn't take care of himself when she did. The mother objected at first because she felt that Ted would miss school. When it was pointed out that Ted still wasn't coming to school regularly even with her help, she agreed that things couldn't get much worse. It was also agreed that when Ted missed school the mother would not write excuses as in the past and that Ted would have points deducted from his grades as a consequence of missing school. It was also decided that the school should not admit Ted when he came to school late, a logical consequence of his tardiness. Ted agreed that these measures were fair and expressed confidence that he could get to school on time.

Chores were discussed next, particularly Ted's approach to them. It was decided that whenever Ted did not complete his routine chores and the mother had to take time to do them, this time would be deducted from time now spent with Ted. One area of contention, Ted's room, was to be left up to his discretion. The only responsibility that Ted was to accept was keeping the door closed so that the mother would not be embarrassed by its condition whenever friends came by.

Attention was then focused on Ted's relationship with his sister. They role-played some of their disputes and then practiced analyzing what each was trying to get the other to do. They decided that each would try to withdraw from power struggles whenever these started to arise.

At the end of this session all agreements that had been made were written out, and the third session was scheduled for two weeks later.

Session Three All three parties arrived on time, and it became very clear that the home situation was improved. Ted had been to school nine out of the past ten days. He indicated that he was having trouble making contacts with other sophomores, however. I suggested that the two of us get together during school time to work on this problem, and Ted agreed.

The mother expressed some concern about the kind of clothes Ted was buying. We then reviewed the principles of encouraging responsibility. The mother agreed that Ted should accept responsibility in this area but admitted concern. When asked if she was concerned about Ted or what others might think of her as a mother, she admitted that it was the latter.

Ted and his sister expressed interest in knowing more about staying out of conflict. The principles of encouragement were reviewed, and they agreed to be more supportive. They also listed some things that had started fights and agreed that whenever any of these surfaced they would withdraw and discuss the situation thirty minutes later.

The mother reported that Ted had been particularly good about keeping her informed about his whereabouts and even came home early many evenings.

A subsequent session was scheduled for two weeks later.

Session Four This was a brief session, lasting only forty-five minutes. The home situation was greatly improved according to the reports and Ted was coming to school regularly. In the session he indicated that there were two boys in one of his classes that he wanted to get to know better and asked if they could stay overnight. His mother agreed but indicated that she hoped he would clean up his room first. She quickly realized what she had said and added that of course it was his decision.

It was agreed that no other sessions would be scheduled unless other problems arose.

SUMMARY

In this chapter two topics, parental consultation and parent education, have been discussed. These have been presented as mutually supportive activities, which can enable parents to function more effectively.

The rationale for parental intervention procedures is quite clear when one looks at divorce rates, the pressures exerted by society, and a variety of other data. Intervention with parents requires understanding of the needs that are present and specific techniques and strategies. Both have been included here.

Finally, two case studies have been presented to illustrate some of the concepts included in the chapter. One deals with involving parents in teacher consultation and the other presents a parental consultation case.

REFERENCES

Auerbach, A. B. *Parents Learn through Discussion.* New York: Wiley, 1968.

Baruth, L. G., and M. D. Jones. "Initiating Child Study Groups for Parents," *The School Counselor*, 23 (1975): 121–126.

Bird, B. "A Mother's Paradoxical Response to Advice," *American Journal of Diseased Children*, 4 (1964): 383–385.

Brandwein, R. A., C. A. Brown, and E. M. Fox. "Women and Children Last: The Social Situation of Divorced Mothers and Their Families," *Journal of Marriage and the Family*, 36 (1974): 498–514.

Brown, D., and S. T. Brown. *Consulting with Elementary Teachers.* Boston: Houghton Mifflin, 1975 (A).

———. "Parental Consultation: A Behavioral Approach," *Elementary School Guidance and Counseling Journal*, 1975 (B).

Brownstone, J. E., and C. J. Dye. *Communication Workshop for Parents of Adolescents.* Champaign: Research Press, 1973.

Carkhuff, R. R. *The Art of Helping.* Amherst: Human Resources Development Press, 1972 (A).

———. *The Art of Problem Solving.* Amherst: Human Resources Development Press, 1972 (B).

Dinkmeyer, D. C. "The Parent 'C' Group," *Personnel and Guidance Journal,* 52 (1973): 252-256.

Dinkmeyer, D., and J. Carlson. *Consulting: Facilitating Human Potential and Change Processes.* Columbus: Charles E. Merrill, 1973.

Dreikurs, R., and V. Soltz. *Children: The Challenge.* New York: Hawthorne Books, 1964.

Evans, E. "Orienting Junior High School Parents," *Personnel and Guidance Journal,* 51 (1973): 729-732.

Frazier, F., and W. A. Matthes. "Parent Education: A Comparison of Adlerian and Behavioral Approaches," *Elementary School Guidance and Counseling,* 19 (1975): 31-38.

Glidewell, J. "Priorities for Psychologists in Community Mental Health." In *Issues in Community Psychology and Preventive Mental Health,* ed. J. Glidewell. New York: Behavioral Publications, 1971.

Gordon, T. *P.E.T.: Parent Effectiveness Training.* New York: Peter H. Wyden, 1970.

Krumboltz, J. D., and H. B. Krumboltz. *Changing Children's Behavior.* Englewood Cliffs: Prentice-Hall, 1972.

Larson, R. S. "Can Parent Classes Affect Family Communications?" *School Counselor,* 19 (1972): 261-270.

Lazarus, A., G. C. Davison, and D. A. Polefka. "Classical and Operant Factors in the Treatment of School Phobia," *Journal of Abnormal Psychology,* 50 (1965): 225-230.

Levitt, M., and B. O. Rubenstein. "The Fate of Advice: Examples of Distortion in Parental Counseling," *Mental Hygiene,* 41 (1957): 213-216.

Luckey, E. B. "Parent Education: A Function of the Elementary School," *Elementary School Counseling and Guidance,* 1 (1967): 255-262.

McWhirter, J. J., and C. Cabanski. "Influencing the Child: A Program for Parents," *Elementary School Guidance and Counseling,* 7 (1972): 26-31.

McWhirter, J. J., and S. E. Kahn. "A Parent Communication Group," *Elementary School Guidance and Counseling,* 9 (1974): 116-122.

Mead, M. "New Designs for Family Living," *Redbook* (October, 1970), pp. 22-25.

Newsweek, March 12, 1973, p. 47.

O'Dell, S. "Training Parents in Behavior Modification: A Review," *Psychological Bulletin,* 81 (1974): 418-433.

Patterson, G., and M. E. Gullian. *Living With Children.* Champaign: Research Press, 1967.

Rettig, E. B. *ABC's for Parents.* Champaign: Research Press, 1973.

Shaw, M. C. "The Feasibility of Parent Group Counseling in Elementary Schools," *Elementary School Guidance and Counseling,* 4 (1969): 43-53.

Sonstegard, M. "A Rationale for Interviewing Parents," *School Counselor,* 12 (1964): 72-76.

Tavormina, J. B. "Basic Models of Parent Counseling," *Psychological Bulletin,* 81 (1974): 827-835.

CHAPTER NINE Organizational Consultation

There can be no doubt that educational organizations are in need of persons and mechanisms that can facilitate orderly adaptation to changing societal demands. The concept of change seems attractive to many educators as school districts vie each year for federal and state funds to create exemplary educational projects. However, few of these projects make a lasting impact, simply because the organization failed to develop broad-based support for the program at the outset, inadequately publicized the project during its operation, could not provide the resources needed to implement the concepts once the project had proven its worth, or neglected a multitude of other activities. Most educational teams engaged in the innovation process look like the blind men who tried to describe an elephant by feeling its various parts. Changes may develop as a result of the attempt, but very often they do not correspond to the reality of the situation. The purpose in this chapter is to continue what has already been begun: that is, to broaden understanding of the process of innovative change and provide some specific suggestions about how consultants may function more effectively in facilitating it. In the section that follows, some issues central to innovative change will be discussed. This discussion will be followed by an examination of two models of organizational change, an exploration of the process of innovation, and, finally, some conclusions drawn for the consultant.

ISSUES IN INNOVATION

A number of issues must be addressed prior to an in-depth exploration of the innovative change process since they impinge on both the semantics of the discussion to follow and the realities with which consultants must cope. Perhaps the most basic of these issues is the definition of the term *innovation*. Tilton (1971) points out that in the planned change literature the term *innovation* is used to denote three separate processes. One usage equates innovation with invention without regard to the adoption or implementation of the process or mechanism which has been created. An extension of the definition is to use innovation to define a process where invention occurs in an organization, but there is also adoption of the new development and it is implemented by its creators. Finally, and most commonly, innovation is used as a descriptive term to denote a process where an organization, such as a school, adopts an idea which is new to that organization but not necessarily new to other organizations. This adoption of an idea or technique new to the organization is followed by an implementation process (Knight, 1967; Mohr, 1969; Zaltman et al., 1973). This latter definition has been adopted for purposes of this discussion.

Another issue which deserves attention is, "What are the indicators that change should occur?" Specifically, how can we know that change is needed? There are those who would perhaps initiate change because "things could be better." This type of vague logic will not suffice if our innovations are to have meaningful outcomes. Zaltman, Duncan and Holbeck (1973) suggest a better approach to determining when the change process should be initiated. They indicate that change is needed whenever a performance gap exists between what an organization is doing and goal related opportunities which are within its environment. Well known critics of educational institutions (Glasser, 1969; Postman and Weingartner, 1969; Hoyt et al., 1974) have been quick to point out that numerous gaps exist between what our schools are accomplishing and what they could be achieving given the nature of their opportunities. When one considers the multiplicity of knowledge bases, skills and attitudes required by individuals in order to take full advantage of the benefits of a technocratic society it is difficult to disagree. In fact, one of the major problems which confronts change agents is that of determining which components of the school should be changed and to meet which needs. Once these decisions are made the innovation process can be set into motion.

If the assumption that performance gaps are numerous and obvious is tenable, the question which arises is "Why is educational change so slow in developing?" Carlson (1965) has suggested that the anachronistic nature of educational change may be due to a shortage of change agents. The students surveyed by Gallup (1974) tend to support Carlson's position as nearly half of them viewed public school officials as not interested enough in innovation while only 13 percent saw them as too ready to try new ideas. However, in the same study, 43 percent of the parents with children in school saw school officials as just about right in their willingness to innovate, while 26 percent said that educators were too ready to try new ideas. Just 21 percent of the parents were of the opinion that educators were not interested enough in innovation. One conclusion which may be drawn from this discussion is that the groups associated with the educational enterprise have contradictory positions about the need for innovation in our educational institutions and these contradictions may in part contribute to organizational inertia.

If one reviews the change literature there seems to be an underlying assumption that the change agent is an individual. Jones (1969) has taken issue with this assumption. He found in his study of "change agents" in business and industrial settings that a group typically fills the role. If Jones's findings can be generalized to education, and we believe they can, it would be an error to recommend that an individual attempt to act as an organizational change agent. Rather, as Havelock (1973) noted, it seems far more advisable for the social activist to identify innovators who can make up a *change team*. The importance of a change team or group approach will perhaps become clearer as the complexities of organizational change are explored in greater detail.

Another consideration is the locus of operation. Murray and Schmuck (1972) indicate that the consultant can work either as an internal process consultant or as a member of an external change team which intervenes in other schools within an educational system. Bennis (1969) and Argyris (1970) seem to be advocating a slightly different position, one favoring only the external change team. Jones (1969) provided support for the idea that the change team can function from within or without. He examined 190 cases of planned organizational change and found that in 106 situations change originated from an internal source and in 84 cases an external change agent was utilized. Havelock (1973), like Murray and Schmuck, believes that change can be initiated either utilizing an internal or external change team. While it is certain that functioning from within alters the perceptions which organizational members have of a change agent, the internal locus of operation appears to present no major barrier to effectiveness.

Baldridge (1971) raises still another important issue in planned change. He asserts that before any intelligent discussion of change can occur we must be ready to discuss the subsystem within the organization which is to be the focus of change. Udy (1965) notes that there are five of these subsystems: (1) the technology of the organization, (2) the staff of the organization, (3) the group processes of these individuals, (4) the administrative structure, and (5) the interaction of the organization with its public. Baldridge's point of the need to specify the area to be changed seems particularly well taken when one examines the innovative change literature. Often the discussion is global in nature with the obvious assumption being that change processes and strategies apply equally well to each subsystem. Baldridge (1971) indicates that this is a doubtful assumption.

In the foregoing discussion we have dealt with a variety of issues which are vital to clear communication in the remainder of this chapter. First, innovation has been defined as the process by which an educational organization adopts a technique, procedure, program or policy which is *new to that organization.* Second, we have said that innovation should occur whenever a performance gap occurs, that is, whenever an educational organization fails to utilize its potential to assist students. Third, while we have not ruled out the possibility of the individual's functioning as a change agent, our own perception is that this role will more typically be filled by a group. Fourth, we have asserted that change may as readily emanate from internal sources as external sources. Fifth, we have indicated that target subsystems must be specified before change proceeds. What has not been set forth is that organizational consultation, like individual or small group consultation, is based upon theoretical assumptions. The next section is designed to assist in the understanding of this premise.

SELECTION OF A THEORETICAL APPROACH

Stiles and Robinson (1973) identified at least three models which they labeled as the political processes model, the research and developmental model, and the systems analysis model. Baldridge (1971) subsumed the systems analysis model into a broader approach, a political systems approach and added a human relations model to the list provided by Stiles and Robinson. These two models, the human relations model and the political systems model, will be discussed in depth in this chapter since they appear to be the most global in nature. The others will be discussed briefly, however.

The selection of a model for organizational change is very much like the process of selecting a theory to undergird the consultation process aimed at the facilitation of individual development. Consultants must familiarize themselves with the various models, assess their own belief and value systems, and make a choice. Bennis (1966) has provided some guidelines for choosing a theory of changing, although he attributes most of his ideas to Robert Chin. These guidelines are:

1. A theory of change must provide the conceptual tools necessary to analyze the process of change and enable us to influence its pace, direction, and quality.
2. A theory of change must identify the role of the change agent and how this individual or group of individuals will interact with the organization.

3. The theory must take the cost of change into consideration.

4. A theory of change must enable the change agent to diagnose those conditions that may either retard or accelerate change.

5. A theory of change must identify the stages of the change process so that the change agent can determine the degree of progress being made.

6. The theory must be so conceptualized and written that it can be communicated effectively.

MODELS OF PLANNED CHANGE: INTRODUCTION

There are at least five theoretical approaches that could have been drawn upon for this discussion. One, the political processes model (Stiles and Robinson, 1973), was eliminated because the locus of change is external and is therefore not germane to this discussion. A second, the diffusion model, was eliminated because it is probably less well known and because it is based upon the assumption that educational change ultimately is the result of educational processes. We have foregone a strict discussion of a conflict approach and a systems approach to change in favor of a political systems approach, which integrates aspects of both. Finally, we have included a discussion of the human relations model because it is undoubtedly the best-known model of planned change and, with adaptation, lends itself to change which emanates from within.

THE HUMAN RELATIONS MODEL

The human relations paradigm of organizational change has been developed and contributed to by a host of organizational theorists and social scientists including Argyris (1970), Bennis (1966, 1970) and Lippitt (1969). Kurt Lewin and Carl Rogers both have contributed heavily to the theoretical base of this model (Gardner, 1974). Lewin's (1951) contribution has been to provide a field theory orientation: that is, a view that the problems of organizations must be solved in a manner that incorporates into the process all those individuals in the organization because of the forces that they bring to bear upon each other. Rogers's postulates regarding the influence of the environment upon personal growth have been adopted also and set the tone for the human relations approach.

Assumptions

The human relationships model has a number of assumptions that serve as its foundation. The first is that conflict among individuals and groups is the basic barrier to effective and efficient organizational functioning. In this regard Bennis (1966) states: "These chronic conflicts probably dissipate more energy and money than any other single organizational disease" (p. 57). These conflicts are presumed to arise from several sources. Poor communication is viewed as a basic reason for group and individual conflict. It stems either from the fact that the individuals in the organization do not possess the skills to communicate properly or that the organization has not established appropriate communication devices. Other causes of conflict are individuals with inadequate personalities, conflicting value systems among either individuals or groups of individuals, lack of information and poor decision-making skills (Bennis, 1966; Baldridge, 1971; Gardner, 1974).

Second, it is assumed that organizations benefit whenever they place the psychological needs of their staff ahead of the bureaucratic concerns of the individuals (Argyris, 1964; Bennis, 1966). This assumption Baldridge (1971) refers to as the "contented cows give more milk" theory. In short, when workers are able to meet their psychological needs, the organization becomes more productive and efficient. A third assumption underlying a human relationship approach to organizational change is that democratic administrative patterns are superior to autocratic approaches (Bennis, 1966). This is of course quite closely related to the concept that the psychological well-being of individuals should be considered ahead of organizational goals, or, perhaps more precisely, individual need attainment is a prerequisite to organizational efficiency and effectiveness.

Focus of Change

Earlier in this chapter it was asserted that planned change cannot be discussed intelligently unless there is some specification of the target area to be changed. The human relations model has as its primary focus individuals and their attitudes and values and group processes in the organization. The group processes of most concern are those involving communication and decision making. Udy's (1965) other subsystems — technology, administrative structure, and the relationship of the organization to its publics — receive relatively less attention. This focus upon individuals and group processes is maintained because of the assumption that changes in these subsystems will result in change in other subsystems.

Baldridge (1971) points out that there are a number of human relationships models of organizational change. Each of these in fact operates upon the assumptions that were enumerated earlier and have a similar focus with regard to the change process. Two of these approaches have been selected for presentation. First, the action training and research approach, as presented by Gardner (1974), will be described. This will be followed by the organizational training model developed by Schmuck and Runkel (1972).

Action Training and Research

Gardner (1974) lists twelve steps in the action training and research model of organizational change. These are:

1. Orientation
2. Contract Setting
3. Reconnaissance
4. Problem and Opportunity Development
5. Aspirations
6. Analysis
7. Experimentation
8. Results Analysis
9. Program Design
10. Implementation
11. Evaluation and feedback
12. Recycling

Let us examine each of these steps rather briefly, beginning with orientation.

Orientation is a phase that is dedicated to trust development between the consultant and those individuals who are to be involved in the consultation process (Glidewell, 1959; Gardner, 1974). It is a time in which communication patterns are developed, when the consultant becomes familiar with the roles of the consultees (Jarvis and Nelson, 1967), and a time for the consultant to share his or her values (Gardner, 1974). The orientation phase in organizational consultation, then, is roughly equivalent to the relationship stage in consulting with individuals.

Gardner (1974) suggests that there are some specific tasks that must be achieved during this initial phase. These tasks are (1) to identify the consultees, (2) to begin to structure the intervention, (3) to determine what resources are required for the intervention process, and (4) to begin to develop a perspective on the nature of organizational effectiveness. This perspective should be developed from the viewpoint of the individual, the organization, and the community. As would be expected, the human relations consultant attempts to establish that the individual requires nurturance and security, that the organization can benefit from the development of the idea that the organization has legitimacy, and that society is entitled to an efficient, effective organization that meets societal norms.

Contract setting follows orientation and is essentially a process of establishing commitments. Will the organization provide the resources necessary to follow through during the consultation process? Will data collected be utilized by the consultees? Will adequate communication devices be established so that all involved will be kept abreast of the activities of the consultant and the interventions that might develop? Gardner (1974) indicates that this contract need not be a written agreement, but suggests that the consultant should do in-depth exploration to ascertain that an agreement does exist. Without a firm agreement in the areas of commitment of resources, the owning of data and the establishment of a communication procedure consultation should not continue (Gardner and McGill, 1970).

Data collection and reconnaissance are synonymous terms. The essential task to be completed during this stage is to develop data about the situation and specifically the problem area(s) that have been identified. Data collection may be done utilizing questionnaires, structured interviews, group meetings, and/or observations (Gardner, 1974). This process should result in a list of questions concerning those aspects of the organization that are functioning well and areas that are potentially in need of change. Once these questions are developed Gardner suggests that they should be reduced to a manageable number and administered to the target group. He labeled this step as problem and opportunity identification.

The ideal way to get responses to the questionnaire that has been formulated is to interview each member of the target population. This would not be particularly difficult if a change team is working in a small school, but if teachers in a whole school district were to be involved in a change process, either a sample would have to be interviewed or the questionnaire would have to be administered through a technique such as a mailed survey.

The next three steps in the change process—aspirations, analysis and experimentation—may be completed in one session with the target group (Gardner, 1974). The word *aspirations* corresponds in a sense to setting objectives. Once a group accepts the data that have been collected about them and their organization they are ready to set goals. Doing so is followed by analysis, a process of determining priorities for action and identifying factors that constrain the attainment of a goal and those that contribute to the achievement of this goal. Eisen (1969) developed a force-field-analysis technique, which is often used by advocates of the human relations model in the analysis stage. Essentially the process is as follows.

1. Describe the situation that you wish to work on, both as it is now and as you would like it to be.
2. List the driving forces: that is, the forces that push toward the solution of this problem.
3. List the restraining forces: that is, the forces that retard the solution of the problem.
4. Identify both driving and restraining forces that you can affect now and draw up a plan of action for dealing with these forces.
5. Determine how you will evaluate your action.

Once the target population has established priorities for changes and identified both driving and restraining forces that affect these areas, they are ready for experimentation. Experimentation provides an opportunity for the group to adopt new ideas or techniques on a trial basis in order to assess their impact prior to full-scale adoption (Havelock, 1973; Gardner, 1974). A school staff might, for example, adopt a new reading program on a tentative basis but agree to try out the approach for a year in three classrooms. After this year, the staff would analyze the results and determine whether or not to proceed. The staff might very well decide that more data are needed or that changes need to be made in the original innovation prior to implementation.

If the experimentation period is a success, as indicated by the analysis of the outcomes of the pilot program, the target group is ready to design a full-scale program, based, it is hoped, not only on the decision-making process but on the data gathered in the pilot study. This program should be implemented and, after a suitable period, evaluated, and feedback provided to the group. These data and the interaction in the feedback session really are the beginning of the recycling process, which entails retracing each of the steps that have been discussed here (Gardner, 1974). In this way innovative change becomes a dynamic, ongoing process.

Techniques and Strategies. Two general techniques are utilized in the action training and research approach to organizational change. These are workshops, where problems are identified and strategies established, utilizing the force-field-analysis approach, and/or course data collection and feedback. These approaches are for the most part rational in nature, and Bennis (1966) has argued that without an affective component, change may not occur. He has suggested that sensitivity or, perhaps more appropriately, T-groups be utilized as the basic approach so that individuals can develop interpersonal competence, trust and cohesiveness can be developed among previously conflicting groups, and other problems associated with organizational functioning can be experienced directly through the microcosm of the small group. There is little evidence that T-groups increase organizational change (Baldridge, 1971; Schmuck and Runkel, 1972), and therefore the approaches suggested by Gardner (1974) appear to have viability.

Implications of an Action Training and Research Approach. First, consultants who expect to use the action training and research approach must be able to define clearly and to communicate their own value systems, particularly as they relate to education. This process is viewed as particularly important in the relationship development phase of the consulting process. Trust, a prerequisite to meaningful action, cannot be developed unless members of the organization are fully aware of the consultant's beliefs and how these might impinge upon actions taken. Once values are articulated, the consultant must behave in ways that correspond to statements made in this area.

The second implication of the human relations model is that the consultant must secure research skills that will enable him or her to develop interview strategies and questionnaires. Skill must also be acquired in analyzing the information gained from these techniques and drawing conclusions about those aspects of the organization that are not functioning.

Third, conclusions must be drawn about areas of malfunctioning in the organization and strategies must be developed with the target group that will have some likelihood of remediating the problem area. This design process requires the ability to use a force-field analysis in the decision-making process. This is done in order to determine the receptivity of the group to change and in order to develop an understanding of the features of innovations under consideration that will make them more or less acceptable to a group. Both of these issues will be addressed later in this chapter.

Fourth, and finally, the consultant must be able either to provide the expertise required to evaluate the change strategies that are developed or to develop the resources needed in this process. Further, the consultant must be able to help the target group utilize the evaluation data to recycle the change process.

Organizational Thinking

This second human relations approach to organizational change will be reported somewhat less briefly in that the assumptions and focus of change are similar to those of the action research and training model. This description will therefore begin by examining the process, then it will focus upon strategies and techniques and conclude by drawing implications for consultants.

The Process Schmuck and Runkel (1972) suggest that the beginning of the change process need not involve the entire system. Indeed, they suggest that there is no group or subgroup that should be focused upon initially, not even the superintendent's office. They note that many change processes are initiated in today's schools by organizing teachers, students, and other groups.

There are a number of tasks which must be accomplished during the initial or entry phase of the change process. One of these is to establish that an entire group or subsystem must be involved in the intervention process. Another of these chores is to work with the most powerful subgroups in order to cultivate their support, but less powerful groups should not be ignored. A third task is to gain commitment from the groups that are to be involved in the change process.

The second phase of the process is to diagnose the functioning of the organization. As was the case with action training and research, this is done largely through formal and informal data collection. Potential problems that deserve particular scrutiny lie in the areas of conflicts between groups, inter- and intra-group communication, decision-making processes, the methods of goal setting, and role definitions that may lead groups into conflict.

Once a diagnosis has been made, a subsystem must be selected to receive the training. Schmuck and Runkel (1972) believe that it is important that the target subsystem should volunteer for the training, if that is at all possible. It should be noted here that if this is to occur, the diagnosis will have to delineate clearly the nature of the problem and the subsystem(s) responsible for that problem. It might, for example, be that second-level administrators (assistant superintendents and directors) are not communicating policy to their subordinates or that lower-level administrators (principals) are failing in this same process. However, Schmuck and Runkel's point that individuals who are made to participate in any endeavor may be resistant seems well taken.

Third, the consultant should demonstrate the nature of the intervention to be attempted. This may simply be a communications exercise or the use of force-field analysis on a simple problem. It might also be a "fishbowl" procedure, where various groups discuss the problems of the organization while others look on. Onlookers would be given the same opportunity at a later time. The purpose of these demonstrations is to familiarize the participants with the techniques of the consultant, thus, it is hoped, lessening resistance to them.

Once demonstrations have been conducted, the organizational training should be planned and sequenced. The process should begin with improving communications skills, followed by attempts to change norms, and finally, initiating structured change. Free and open communication is essential for organizational functioning, as is a norm that promotes staff cooperation in all areas, particularly problem solving. Structural change involves developing new job functions, restructuring roles, initiating new policies, et cetera. Restructuring, then, is actually the process of institutionalizing the change that has been planned, modeled, and practiced.

Fourth, the outcomes of the intervention must be assessed through both formal and informal means. If the intervention has been a success, the change agent can take the fifth and final step, withdrawal.

Strategies and Techniques Four strategies are listed by Schmuck and Runkel (1972). These are:

1. Working with the subsystems of the organization as groups
2. Developing communications skills
3. Working with groups (subsystems) to develop problem-solving skills
4. Developing a series of training exercises, which start with simulation and evolve to a point where the real issues of the school are the focus.

Let us look at each of these in more detail.

All training, whether it be in the area of communications or problem solving, is done with intact groups (Schmuck and Runkel, 1972). This means that intervention would be made with teachers, administrators, counselors, or other working groups. To be sure, more than one of these groups might be involved at the same time, but it is important that each member of each subgroup should be included. Schmuck and Runkel stress that personality change is not the goal of the group meetings and indeed indicate that individuals who have been involved in personal growth groups may hinder the task groups that they develop because they mistake the purpose of the latter. The groups are brought together to enhance communication, to learn more effective means of problem solving, and to restructure roles as a result of these processes. These groups are appropriately termed *task groups*.

The techniques utilized in the organizational training model to develop communications skills are similar to those described earlier in this volume. In fact, the Carkhuff model could be used quite appropriately to help the various groups in the school learn to communicate more effectively with each other and with other subgroups. Schmuck and Runkel (1972) recommend that individuals be able to paraphrase the communications of others, be able to describe accurately the behaviors of others, be able to describe personal feelings, and be able to interpret accurately the feelings of others. Only the process of accurately describing human behavior is not included in the Carkhuff model.

Schmuck and Runkel (1972) are not specific about the strategies that they use to restructure the organization, although it is presupposed that the increased gains in communication and problem-solving ability will lead to this restructuring. Certainly the more operational specification of organizational goals is expected to provide cues about what restructuring is necessary. However, as we indicated earlier, the task of restructuring is crucial.

Implications. Obviously the consultant who hopes to use organizational training must have the ability to teach, through modeling and other means, communication and problem solving skills. These are crucial to the process. Additionally the consultant must be able to diagnose institutional problems through the use of research and systematic interviewing procedures. This, like the need to be able to evaluate the process, is a similar implication to those which evolved from the action training and research model.

THE POLITICAL SYSTEMS MODEL

The political systems model of organizational change has its roots in two schools of thought. The first of these is the sociological school of thought usually labeled *conflict theory*. Karl Marx is viewed as the individual who provided the impetus for this theory, and Lewis Coser (1967) and Rolf Dahrendorf (1959, 1968) are modern advocates of this particular school of thought. The tenets of this perspective are, first, that conflict, whether it be in society or in an organization, is natural and is not necessarily a debilitating phenomenon. Conflict arises because of the competition for scarce resources and the values of sub-groups concerning how these resources should be utilized. The second tenet of this theoretical position is that groups vary in power and there is a continuous struggle for supremacy and domination among various groups (Dahrendorf, 1959). Third, the process of change can best be understood by examining the nature of the conflicts that arise and the outcomes of the conflicts. Fourth, not only is conflict not viewed as debilitating; it is viewed as the crucial element in ascertaining that a system or an organization retains its vitality. Growth and change occur as a result of conflict (Coser, 1967). Fifth and finally, a social system or an organization develops mechanisms designed to maintain the level of conflict at a workable level. Role separation, physical distance, and evaluation are three of these mechanisms commonly used in education, although Litwak (1961) lists others. Administrators, as members of one subgroup, hire teachers and other educational practitioners and as a result are continuously inserting into competing subgroups individuals with their own perspective. The physical location of principals, educational specialists, and other upper-echelon administrators also can reduce the conflict between these groups, since they characteristically interact in a controlled situation. Further evaluation of the school program provides a means of reducing conflict, in that this process provides an orderly process for conflict resolution.

The second theoretical basis for the political systems model is the systems theory. While systems theory developed originally in the biological sciences, Katz and Kahn (1966), and more recently Kast and Rosenzweig (1974), have contributed heavily to the application of these ideas to organizations. Systems theorists view organizations as constantly in dynamic interactions both internally and with their environment (Kast and Rosenzweig, 1974). Of particular importance to the survival of the organization is its relationship with the environment, for it is from the environment that it receives its resources and, to a large extent, particularly in the case of public education, its value system. However, Kast and Rosenzweig (1974) indicate that each organization establishes certain boundaries that serve as a selective screen to environmental input.

The reader will recall that early in the chapter Udy's (1965) five organizational subsystems were enumerated as technology or the means by which a group accomplishes its goals, staff, group processes, administrative structure, and the interaction of an organization with its environment. Kast and Rosenzweig (1974) adopt essentially these same subsystems when they discuss an organization, but they use somewhat different labels. Instead of technology they refer to a technical subsystem, which is the knowledge needed to perform a task. Knowledge, for these authors, includes skills and techniques. Udy's staff and group processes are grouped together in a "... psychosocial subsystem which is composed of individuals and groups in interaction" (p. 111). Udy's concept of administrative structure is termed a *managerial subsystem* by Kast and Rosenzweig (1974). This subsystem has the pervasive functions of assisting the organization to relate to its environment, establish goals, design structure, and establish control processes. Kast and Rosenzweig (1974) set forth two additional subsystems: goals and values, and structure. The goals and values subsystem is somewhat analogous to Udy's idea of environmental interaction but is more specific in that Kast and Rosenzweig posit that goals and values are developed as a result of the environmental forces that are brought to bear on an organization. Structure involves both the formal role relationships often seen on organizational charts and the informal structure that develops because of personal interactions.

Systems theorists pose that two types of mechanisms develop within each organization. These are adaptive mechanisms, which enable the organization to change as a result of both internal and external input, and maintenance mechanisms, which tend to counteract change, at least rapid change, which will disrupt the organization. These mechanisms are often in conflict, but like conflict theorists, systems theorists do not view this as necessarily a negative situation (Katz and Kahn, 1966; Kast and Rosenzweig, 1974). A systems theorist's view of an organization is depicted in Figure 9.1.

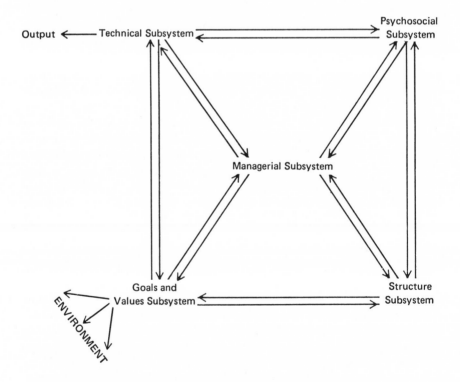

FIGURE 9.1. A systems view of organizational functioning

As can be seen in this rather brief background of the theoretical underpinnings of the political systems approach to innovative change, organizations are viewed as complex entities. Hence, their change is viewed as a more complex process than that posed by the human relations school of thought. Let us look now at the specific assumptions underlying the political systems approach to organizational change.

Assumptions Baldridge (1971) presents five assumptions that he views as central to the political systems approach. These are paraphrased below:

1. Conflict within an organizational structure is neither unnatural nor necessarily a symptom of organizational dysfunctioning. Conflict is an expected phenomenon in organizational functioning.
2. The various power blocs within an organization will attempt to influence the development of policy. The goal of this influence process is to assure that the subgroup's values and goals will be considered.
3. In most organizations, decisions are made largely by small power blocs. However, different groups may control different decision-making processes.
4. The often-held view that decisions are simply bureaucratic orders is untenable. Those individuals in formal power are influenced by power blocs as a result of political processes. Most officials attempt to build compromises between the goals of these power blocs.
5. External groups also comprise power blocs that must ultimately be considered in the formulation of policy. Internal power groups cannot make decisions without considering these groups.

These assumptions have quite naturally been derived from both conflict and systems theory.

Focus of Change Baldridge (1971) indicates that there are at least three concerns that should receive scrutiny in the change process. These he enumerates as the social structure, interest articulation, and decision making. In looking at the area of social change, our concern should not only be the various groups (the social structure) that exist within a school but also the values held by various members in each of the groups. Teachers may value smaller class loads, increased clerical assistance, and more instructional aides. On the other hand, counselors and resource teachers may value other aspects of the educational process, such as individualized instructional patterns or increased cooperation between home and school. By knowing the values of a given group, a consultant can begin to predict how that group will function.

Interest articulation is the means by which a group exerts political influence in order to insure that its values and goals receive attention. One example of this process is the formation of professional associations or unions to exert pressure upon decision makers. Another example of interest articulation is social influence resulting from interpersonal relationships. Many consultants have established relationships that have resulted in their becoming more influential in the decision-making process. Still another means by which interest articulation occurs is aligning with other pressure groups. Special educators have become involved with, and indeed have formed, parent action groups to make certain their views are heard. Each subgroup within the school organization has a variety of devices designed to insure that it influences the decision-making process. The change agent must be aware of this articulation and actually participate in it.

Baldridge (1971) also suggests that the decision-making process itself should receive increased attention. The change agent should be aware of the political coalitions that exist, pressure groups that impinge upon the process, and the idiosyncrasies of decision makers who influence decision making. There is a particular need to become familiar with the external forces that impinge upon the decision-making processes in the school setting, such as voting blocs. This influence deserves particular importance when one considers that school boards are elected and upper-echelon administrative staffs are appointed directly by the board.

It is important to note that the action designated to bring about innovation will focus upon a subgroup such as administrators or teachers. It is also worthy of mention that the specific goals of change may involve any of the subsystems of the organization. A change in any program may, for example, focus upon technology — that is, the knowledge and skills required to perform the task — or upon the structure or organization of the program. Similarly, the change process may have goals that focus upon the management, goals, and values, or on the psychosocial subsystem. However, since each of these subsystems is in dynamic interaction with the others, a change in one will impinge upon the others. For example, a change in teaching methods (technology) may lead to a need for more expertise in the managerial subsystem, thus causing either a change or more conflict. Similarly, a change in goals and values of pupil personnel workers toward prevention and away from remediation would surely influence technology and perhaps structure, in that different leadership patterns would be required. Because of this dynamic interaction, the change agent needs to consider carefully all of the implications of a particular innovation.

Finally, the political systems model dictates that the consultant look at a variety of sources that may provide an impetus for change. Kast and Rosenzweig (1974) list six such sources: the environment, the goals and values of staff members, technology, the structure of the organization, the psychosocial subsystem, and management. The environment and various subgroups within the environment are obviously potential instigators of educational change. Local, state, and federal governmental agencies are constantly exerting pressure for change and in some instances demanding change through legislative channels.

Pressure groups, some of which are ongoing and some of which are ad hoc in nature, constantly exert forces upon the school. These forces, like those from within, influence policy development. Some effort needs to be made in some instances to anticipate these forces so that change will be orderly and in other cases so that the forces brought to bear can be either accelerated or decelerated depending upon the nature of the pressure.

Goals and values held by staff members can be influenced by external pressure as well as the dynamics of internal factors. The consultant must be able to determine those forces that influence goals and values and in some instances act to influence these directly.

Obviously, advances in technology will provide an impetus for change. New teaching methods, computer-assisted counseling techniques, computerized record-keeping systems, and management by objectives are but a few technological advances that require organizational change. Here again the consultant needs to be aware of these advances and how they may have an impact upon the organization.

Structure is essentially the means by which an organization divides up its various tasks. Dysfunctional organizations or suborganizations often attempt to restructure themselves in order to gain efficiency or effectiveness or, in some instances, both. The organizational consultant needs to gain some understanding of the relationship of structure to function and how function can be facilitated by appropriate structure.

The assumption of the political systems model is that the psychosocial subsystem *will* provide impetus for change which will enhance human satisfaction and functioning. Low staff morale and intragroup conflict are indicators of need for change in the psychosocial subsystem. So is failure to accept and implement programs, procedures, and techniques that have been initiated by other subsystems.

Finally, management is a source of change and has the responsibility not only for change but for interrelating that change to all subsystems (Kast and Rosenzweig, 1974). Failure to carry out this coordination function can result in the failure of an organizational innovation that has been adopted. This subsystem also has responsibility for establishing control mechanisms that regulate the life of the organization but that can effectively kill an innovation. Perhaps the most obvious regulatory function controlled by management is the budget. Unless resources are provided, no innovation can survive.

Up to this point, the discussion has focused upon some rather abstract ideas regarding the political systems change model. Attention will be directed now to some specific techniques and strategies needed to implement this type of change.

Techniques and Strategies. Baldridge (1975) lists five rules for the agent of political systems change. First, he suggests that the energy of the change agent be carefully focused on concentrated efforts. Many individuals and groups dissipate their energies by becoming involved in too many struggles, and this is a serious error. A change agent must learn to identify those issues that are worth pursuing and those that make very little difference. The change agent needs not only the wisdom to discern when changes can and cannot be made, but the ability to concentrate on the few areas of potential change that will make a difference.

The second and related rule that Baldridge proposes is: Know when to fight. Generally he recommends that change be attempted when there is a good chance of getting something accomplished. He also suggests, and the authors agree wholeheartedly, that there are times when action should be taken even when there is certainty that no change will occur. Let us take a hypothetical case where a school is obviously giving too many standardized tests, but it is a certainty that the committee reviewing the matter will recommend continuation of the status quo. The change agent may wish to voice opposition to the present testing program as a first step in developing awareness of the need to change. This initial battle may be lost, but the war will continue.

Rule three is learn the history of the situation (Baldridge, 1975). Baldridge suggests that individuals who are historically naive about issues are usually unable to make changes. He suggests that whenever a crucial issue arises, the change agent look into what happened the last time the issue arose and who was responsible for the action taken. Many change agents have wasted countless hours working to influence individuals who already agreed with their particular view. That time would have been better spent attempting to influence individuals who were on the opposite side of the issue. In addition, in almost every debate there are those who are strongly for and against issues and individuals who are in the middle of these extremes. Knowing who is on the fence and thus open to influence may be the best way to get policies and procedures altered.

It is perhaps obvious from the tone and content of this entire section that internal power blocs join forces to influence decision making. Rule four is build coalitions. Counselors, school psychologists, and/or resource teachers are rarely in a situation where (1) they represent the power structure or (2) they are in the majority. It is, therefore, necessary for them to join forces with other smaller groups in order to achieve goals of change or to persuade more powerful groups of the viability of their position.

Rule five is very much like rule four in that Baldridge recommends that change agents join external constituencies. There can be little doubt, particularly when change in the educational setting is at stake, that external forces are a major factor.

In addition to the foregoing rules Baldridge (1975) makes two other suggestions that seem to be of particular value to the change agent. The first of these has to do with the effective use of committees. As we have seen, decision making is viewed primarily as a political process shaped by the various forces that power blocs can exert upon it. Baldridge suggests that ultimately decision making is the result of committee action and that the change agent should work to have persons appointed to key committees. This is only the first step, however. Once on the committee, an individual must attend regularly and do the homework needed to be an effective committee member. The homework usually involves both looking into the history of the issue and developing personal expertise in the issue at hand. If the mission of the committee is to study budget allocation for special services personnel, the committee member should know (1) what the state contributes, (2) what comes from local taxation, (3) any additional source of revenue that supports these individuals, (4) how much money is needed for new personnel, (5) how this expense would affect taxes, (6) how this relates to the rest of the school budget, et cetera. In short, if committees are to be influenced, the committee members must function at a higher level than other members of the organization.

Baldridge makes one additional general suggestion: to use the formal organization. His suggestion is that officials in the administrative structure are eager to please and minor innovations can occur simply as the result of a simple request. There are, of course, times when no grand change strategy is required to bring about change, but usually true innovation requires greater effort.

Implications. The political systems model has some far-reaching implications for the consultant. Not the least of these is that there is a need for professionals to politicize their actions and thinking. Doing so means taking an active role in committees, professional societies, and community endeavors. By participation in these and other types of activities, a perspective can be gained regarding the values and goals of the various subgroups that exert pressure on the decision-making process and the consultant can begin to build viable coalitions that can have a decisive impact upon the process.

Still another implication of this model is that the consultant must become intimately familiar with the formal and informal power structure so that when requests for change are initiated they can be channeled to the appropriate official or officials. The formal power structure is normally depicted in organizational charts and job descriptions available in the superintendent's office. The informal power structure is less easy to discern. Most of us are aware that certain individuals hold a disproportionate amount of power in the decision-making process, for reasons that are not always clear. In some instances power is derived from "political connections" in the community, in others from length of tenure and expertise that has accrued, and in still others power results from association with decision makers. Superintendents' secretaries at times assume considerable power, since they control telephone communications and appointments. Perhaps the only real means of becoming familiar with the informal power structure is through experience and participation in the school organization. Nevertheless, being able to diagnose accurately the informal power structure is essential to the success of the political systems change agent.

Just as the change agents must become familiar with the administrative structure, so must they familiarize themselves with the division of tasks within the organization. Substructures often comprise power blocs with divergent goals and values. In one school district the director of transportation effectively blocked an instructional program that required more field trips, because it required more work in his division. An effective change agent could perhaps have anticipated this consequence and would have worked to exert influence to overcome it.

Since the school cannot operate without economic resources, which flow in from the community, the state government, and federal agencies, change agents must thoroughly familiarize themselves with the nature, amount, and expenditure of these resources. Of particular interest in this area should be that portion of the budget that is not dedicated to existing, ongoing endeavors and is thus available for the development of new programs. The local tax laws, including the tax base of the school district, should be scrutinized, along with how taxation compares to that of other districts and the views of the community on taxation for education.

Another source of input to schools comes from accrediting agencies and state departments of education, both of which influence decision making through standards and regulations. Being familiar with the guidelines of these groups, along with the economic situation of the school district, can help the change agent determine which innovations are possible and which, because of either external policies or fiscal deficits, are impossible.

Evaluation was posed early in this section as one means used by organizations to manage conflict, or at least keep it at a tolerable level. Certainly the change agent must be able to interpret data and help focus them to bring about organizational change. This does not mean that the consultant must be an expert in the area of evaluation. However, meaningful interpretation of the data must be made so that this can be one source of input to the decision-making process. The consultant should not expect that objective data will insure that the decision-making process will proceed in a rational manner, however. Political forces that are often irrational will still strongly influence the process.

Perhaps the most important skill needed by the political systems change agent is the ability to analyze existing forces with regard to an issue and decide whether or not an effort should be made in the particular area under study. Once a decision to act has been made, groups and persons who can have a positive effect upon the outcome must be marshaled and their efforts focused so that a desirable outcome will be reached.

One warning should be inserted at this point about the risks associated with the change agent role described in these sections. Even if all of the steps listed are followed carefully, there can be no assurance that change will be initiated. In addition, any individual associated with this type of activity may be open to political retribution in the form of reassignment or even dismissal if untenured. Therefore, a consultant considering the political action approach to change should consider carefully his or her personal situation and make certain that he or she is willing to take the risks required. There is also the risk that, once changes are made, the situation that exists may at best remain the same or at worst deteriorate. A loss of professional credibility and influence may result. To some, this may be a worse fate than dismissal or reassignment.

SOME GENERAL FACTORS IN ORGANIZATIONAL CHANGE

To this point the main thrust of this chapter has been to look at some of the issues in planned change and to examine two theoretical models that may provide a guide for the consultant in this area. Let us now turn to some general organizational factors that should be considered in the planned change process, some features of innovations that can make them more acceptable to organizational members, some of the barriers to innovation, and, finally, to drawing some conclusions for the consultant about these notions.

Organizational Characteristics

Organizational theorists have hypothesized and to a degree provided support for the idea that quite apart from theoretical approach or change agent style, certain organizational characteristics affect the capacity of the organization to innovate. Hage and Aiken (1970) assert that the professionalism of the staff is one of these characteristics. Their hypothesis, for which they provide support, is that the greater the length of educational preparation (professionalism) engaged in by the staff of an organization, the more apt that organization is to innovate. Most educators engage in rather lengthy educational preparation and thus possess a relatively high degree of professionalism. By this single yardstick, most educational institutions would innovate freely.

Sieber (1975) sheds some additional light on educators as prospective innovators when he asserts that since educators have not reached professional status, their quasiprofessional status actually acts to retard their participation in innovation. Sieber defines a profession as one in which individuals perform a service highly valued by society, function autonomously, and possess a great deal of technical competence. Educators seem to meet only the first of these criteria but identify themselves with those who are truly professionals in our society. This discrepancy between what educators are and what they wish to be leads to status insecurity, according to Sieber. This insecurity, in turn, causes educators to reject new ideas from within and without in order to preserve authority, expertise, and status. Further, Sieber believes that status insecurity causes educators to avoid educational innovation because energies that might be expended in this area are expended in status enhancement activities such as participation in professional organizations. Sieber makes other points, but if he is correct, the state of the education "quasiprofession" may be a major barrier to change.

To summarize, it would still be expected that the higher the degree of education possessed by the educational staff, the greater the likelihood that they will innovate. The implication of this is clear. In-service education, pay scales that promote increased education, and informal educational experiences are all potentially useful as tools to foster institutional innovation.

A decentralized power structure — that is, one where decision making is distributed to groups and individuals — also seems to be a positive factor in producing innovative change (Hage and Aiken, 1970). Perhaps this is true because, as Shepard (1967) pointed out, organizations with rigid, centralized power structures can change only from the top down. Not only does a centralized power structure tend to retard innovation, so does a structure that is highly formalized (all positions have rigid job descriptions). The military is an example of this type of organization, and unfortunately many school organizations are patterned after this system. If it becomes clear that the organizational bureaucracy is the basic reason for lack of innovation, it may well become the target of change, probably using external groups as the basic initiator.

Hage and Aiken (1970) also put forth the notion that the focus of the organization upon efficiency also is an important variable in determining whether or not an organization is innovative. If an organization emphasizes efficiency, or holding costs to a minimum, change is deterred because innovation is often coupled with greater expenditures. With the present trend in educational funding, it might well be expected that, given this as correct, innovation will become less frequent rather than occurring more often, as many educators hope.

The clarity of organizational goals appears also to be a major factor in the innovative capacity of an organization. Miles (1965) and Sieber (1975) argue that the goals of some educational organizations are so diffuse as to prevent innovation simply because it is difficult to ascertain the direction in which the organization is attempting to go. Goal diffuseness also seems to contribute to professional insecurity because with unspecified goals it is hard to define the technical competence needed by teachers, pupil personnel services workers, and others. As was indicated earlier, professional insecurity is also a barrier to change. Assuming that Miles and Sieber are correct — and their idea seems viable — institutional goal setting may need to precede all other innovation.

Miles (1965) and Sieber (1975) have listed some other special characteristics of educational organizations that make them particularly resistant to change. Among these are vulnerability to the demands of society and role invisibility. One need only look at the last fifteen years in education to find support for the idea that educational organizations are often overwhelmed by society. Modern mathematics and the return to conventional mathematics, infusion of science into the curriculum, career education, ecological education, and many more programs have been developed at the behest of a concerned society. The result is much unplanned and at times chaotic change. These changes are often incompatible with the stated goals of the school and, because they work at cross purposes with the organization, retard planned change. Miles (1965) suggests that many tactics have been adopted to offset these external forces, such as policies about classroom visitation, using the PTA as a buffer, and attempts to "brainwash" board members. Public relations programs are also utilized for this purpose. It may well be that the consultant may need to suggest these and other techniques to reduce the vulnerability of the particular school or system.

Most educators perform their role in a relative vacuum, since others do not have a chance to observe their functioning. Miles (1965) has suggested that since there is little evaluation, at least meaningful evaluation, most educators can avoid change without fear of negative feedback. What is clearly needed is an evaluational system that rewards innovative practice. The avoidance of merit pay by all groups involved with education makes such a system unlikely to occur in its best sense. However, innovativeness can become a criterion in the evaluation process, and this may help.

In summary, there are many characteristics of organizations that make them accepting or rejecting of innovations. The active change agent will address these at the outset. Let us turn now to the characteristics of innovations that make them more or less acceptable.

Acceptable Characteristics of Innovations

Not surprisingly, many of the characteristics of desirable innovations interact with organizational concerns. For example, innovations that require greater expenditures are less likely to be selected and adopted when individuals are speaking in a general sense, but this idea ultimately must be considered in the context of a given organization. While Ostlund's (1969) position that the crucial question in innovation should be the impact upon students, this question is often not considered as carefully as the cost.

Another important aspect that influences the adoption of an innovation is the extent to which it increases or decreases the comfort of those concerned. Havelock (1973) indicated that teachers in particular tend to resist those innovations that increase their work load. There seems also to be resistance to innovations that threaten traditional roles (Shephard, 1967) and require the acquisition of additional skills or knowledge.

To be maximally acceptable, an innovation must be definable in such a manner that it can be communicated clearly to the staff members of a school system. Lin and Zaltman (1973) have pointed out that less complex innovations are accepted more readily than those of greater complexity. This fact is, of course, in part tied to the communication process just referred to, but complex innovations are more likely to require more money and cause personal discomfort among those affected, two additional deterrents to adoption.

Finally, an innovation must have a perceived advantage over other alternatives if it is to be accepted. It is also helpful and perhaps mandatory if the innovation is to be compatible with existing programs and can be demonstrated to supplement or complement them in some manner. Here again, the nature of the innovation and the characteristics of the innovating organization come into dynamic interaction and influence the outcomes of the change process.

Additional Barriers to Change

We have already seen that certain organizational characteristics are in and of themselves barriers to change, as are poorly designed innovations. However, there are a variety of other factors which may retard change.

Kast and Rosenzweig (1974) list five major sources of resistance to change. These are sunk costs, miscommunication, group norms, threats to the balance of power, and great diversity among the subgroups within the organization. In an earlier publication Kaufman (1971) had listed some additional barriers to change. He indicated that there are benefits that result from stability, at least to certain groups, and thus resistance to change arises. Kaufman also notes that there are psychic costs associated with change because of the stresses involved in the process. Further, he notes that human behavior becomes routinized, and these habits provide still another obstacle to change. Let us look at some of these sources of resistance to change in more detail.

Sunk cost is a business term used to denote the time, energy, and money required to establish existing programs (Kast and Rosenzweig, 1974). However, the concept is equally applicable to educational institutions. Teachers often spend long hours in conceptualizing a curricular design and in developing instructional patterns to deliver its concepts. These are the psychic costs referred to by Kaufman and are a part of the sunk costs. The implementation of such a planned program usually requires the acquisition of textbooks, library materials, equipment, and other similar items, which sometimes require the expenditure of large amounts of money. All those associated with this type of development, whether they be teachers or other professionals, remember all too well the investment required and are often not anxious to embark upon another such venture.

Effective communication has been characterized as the essence of interpersonal and organizational functioning. Kast and Rosenzweig (1974) point out that often individuals who are aware of situations that need to be changed fail to communicate them in a manner that is accepted or understood. It is therefore recommended that all communications of problems should be made in the clearest possible language and that insofar as is possible, the problems be data-based. By this is simply meant that objective support should be provided for the opinions held by the change agent. A variety of data in the form of teacher reports, standardized test results, community surveys, follow-up studies of dropouts and graduates, and systematic records of numbers and types of problems existing in the situation can serve as the basis for recommending changes. "Opinions supported by data are more likely to be accepted" is the rule offered here.

Tradition that has been institutionalized in the form of group norms serves as a major form of resistance to change. Many consultants interested in change have been stopped cold by the statement "We've always done it this way and it works pretty well." This response is to a certain extent the result of sunk costs alluded to earlier. It also grows out of the concern that change may worsen the situation, thus eroding the quality of existing practices (Kaufman, 1971). This concern is certainly a legitimate one, and it seems that the burden of proof for validity of change should rest with the change agent. Perhaps the best attitude to take in the face of this type of opposition is to assume that present practice may be better than available alternatives, but also take the stance that experimentation is necessary to test the assumption that the status quo is superior. In this way the change agent presents a case that is neither for nor against present practice but in favor of investigations that may in fact affirm that present practice is superior.

Kast and Rosenzweig (1974) suggest that innovation may upset the balance of power between various factions which exist in the organization. This could, of course, prove harmful to certain groups, and thus they resist changes that threaten their particular position. While it would be best to adopt only those innovations that would be helpful to everyone, doing so is not always possible. However, it is mandatory that those innovations that will threaten the positions of others be considered carefully before action is taken. The question that must be answered is whether the innovation is worth the conflict that is certain to result.

Diversity among groups may become a barrier to change. Some school districts have erred by hiring highly educated superintendents and expecting them to work with principals and teachers who were on a much lower educational plane, an expectation that was not realized. Diversity can also result in resistance to innovation when teachers and those who work with them hold different theoretical points of view. Most of us are aware of the classic fight between behaviorists and humanists, and these conflicts can occur among groups in an individual building or in an entire school district. Another type of diversity, race, has also stymied, because of differing perceptions of the problem, many school districts that wanted to innovate. Whenever these and other types of diversity prevent innovation, staff development procedures that focus upon communication are probably needed. In addition, the hiring procedures of the school need close examination.

Mahan and Chickedantz (1977) surveyed 168 elementary school educators in an attempt to determine some of the specific deterrents to innovation. Their results are shown in Table 9.1.

TABLE 9.1. Deterrents to elementary school innovation

Factors That Can Endanger the Quality of Elementary School Innovation	Mean Rating Received (0 to 3 scale)	Rank Order as Back-Home Impediment
Lack of teacher and principal knowledge on how to use and evaluate innovations	1.48	3
Conflicting educational attitudes, beliefs, and values of those involved in innovations	1.43	1
Fear of incompetence with new ideas	1.21	7
Realization that an innovation means more work	1.16	2
Minimal communication among all the involved implementers	1.13	5
Nondecisiveness of evaluation: i.e., findings rarely answer important questions	1.07	8
Insufficient financial resources to support the innovative effort	.98	6
Failure of building administrators to provide change-oriented leadership	.92	4
No representative decision-making process involving all people affected	.87	11.5
Failure to determine educational needs before launching an innovative effort	.85	9
Feeling that as one supports an innovation one confesses that the old way is a failure	.80	10
Lack of a specific, detailed, predesigned installation strategy	.79	11.5
Poor conception and poor design of the innovation itself	.59	14
Too much decentralization and dispersal of decision-making power	.55	14
Resistance of the citizens of the school community	.51	14

The elementary school curriculum coordinators, subject matter specialists working out of the central office, teacher team leaders, building principals, and associate superintendents provide two pieces of data. First, they rated the deterrents to innovation according to their own perceptions, using a three-point scale. Then they conducted an informal survey in their home school districts to ascertain the perceptions of colleagues of factors that constituted barriers to communication. As can be seen in Table 9.1, those surveyed rated lack of knowledge about the use of innovation, conflicting educational attitudes and values, fear of lack of competence with new ideas, concern that an innovation would require more work, lack of communication, and inadequacy of evaluation as the top six deterrents to innovation. However, their informal survey in their school districts resulted in slightly different rankings. Of particular interest was the perception that failure of building administrators to provide change-oriented leadership is a major deterrent to innovation, since this observation supports some of the speculation about lack of innovation in education. Generally the data collected by Mahan and Chickedantz (1977) support Kast and Rosenzweig's (1974) contentions that sunk costs (concern about work), miscommunication (minimal communication), and group norms (conflicting attitudes and values) inhibit innovation. There is little direct support for their ideas that group diversity and threats to the balance of power are deterrents to innovation, although some of their findings might be interpreted as such.

There are other barriers to organizational change. Through practice the consultant will learn to recognize and cope with them. It should be noted that these barriers are not necessarily bad, however. None of us would like to be associated with an organization that was constantly changing. These sources of resistance can, in addition to preventing change, insure that change is planned and orderly.

ESTABLISHING AN ELEMENTARY SCHOOL GUIDANCE PROGRAM: A CASE STUDY IN CHANGE

Background The school district had received a federal grant to establish a combined elementary guidance and reading program, which it was believed would run for three years. However, at the end of one year it appeared that the grant would not be refunded. The superintendent asked the school principals to establish their priorities with regard to providing local money to support the nine elementary counseling positions and the nine reading teachers. The principals voted almost unanimously to put reading teachers as their number one priority. The federal program was subsequently refunded for the second year, but it became a certainty that it would not be refunded thereafter. Three of the nine elementary school counselors formed a committee with the explicit goal of influencing not only the principals' thinking but ultimately the school board's decision with regard to funding the positions.

Strategy The first decision of the committee was that they were in and of themselves relatively powerless. They therefore decided that a liaison with other individuals would have to be developed. It was decided to expand the committee to include a highly respected businessman, a chairwoman of one of

the local PTA's and a professor from the local university, all of whom supported the concept of elementary school guidance.

Once the change committee was fully developed a number of steps were
decided upon. These were:

1. The data from the project showing that the counselors made a significant
impact upon the outcomes of the project would be made available to parents,
teachers, and the news media.

2. Petitions would be placed in all schools on the night of the first spring PTA
meeting to solicit parent signatures. The petitions stated that elementary school
counselors should be included as a part of the elementary school education
program. Several hundred signatures were secured.

3. School board members would be contacted to determine whether or not
they had formulated an opinion on the issue of counselors and reading teachers.
It turned out that four of the seven had not; two favored counselors and two
favored reading teachers.

4. The three lay members of the committee would attend board meetings and
speak in favor of elementary school counselors. Further, it was decided that the
school budget would be studied in detail and that recommendations would be
made for cuts in existing programs if no new money should become available to
the school district. This latter step was a contingency plan, but ultimately it had
to be taken.

5. A highly respected former school board member would be contacted to
present the petitions once signatures had been collected.

6. It was decided that a meeting would be held with the superintendent, the
assistant superintendent, the principals, and the counselors to discuss this
problem. The purpose of this meeting was to get principals to communicate
that they wanted elementary school counselors even though they had placed
reading teachers as their first priority.

Actions Taken   At a school board meeting held in the early spring, the former
school board member presented the petitions, which were signed by parents who
supported elementary school guidance. The president of the school board
accepted the petitions but reaffirmed her support of the reading teachers. The
next item on the agenda was consideration of the school budget for the forth-
coming year. At this point a member of the committee asked for the floor to
comment on the budget. Permission was granted.

The committee had discovered that two administrative teachers who had
recently been hired had not been able to function effectively because principals
saw them as usurping their role of supervising new teachers. It was also learned
that the size of the superintendent's staff had been challenged by a number of
persons and groups within the community, including one of the board members
who favored the reading teachers. The committee member suggested that the
two administrative teachers and one administrative assistant to the superinten-

dent be deleted from the budget to make room for four counselors. It was also suggested that professional travel and fees for consultants be reduced to make room for an additional counselor. Finally, it was suggested that the four additional counseling positions rather than four teachers for the emotionally disturbed be funded. The crux of this argument was that since these classes were not really to be formed for the emotionally disturbed but for children with discipline problems, damage would result because of the labeling. It was also known that most of the board members believed that teachers should handle their own discipline problems, and this point was emphasized in the presentation.

After the board meeting the committee members who had made the presentation on the budget gave an interview to a local radio station about the waste in the proposed school budget and provided a rationale for elementary school counselors. Portions of the interview were played throughout the next day on local newscasts.

Finally, each school board member was contacted by a counselor to determine whether or not he or she had any questions about the presentation, the data that had been presented, or any of the issues that had been raised.

The outcome of all of this was that while not all of the budgetary recommendations that were made were adopted, the budget was altered to include the elementary school counselors.

SUMMARY

The chapter has been devoted in its entirety to organizational change and the role of the consultant in the change process. At the outset some of the various issues associated with change, including the definition of innovation, the locus of the change agent, the change group versus the solitary change agent, and others were enumerated. This was followed by a presentation of two models of organizational change: the human relations model and the political systems model. Implications for the role of the change agent were drawn from each of these. Finally, several general considerations regarding the change process were perused. Some of these included a discussion of the features of organizations that make them susceptible or resistant to change, the nature of acceptable innovations, and various sources of resistance, with some guidelines to overcoming them.

REFERENCES

Argyris, C. *Integrating the Individual and the Organization.* New York: Wiley, 1964.

_____. *Intervention Theory and Method*. Reading: Addison-Wesley Publishing Company, 1970.

Aspy, D. "The Helper's Tools: Chicken Soup or Rifles," *Personnel and Guidance Journal,* 49 (1970): 117–118.

Baldridge, J. V. "The Analysis of Organizational Change: A Human Relations Strategy versus a Political Systems Strategy." Palo Alto: Stanford Center for Research and Development in Teaching and Research, Memorandum No. 75, September, 1971.

_____. "Rules for a Machiavellian Change Agent: Transforming the Entrenched Professional Organization." In *Managing Change in Educational Organizations,* ed. J. V. Baldridge and T. E. Deal. Berkeley: McCutchan Publishing Corp., 1975, pp. 378–408.

Bennis, W. *Changing Organizations.* New York: McGraw-Hill, 1966.

_____. *Beyond Bureaucracy.* New York: McGraw-Hill, 1970.

Brown, D., and D. J. Srebalus. *Contemporary Guidance Concepts and Practices.* Dubuque: Wm. C. Brown, 1972.

Carlson, R. O. *Change Processes in the Public Schools.* Eugene: Center for the Advanced Study of Educational Administration, 1965.

Chin, R., and K. D. Benne. "General Strategies for Effecting Change in Human Systems." In *The Planning of Change,* 2nd ed., ed. W. G. Bennis, K. D. Benne, and R. Chin. New York: Holt, Rinehart & Winston, 1969.

Coser, L. A. *Continuities in the Study of Social Conflict.* New York: Free Press, 1967.

Dahrendorf, R. *Class and Class Conflict in Industrial Society.* Stanford: Stanford University Press, 1959.

_____. *Essays in the Theory of Society.* Stanford: Stanford University Press, 1968.

Eisen, S. *A Problem Solving Program.* Washington, D.C.: NTL Institute for Applied Behavioral Science, 1969.

Gallup, G. H. "Sixth Annual Gallup Poll of Public Attitudes toward Education," *Phi Delta Kappan,* 56 (1974): 20–32.

Gardner, N. "Action Training and Research: Something Old and Something New," *Public Administration Review,* 34 (1974): 106–115.

Gardner, N., and M. E. McGill. *Guidance for the Training of Professional and Technical Personnel in the Administration and Management of Developmental Functions.* New York: Public Administration Division, Department of Economic and Social Affairs, United Nations, 1970, pp. 192–195.

Glasser, W. *Schools without Failure.* New York: Harper & Row, 1969.

Glidewell, J. C. "The Entry Problem in Consultation," *Journal of Social Issues,* 15 (1959): 43–50.

Hage, J., and M. Aiken. *Social Change in Complex Organizations.* New York: Random House, 1970.

Havelock, R. G. *The Change Agent's Guide to Innovation in Education.* Englewood Cliffs: Educational Technology Publications, 1973.

Herr, E. L. "The School Counselor as a Social System: Some Elements of a Change Agent's Role." In *Group Guidance and Counseling in the School,* ed. J. C. Hansen and S. H. Cramer. New York: Appleton-Century-Crofts, 1971.

Hoyt, K., R. N. Evans, E. F. Mackin, and G. L. Mangum. *Career Education: What It Is and How to Do It,* 2nd ed. Salt Lake City: Olympus Publishing Company, 1974.

Jarvis, P. E., and S. E. Nelson. "Familiarization: A Vital Step in Mental Health Consultation," *Community Mental Health Journal,* 3 (1967): 343–348.

Jones, G. N. *Planned Organizational Change.* New York: Frederick A. Praeger, 1969.

Kast, F. E., and J. E. Rosenzweig. *Organization and Management: A Systems Approach,* 2nd ed. New York: McGraw-Hill, 1974.

Katz, D., and R. L. Kahn. *The Social Psychology of Organizations.* New York: John Wiley & Sons, 1966.

Kaufman, H. *The Limits of Organizational Change.* Tuscaloosa: University of Alabama Press, 1971.

Knight, K. "A Descriptive Model for the Intra-Firm Innovation Process," *Journal of Business,* 40 (1967): 478–496.

Lewin, K. *Field Theory in Social Science.* New York: Harper, 1951.

Lin, N., and G. Zaltman. "Dimensions of Innovations." In *Processes and Phenomena of Social Change,* by G. Zaltman. New York: John Wiley & Sons, 1973, pp. 93–115.

Lippitt, G. *Organizational Renewal.* New York: Appleton-Century-Crofts, 1969.

Litwak, E. "Models of Bureaucracy Which Permit Conflict," *American Journal of Sociology,* 67 (1961): 182.

Lowe, M., "The Need of Counseling for a Social Frame of Reference," *Journal of Counseling Psychology,* 15 (1968): 486–491.

Mahan, J. M., and M. Chickedantz. "Deterrents to Fully Effective Innovations in Elementary Schools," *Phi Delta Kappan,* 59 (1977): 131.

Miles, M. B. *Change Processes in Public Schools.* Eugene: Center for the Advanced Study of Educational Administration, University of Oregon, 1965, pp. 11–34.

Mohr, L. "Determinants of Innovations in Organizations," *American Political Science Review,* 10 (1969): 193–197.

Murray, D., and R. Schmuck. "The Counselor-Consultant as a Specialist in Organization Development," *Elementary School Guidance and Counseling,* 7 (1972): 99–104.

Ostlund, L. "The Role of the Product Perceptions in Innovative Behavior." In *Fall Conference of the American Marketing Association,* ed. P. R. McDonald. Chicago, 1969.

Postman, N., and C. Weingartner. *Teaching as a Subversive Activity.* New York: Delacorte Press, 1969.

Schmuck, R. A., and P. J. Runkel. "Organizational Training." In *Handbook of Organizational Development in Schools,* ed. R. A. Schmuck et al. Palo Alto: Mayfield Publishing Company, 1972, chap. 2.

Shepard, H. A. "Innovation-resisting and Innovation-producing Organizations," *Journal of Business,* 40 (1967): 113–118.

Sieber, S. D. "Organizational Influences on a Demonstrative Role." In *Managing Change in Educational Organizations,* ed. J. V. Baldridge and T. E. Deal. Berkeley: McCutchan Publishing Corp., 1975, p. 97.

Stiles, L. J., and B. Robinson. "Change in Education." In *Processes and Phenomena of Social Change,* ed. G. Zaltman. New York: John Wiley & Sons, 1973.

Tilton, J. E. *International Diffusion of Technology: The Case of Semiconductors.* Washington, D.C.: The Brookings Institute, 1971.

Udy, S., Jr. "The Comparative Analysis of Organizations." In *The Handbook of Organizations,* ed. J. G. Marsh. Chicago: Rand McNally, 1965.

Zaltman, G., R. Duncan, and J. Holbek. *Innovations and Organizations.* New York: John Wiley & Sons, 1973.

CHAPTER TEN Consulting in the Community

Consultants are focusing their attention increasingly upon the larger community, for it is recognized that both the source of and solution to many problems experienced by students reside outside the walls of the educational institution. Also, as the concept of prevention becomes an integral part of our professional perspective rather than a trite cliché to be trotted out at professional meetings, the community assumes added significance. In order to develop a truly preventive, developmental program, one must start in the community. To muster an effective remedial system, the resources of the community must be tapped. The community as both the cause and cure of students' problems will be examined in this chapter. So, too, will techniques for entering and mobilizing the vast resources available to all consultants.

Community Consultation and Prevention

Direct service, whether in the form of counseling, therapy or remedial education, is not only expensive but is minimally successful. Drum and Figler (1973) assert that one means of decreasing direct service is through involvement in the community. They suggest that we focus upon those conditions that cause the problems and attempt to eliminate them. Menacker (1974) makes a similar suggestion.

But what are these conditions that contribute to student dysfunction? The family? Certainly! Substandard housing? Yes! Community discrimination? Absolutely! Poor welfare systems? Of course! Lack of health services? Most certainly! This list could be continued but it is hoped that the point has been made. Conditions that exist outside our school impinge upon students, often in a manner that detracts from their psychological development. The result is a student who is less educable and one who is eventually less educated. The amelioration of these conditions should be the cornerstone of educational practice.

Community Consultation Enhancing In-School Programs

There are literally dozens of programs that could either be begun or enhanced if more personnel were available. In these days of tight educational budgets, it seems unlikely that these personnel will be provided by hard-pressed school boards. Therefore, it becomes essential that persons from the community be recruited and trained to assist us in our efforts. Volunteers can be used for this purpose. So can staff members from community agencies. By tapping these resources, services not available can be offered to students.

Community Consultation and Remediation

Prevention and developmental programs will never completely eliminate problems and thus remediation will continue to be important. The community can and should provide health services, mental health programs, correctional services, and others. What is necessary is that community agencies be made fully aware of the needs of students and develop the capability of meeting these needs. The school-based consultant should act to insure that this occurs.

A MODEL FOR COMMUNITY CONSULTATION

Lewis and Lewis (1977) have provided what is undoubtedly the most comprehensive model for what they term *community counseling*. Let us hasten to add that they do not use *counseling* in the traditional sense and include everything from educational programs to political activity aimed at community change under the rubric of community counseling. They go on to identify (p. 16) four types of program that can be used by the community counselor or, in our case, the school-based consultant. These are:

1. Extensive experiential programs; programs that provide direct experiences available to the population as a whole.
2. Intensive experiential programs: programs that provide special experiences to individuals or groups that need them.
3. Extensive environmental programs: programs that attempt to make the community more responsive to the needs of its members.
4. Intensive environmental programs: programs that intervene actively in the environments of specific individuals or groups so that special needs can be met.

In Table 10.1 are listed several community-oriented activities that might be pursued by various types of school-based consultants and that fall under the categories outlined by Lewis and Lewis (1977). This listing is, of course, not exhaustive, nor should the activities listed for each consultant be considered to be the exclusive prerogative of that professional. In fact, it seems quite likely that some school psychologists, school counselors, and special educators would be involved in many of the activities listed.

A DEPARTURE FROM TRADITION

Some educational programs are preparing their graduates to become community consultants. However, for most school-based consultants, the idea is a departure from tradition, which indicates that educational personnel should confine their activities to the building or, at the very least, the school district. This tradition may make school administrators wary of endorsing community-oriented activities because they fear political repercussions. This fear is not without some foundation in reality. A community action program aimed at raising taxes to provide recreational facilities will have powerful opponents. So will efforts to change regulations governing welfare or attempts to alter the functioning of community agencies. Any opponent may use whatever political clout he or she possesses to strike back at the school.

Perhaps the only concern for the consultant should be that no community-oriented program be initiated that will result in overall lowering of services to students. It will be of little value if a bond issue is passed to build a new day-care facility if the school board takes a hard line against innovations in the school. It is usually hard to predict these occurrences, however. If they can be predicted, caution should be used in pursuing community-oriented programs.

TABLE 10.1. Possible community activities for school-based consultants

Type of Activity	School Counselors	School Psychologists	Special Educators
Extensive Experential	1. Development of courses on listening and helping skills 2. Developing career exploration groups open to all	1. Training crises intervention workers 2. Developing a peer counseling service	1. Developing a public relations program that would develop an understanding of the needs of the handicapped 2. Developing courses on parenting
Intensive Experential	1. Implementation of racial conflict programs 2. Establishment of rap groups for teenagers, using community members	1. Developing programs to assist individuals to make appropriate referrals to community agency	1. Developing tutoring skills in volunteers as a means of increasing services to handicapped

Extensive Environmental	1. Working to increase community recreational facilities	1. Working to increase community mental health facilities 2. Consultation with teachers 3. Consulting with law enforcement officers about the needs of juvenile delinquents	1. Involvement in programs aimed at increasing health care in the community
Intensive Environmental	1. Working in a program aimed at upgrading housing for the poor	1. Organizing child advocacy groups	1. Participating in programs aimed at developing separate facilities for institutionalized handicapped 2. Developing a sheltered workshop

THE PROCESS OF COMMUNITY CONSULTATION

Determining Needs

There are at least three approaches to determining student needs: gather self-perceptions, ascertain the perceptions of others, and utilize objective data. Each of these methods will be discussed.

One of the most comprehensive sources of data regarding the perceptions of adolescents about their own needs is the Purdue Opinion Panel, a survey conducted periodically by the Measurement and Research Center, Purdue University, Lafayette, Indiana. One of the recent surveys (Purdue Opinion Panel, 1973) focused upon the educational needs of adolescents perceived by adolescents. In Table 10.2 a summary of the data found in that survey is provided. One fact that becomes clear from these data is that the areas of concern are similar for both sexes. Having one's own money was a concern of 40 percent of the boys and 42 percent of the girls. Similar proportions of boys and girls were also greatly concerned about jobs, friendships, self, relationships with adults, values, skills, abilities, and behavior. Considerable differences in concerns arose in only two areas: physique and family life in the future. Perhaps the greatest implication that can be drawn from these findings, if they can be accepted at face value, is that remedial and/or developmental programs should contain similar elements for boys and girls.

While data such as those collected in the Purdue Opinion Poll can provide

TABLE 10.2. Problems rated as of very much concern by adolescent boys and girls

	Boys		Girls	
Problem Area	Rank Order	Percentage Concerned	Rank Order	Percentage Concerned
Having Own Money	1	40	3	42
Job or Occupation	2.5	37	4	39
Family Life in Future	2.5	37	1	53
Friendships	4	33	8	32
Myself (Who Am I?)	5	29	5	38
My Physique	6	26	2	44
Relationships with Parents/Adults	7.5	25	6	34
Values	7.5	25	7	33
Skills and Abilities	9	20	9	18
My Behavior	10	17	10	17

Based on the Purdue Opinion Panel, *Counseling and Educational Needs of Adolescents,* Report No. 90. Lafayette: Measurement and Research Center, January, 1973.

some general guidelines for understanding the needs of adolescents, it is important to collect local information. A questionnaire such as the one shown in Table 10.3 can be used for this purpose. Students are asked not only to check their own concerns but to indicate the problems which they are aware of being experienced by others. It has been found that even on an anonymous questionnaire students are reluctant to identify their own concerns. However, they are much less inhibited about reporting the concerns of others. While there are certainly some problems with interpreting column two (five students might report that one of their mutual friends is pregnant), the information can provide an interesting check against self-reports.

This same type of questionnaire can be adapted to serve as a means of collecting information from parents, teachers and members of the community. In this type of adaptation the introduction would be rewritten. A suggested rewrite for parents is as follows:

Parent survey of student needs

Please indicate the extent to which the following are problems experienced by your children and by the children known to you. *Please do not put your name on this questionnaire unless you wish to be contacted by a member of the student services team.*

Problem Area	*Column One*	*Column Two*
List Problems	Your children are experiencing.	The children of others are experiencing.

Here again, parents are more likely to identify the problems experienced by children other than their own, and thus column two provides a source of some interesting data.

Objective data can come from a variety of sources. Health information may come from state and local reports, from census and other data. For example, the topics of abortion, birth control, and venereal disease received much attention from a presidential commission. *The Report of the Commission on Population Growth and the American Future* (1972) pointed out, among other things, that the law is a barrier to providing both information about contraception and services to adolescents. The commission cites as the major barrier those laws that bar physicians from examining minors without parental consent. Members of the commission went on to make the following recommendations:

Because of the serious social and health consequences involved in teen-age, out-of-wedlock pregnancy and venereal disease, the Commission urges the elimination of legal restrictions on access to contraceptive and prophylactic information and services to young people [p. 170].

TABLE 10.3. Student problem checklist

The following is a listing of problems experienced by many boys and girls. Please place a check in column one beside each problem area which you are experiencing. Also, place a check in column two if you know other students who are experiencing this problem. *Do not place your name on this questionnaire unless you wish to be contacted by a member of the student services team.*

Problem Area	*Column One* *You are* *experiencing*	*Column Two* *Others you know are* *experiencing*
1. Want part-time employment to make money.	___	___
2. Need to improve relationships with adults, including parents.	___	___
3. Need to improve relationship with peers.	___	___
4. Need to develop skills in dealing with opposite sex.	___	___
5. Drug Abuse— a. drink too much b. smoke pot c. take other drugs	___	___
6. Need help with academic skills, study skills, etc.	___	___
7. Pregnant	___	___
8. Has health problem	___	___
9. Considering dropping out of school.	___	___
10. Need premarital counseling.	___	___
11. Breaking the law.	___	___
12. Has psychological problem, such as depression.	___	___
13. Need someone to talk to.	___	___
14. Money management.	___	___
15. Credit counseling.	___	___
16. Selecting a career.	___	___
17. Use of leisure time.	___	___
18. Not having enough to eat.	___	___
19. Other (please list)	___	___

Let us look in more detail at the problems addressed by the commission: premarital pregnancy and venereal disease. The United States Bureau of the Census (1971) reported that in 1965 there were 125,000 children born to teenage mothers. This figure had risen to 160,000 by 1968 and 180,000 in 1970. Sheer numbers make teenage pregnancy a problem, but Shertzer and Stone (1974) add another dimension to the problem of teenage pregnancy when, after a review of the literature, they conclude that these pregnancies undoubtedly lead to many early marriages. They correctly state that marriages among teenagers are far more likely to end in divorce than those between individuals who are older. Goode (1971) further illuminated the problem of the earlier marriages when he enumerated those factors associated with divorce. Among those listed were low socioeconomic status, low educational level, short courtship, marriage at an early age, and economic instability. It is interesting to note that all of these are likely to be characteristic of the teenage marriage precipitated by an untimely pregnancy.

The fact that sexual activity among unmarried persons seems to be increasing* has led to a spiraling out-of-wedlock pregnancy rate. This activity, along with what appears to be increased promiscuity at all levels, has resulted in an epidemic of venereal disease in our society. One estimate by the American Social Health Association made in 1970 was that 14,000,000 persons had some form of venereal disease, and all indicators are that this problem has increased dramatically since 1970, particularly among teenagers. While so-called wonder drugs have made the treatment of most venereal diseases much simpler, many teenagers are unaware of the availability of services that can help them deal with these diseases once they are infected.

Drug abuse is another problem that has received much attention, and thus objective data are available. The United States Bureau of Narcotics and Dangerous Drugs (1970) reported that 1,352,000 persons under the age of twenty-one were addicted to narcotic drugs. Although this figure is alarming, it is only a small indicator of the extent of the problem. In a study of drug use in New York City Schools, the Fleischman Commission on Education (APGA, 1973) reported that 45 percent of the high school students were using some form of "psychoactive" drugs. This same commission also reported that 20 percent of the students in lower grades were using some form of drugs. Interestingly, the researchers found that the percentage of drug users had declined in New York schools outside New York City. Drug abuse is not solely a New York problem, however.

Research reports such as the one conducted by Hager, Venes, and Stewart (1971) give us objective data on the use of various types of drugs among a

*One estimate is that 27 percent of all unmarried girls between ages fifteen and nineteen have had sexual intercourse. Commission on Population Growth.

sample of midwestern thirteen-to-seventeen-year-olds. They found that 5 percent of the thirteen-year-olds, 6.5 percent of the fourteen-year-olds, 10.3 percent of the fifteen-year-olds, 18.2 percent of the sixteen-year-olds, and 22.1 percent of the seventeen-year-olds had used marijuana at least once. The drugs most often used next to marijuana were the amphetamines. The percentage of thirteen-to-seventeen-year-olds reported using these amphetamines was 3.3, 4.8, 5.8, 9.3, and 11.1 respectively. Hallucinogens were reportedly used at least once by 3 percent of the thirteen-year-olds, 5 percent of the fourteen-year-olds, 6 percent of the fifteen-year-olds, 9.6 percent of the sixteen-year-olds, and 9.5 percent of the seventeen-year-olds. Only about 2.5 to 3.0 percent of the various groups had tried so-called hard drugs. It is clear that the proportion of individuals in the various groups who had used drugs at least once increased with age. The researchers also reported that the extent of use — that is, the number of times various drugs had been used — increased with age.

The abuse of alcohol is receiving increasing attention from authorities throughout this country. Although the use of narcotic drugs seems to be abating, the abuse of alcohol among adolescents is dramatically on the upswing. This rise can be accounted for because alcohol is readily accessible to most adolescents and its use in our society is readily accepted. However, the results of alcohol abuse can be just as dramatic as the use of heroin or cocaine.

Objective data about crime are also available. For example, *Uniform Crime Statistics* (1972) shows that somewhat over one-quarter of all persons arrested were under the age of eighteen and that approximately 10 percent were under the age of fifteen. While these figures are already alarming, they continue to rise daily. Clearly juvenile delinquency and the aforementioned problems of drug abuse, premarital pregnancy, and venereal disease must be of concern to the consultant.

Only two other concerns will be mentioned in this section, although the list considered here is not exhaustive. These problems are school dropouts and youth unemployment. *The President's Manpower Report* (1975) reports that dropout rates of blacks and whites is approximately 23 and 17 percent respectively. In certain regions such as the South, these figures are much higher. This same report indicates that unemployment among individuals who are between sixteen and nineteen years of age is approximately four to five times that of adults. To clarify this last figure, at the time of the writing of this material the national unemployment rate was approximately 6.0 percent. From this figure we would expect the unemployment rate for sixteen-to-nineteen-year-olds to range from 24.0 to 36.0 percent.

That dropping out of school and unemployment are related can be well documented. However, it is also true that prospective young workers do not possess the skills needed to assume the jobs which are available in our technological society. It is also probably true that employers discriminate against younger workers because of concerns about stability and maturity.

The Local Situation

While the foregoing statistics are representative of particular problems on a national scale, each consultant is confronted with a somewhat different problem: getting data about his or her area. However, much of the information presented is available from local governmental agencies such as the police department, employment security offices, municipal libraries, and public health departments. Ferreting out this information will, of course, be somewhat time-consuming, but in many instances the aforementioned agencies have reports already prepared depicting the local situation.

Statistics regarding school dropouts are often available from the administrative offices of a school district. Other information about particular student needs can be determined by surveying students in relatively unsophisticated ways. Consultants often lament the amount of time spent in data-collection activities, for it detracts from their direct service time to students. However, the purpose of the data collection is to allow the consultants to set priorities intelligently and to be able to communicate to various community agencies the extent and severity of the problems in a particular school population. These data can also be useful in beginning to design community-based programs that will prevent problems from arising in the future.

Step One: Assessing the Availability of Services

Once a well-defined set of student needs has been identified, a survey of community agencies that might be of assistance in either remediating existing problems or providing developmental experiences should be compiled. *Community agencies,* in the sense that the expression is used here, go far beyond the traditional concept, which has often been limited to health, placement, welfare, and related socially oriented agencies. A community agency can be any governmental, business, or private establishment that has the potential to offer services and/or experiences that will facilitate the psychological growth of students.

Drum and Figler (1973) suggest that the following types of information be collected about community agencies.

1. Name of agency and location
2. Purpose
3. Services and numbers of people who can be served
4. Delay of service or expected waiting periods
5. Hours when services are provided
6. Fees
7. How to get help, including contact persons, telephone numbers, and application procedures

Many school districts already have files that have been developed within the individual schools or on a district-wide basis and that list social agencies. These files or publications typically provide the information that Drum and Figler suggest be collected and therefore need not be duplicated. Information that might not be so readily available is listings of governmental agencies and/or officials who might influence sanitation, housing, and law enforcement in the community. Data about businesses and industries that might provide developmental career exploration experiences, part-time jobs, or future employment opportunities also need to be collected if they have not been compiled previously. Probably more guidelines are available for collecting this type of information than any other.

Hoppock (1967) and Norris et al. (1972) have addressed themselves specifically to the problem of conducting a community occupational survey. Norris and her associates suggest that there are generally three types of information sought in these endeavors: "(1) an overview of the local occupational pattern at a particular time, (2) specific information about particular occupations; and (3) indications of changes and trends both in occupational distribution and in occupations themselves" (p. 300). Although this information is undoubtedly useful in career planning and placement and should be collected, so should other types of information. Data such as the availability of resource persons who can make presentations to student groups, the willingness of the business or industry to accept groups of students on field trips, the availability of short-term placement opportunities for job exploration, and the availability of films and filmstrips that describe the particular business and/or industry will also be of great utility in helping teachers and others develop needed experiences for students.

Earlier it was mentioned that along with more typical information about community agencies, data regarding key persons or agencies that influence the quality of community life should be collected. It should be quickly mentioned that this kind of information may not be readily attainable through traditional means or surveys. Anyone who has tried to have a streetlight installed or get enforcement in a speed zone has encountered the bureaucracy of local, county, or state government, and if their encounters are similar to ours, the experience was frustrating. Therefore, the individual who hopes to become involved with governmental agencies needs to acquire whatever publications are available that set forth the duties and responsibilities of the various agencies in a particular branch of government. It is also extremely helpful to have several personal contacts within government who can provide more direct information.

At this point let us move from the general consideration of community agencies to a specific listing of some rather common ones, so that the reader can gain a better understanding of both the wealth of resources available and the complexity of the task of data collection. The listing provided here is limited.

COMMUNITY HEALTH AGENCIES
Public health program
Maternal and child health
Vaccination assistance project
American Cancer Society
American Dental Society
American Public Health Association
Cerebral Palsy Foundation
Multiple Sclerosis Society
American Heart Association
American Red Cross
American Association of Mental Deficiencies
Mental health centers
Local physicians
Free clinics
Hospital administrators

SOCIAL AND WELFARE AGENCIES
Crippled children's services
Day care services
Foster care program
Family services
General assistance programs
Aid to Families with Dependent Children
Aid to the blind
Services to unwed mothers
Local Council of Churches
American Friends Service Committee
Catholic Charities Bureau
Catholic Welfare Bureau
Jewish Family Service
Lutheran Welfare League
National Jewish Welfare Board
Salvation Army
YMCA
YWCA
American Red Cross
Travelers Aid
Mountain Mission
Union Mission

EDUCATIONAL RESOURCE AGENCIES
General Educational Development Testing Program

Guaranteed student loans
Scholarship programs
Vocational rehabilitation
Community colleges
Adult basic education program
Private trade schools
Unions

GOVERNMENT AGENCIES
Law enforcement
Juvenile court
Detention homes
Halfway houses
State Department of Education
Probation officers
Sanitation Department
Department of Housing and Zoning
City Solicitor or Attorney
State schools for the deaf and blind

BUSINESS AND INDUSTRY
Chamber of Commerce
Labor unions
Individual businesses

YOUTH ORGANIZATIONS
4-H Clubs
Child Study Association
Camp Fire Girls of America
Catholic Youth Organization
Boys Clubs of America
Big Brother Program
American Junior Red Cross
Girls Service League of America
American Youth Hostels
Boy Scouts of America
Girl Scouts of America

It was suggested earlier that before beginning community consultation it is necessary to determine the nature and extent of student concerns and arrange these in order of priority. Once data are collected about community resources that may be helpful in meeting these needs, a matching process should occur. In this process, what the consultant attempts to do is identify agencies that hold the promise of providing the greatest assistance to students whose problems have been identified as priority number one, priority number two, and so forth. Once this task is completed, it is time to begin contacting various agencies.

Step Two: Entry

The consultant to community agencies will often be in an unfamiliar role and thus be uncomfortable in this activity. This discomfort may be compounded by the attitude of various professionals encountered in the community, who often view school-based personnel as somewhat less effective than other groups of specialists. Therefore, a major problem in community-based consultation is to make entry into the agency and be accepted by the staff of that particular agency.

Glidewell (1959) suggests that one of the first steps that school districts should take in developing a relationship with a particular agency is to designate an individual who will be responsible for working with that agency. While this may seem like a simple idea, it does suggest that perhaps some consideration of community consultation be given on a school-system basis and that individual consultants be assigned the responsibility for working with various agencies and groups. Imagine the confusion that would result if three consultants from three different schools appeared at the local employment security office to discuss placement problems!

Jarvis and Nelson (1967) made another valuable suggestion, which seems vital for entry into an agency as a consultant. It was that the consultant gain some firsthand knowledge of the agency with which he or she expects to work. This familiarization process also seems crucial if one expects to be accepted.

Let us consider the problem of familiarization further and look at how it might be accomplished. In the foregoing paragraph it was suggested that one consultant be given the responsibility for working with a single agency, in order to avoid confusion. In making the decision as to which consultants will work with agencies, the primary factor should be the individual's knowledge of that particular agency. Increasingly, consultants come from varied backgrounds, and it is conceivable that a single school district might have individuals who have been formerly associated with welfare agencies, Employment Security, government, industry, law enforcement agencies, and other target groups. Needless to say, this type of experience would not only have provided the knowledge to understand the workings of an agency but would give increased credibility to the consultant.

It is not likely that all consultants will have an experiential background that will enable them to understand the functioning of a community agency. It therefore becomes important for that individual to tap those resources that are available to gain the knowledge. Most government agencies have policy manuals, organizational descriptions, and evaluation reports, which can serve as an invaluable source of information. Business and industries also have year-end reports for stockholders and other similar documents. However, with private institutions of all types it may be necessary to spend a great amount of time with the personnel involved in order to gain a full understanding of the functioning of the particular institution.

Glidewell (1959) makes an additional suggestion, which should be given careful consideration in the entry process. He recommends that while a consultant should spend time with all members of a client group, careful attention should be paid to the amount of time spent with status leaders. Most of us are aware that businesses, community agencies, and other social institutions have a distinct power hierarchy. Glidewell is merely suggesting that to spend more time with individuals who are in low status positions may be less productive and may have the effect of alienating those individuals who make decisions.

Another important aspect for consultants of making a successful entry into a community agency is to have clearly in mind the objectives that they hope to accomplish and the ways in which the particular agency can be of assistance in achieving the goals that have been set forth. In addition, when possible the consultant should be prepared to demonstrate how achieving the goals that have been laid out can contribute to the functioning of the agency being approached. For example, can different techniques, particularly those conducted in collaboration with the school, be more effective in keeping students of parents on welfare in school? Can participation in a work release program assist a business or industry to recruit better qualified, more enthusiastic workers? Will cooperation with the school enable local Employment Security officers make not only more placements but placements that are mutually satisfying to the employer and employee? These and related questions, if answered affirmatively, can greatly facilitate the entry process.

Step Three: Goal Setting

Once the consultant is accepted by the staff of the target agency, goal setting should occur. Goal setting, like that in other consultation interactions, must be conducted mutually and in a manner that recognizes the institutional goals of the school and the community agency. Examples of goals which might be established are as follows:

1. To provide each high school student seeking employment an entry-level job within six months after graduation.
2. To provide sex education programs for each student in the school.

3. To make available a work release program for students who are experiencing financial need.

4. To develop values rap groups for all students who express an interest in them.

5. To provide group work for students of alcoholic parents with the end result being that students (1) understand the dynamics of alcoholism and (2) develop skills that will enable them to cope more effectively with their parents.

6. To develop delinquency prevention programs that involve out-of-school leisure-time activities, formal and informal values clarification groups, and more involvement in school activities.

The reader should quickly note that the term *goal* rather than *behavioral objective* has been used for the foregoing. Each of these could be specified much as number one has been. However, this needs to be done from the perspective of the local situation. Questions such as what type of out of school activities should be conducted to achieve what behavior and the extent of that behavior expected to occur must be specified locally.

The senior author has often sat in community mental health staff meetings where the various problems of providing mental health services to youth was the theme. Invariably the topic centered on how this particular group of specialists could more effectively have access to the school and work cooperatively with school officials. In conversations with personnel managers for corporations of various businesses and industries similar concerns are heard. However, the theme among industrial leaders is more likely to be a concern for the types of workers that are being "produced" by our schools and a desire to provide some input into the educational process. Officials of vocational rehabilitation agencies, Employment Security offices, and various other community groups sound similar notes. For those of us who have spent many years working with educational institutions, those concerns initially sound ridiculous, but nonetheless are real.

The consultant can help community groups enter into productive, collaborative relationships by (1) acting as the liaison to a group or by (2) assisting it to understand better the interworkings of a school system and methods of having access to the system. Community groups need to understand the power structure, the nature of classroom activities, the functioning of special programs, rules, and regulations that govern the operation of a school system, such as the number of minutes of instruction required and a myriad of other facts. These groups also need to realize that many educators feel that past efforts with groups such as probation officers, mental health workers, and social welfare workers have not been particularly productive for them in an educational sense. Providing this type of information plus developing the skills that will enable staff members of community agencies to take advantage of the information that they have gained may be the most important service that a consultant can provide to a community agency staff.

Many community groups have attempted to offer drug abuse workshops, leisure activities, community service programs, et cetera, that involve students at various levels. The outcomes of these efforts have often been disappointing to these agencies or groups, but they are often at a loss to explain their failure. Perhaps the major reason for students' not becoming involved is that many of these programs have been designed to advance the goals of the group rather than to meet the needs of the students; at least the needs as students saw them. Community groups need to learn needs assessment techniques so that their programs can be designed to correspond with student perceptions. Doing this may pose a problem for some groups because funding is provided so that a specific service can be provided. However, a home for unwed mothers perhaps should be involved in sex education programs just as an employment agency should be involved in career development experiences for preplacement prospects, even though in both instances agency members may be reluctant to become involved in these activities because of various constraints.

Community groups are increasingly aware that parents need to be involved in both preventive and remedial programs aimed at youth but are often at a loss as to how this can be accomplished. Consultants can assist these agencies to develop means of involving parents in their activities. Again, the key here seems to be meeting the needs of parents rather than placing the emphasis upon advancing the goals and objectives of the particular group.

Step Four: Evaluation

In the sense that objectives may be somewhat less clear for community evaluation and their outcomes confounded by other programs, evaluation of community-based consultation is difficult. This matter will be taken up in more detail in Chapter Eleven.

DEVELOPING A VOLUNTEER PROGRAM

Volunteers have long been a part of the educational process. Typically they have been assigned menial tasks that teachers and others did not wish to perform. Fortunately we are now recognizing that volunteers can provide a rich resource, which can greatly enhance many aspects of our schools if they are recruited, trained, and oriented in an appropriate fashion. This recognition has come simultaneously with the realization that volunteers can perform a variety of tasks.

Jon Carlson, an elementary school counselor at Nova University, trained ten parents in Adlerian theory and child-rearing methodology. These parents were then asked to contact and train ten parents each and, after these parents completed the course, they were asked to train ten others. The results of this one effort was that literally hundreds of parents received training in the use of Adlerian psychology in child rearing. A school psychologist in North Carolina recruited and trained twenty volunteers, who took over classrooms so that teachers could attend consultation sessions. A resource teacher in West Virginia used volunteers to deliver reinforcers such as games and oral reading as part of her behavior modification program. A secondary school counselor in Iowa used retired community members to lead vocational exploration groups for all students in a high school. Volunteers have been used as test proctors, tutors, substitute teachers, counselors, discussion group leaders, job placement officers, confederates in monitoring children's behavior, and in many other ways. In short, volunteers can be used to meet many existing needs in our schools. Our own imagination and ingenuity is the major restriction to their use.

Recruitment

Volunteers should be recruited in much the same manner as any professional person. First, there must be a determination of the job to be filled. This should be followed by a consideration of the characteristics of the person who could successfully fill the position. Newspaper articles, radio spots, announcements at PTA meetings, and fliers sent home with students can carry the message into the community. These announcements should list any special qualifications, the number of volunteers needed, the nature of the training program (if any), the expected service, and information about making application.

Screening

Lewis and Lewis (1977) suggest that volunteers be encouraged to examine their own needs and work in programs that will allow them to meet those needs. It is suggested here that each volunteer be interviewed individually and an attempt be made to start this examination process. Also, the screening interview should attempt to ascertain whether the volunteer has those characteristics demanded by the program. For example, a great deal of patience is required by individuals who work with trainable mentally retarded children. A volunteer for this area who is highly impatient will experience frustration and probably drop out, thus disrupting the program. The following is a list of questions which might be posed in a screening interview.

1. Why did you volunteer? What do you hope to gain from the program?
2. What can you offer? What are your strengths? Weaknesses?
3. Have you ever volunteered before? In what type of program? With what result?
4. What is your current schedule? How much time can you give to the program? Will there be interruptions in your services? How often?
5. What is your philosophy of education? How can we best educate children? How would you like your own children, if any, to be educated?
6. How do you see yourself fitting into the program as described?

Provision of Status

Volunteers often feel, and rightly so, that they have little status in the school setting. This must be remedied. One school district dubbed their volunteers V.I.P.'s. The volunteers were introduced in staff meetings as "our very important persons." Another district sponsored a volunteers' banquet and awarded a plaque to the volunteer of the year. In this same district, a personal letter was sent to each volunteer by the building principal at the end of each year thanking him or her for his or her services. Certificates, plaques, awards, and, most of all, treatment with respect are important means of giving volunteers the status they deserve.

Training

The training program will, of course, be tailored to the purpose for which the volunteers were recruited. Lewis and Lewis (1977) suggest that initial training be followed by in-service education that grows out of the questions that they raise during their tenure. They go on to suggest that the creativity of the volunteer be tapped in determining the role to be assumed in the program and in developing the program itself.

Provision for Career Development

Many persons who volunteer do so as a first step toward the development of a career. Work experience gained in a volunteer program should be geared to promoting career development when possible (Lewis and Lewis, 1977). Doing this can be facilitated by identifying jobs that require skills similar to those acquired in the program, making lists of jobs within the school district available to volunteers, providing informal career counseling, and making referrals for more formal counseling and by providing feedback to individuals about their strengths and weaknesses as they function in the program.

DEVELOPING A VOLUNTEER PROGRAM: SOME EXAMPLES

Developing Leisure Activities

A counselor in a rural North Carolina school district became aware that a substantial drug problem was developing in her small town. Her first effort to cope with the problem was an extensive values clarification program, which had little effect, according to her informal evaluation. She did learn from these sessions that students felt that there was very little for them to do in the local community and that they often went to a neighboring community for entertainment. It was in the neighboring community that the drugs were acquired. At this point the counselor decided upon a course of action that involved (1) surveying the students' perceptions of the leisure needs in the community, (2) surveying the availability of leisure activities and resources, and (3) contacting local groups to determine their willingness to develop solutions to the problem.

The two surveys revealed that there were indeed few recreational activities and/or resources, particularly in the evening, and that students believed that there were fewer leisure resources and activities than were actually available and that they expressed a desire for more activities.

The counselor next presented three types of data to the county commissioners, the group empowered to expend public monies. First she presented an estimate of the drug problem and her views on its basis and second, the results of the two surveys were reported. The county commissioners expressed an interest in assisting with the resolution of the problem and asked the counselor to work with them. The counselor and the commissioners designed a survey, distributed to all high school students, which was designed to determine what types of leisure activities would be most acceptable and used. From these data it was determined that a swimming pool, tennis courts, and basketball courts were in greatest demand. Two years after the first meeting, the county commissioners appropriated enough money to build and operate a swimming pool, two lighted tennis courts, and two lighted basketball courts.

Two concurrent efforts had been conducted to enlist school support and community support for additional leisure activities for students. One of these was directed at making school facilities available during winter months for sports activities. The other was directed at the local clergymen's association in order to get community churches to underwrite a film series. The effort with the school board was successful, but the clergy refused to become involved.

A Sex Education Program

A school psychologist in a high school of 1,200 had firm data that showed that an average of at least 3 percent of the 625 girls in the school became pregnant each year. He recognized that he had neither the time nor expertise to provide programs for the girls on health care during pregnancy and/or on adoption procedures if the girls decided to give up their children. He decided to attempt to involve the county health department and the local adoption agency in a program for all tenth-grade girls and boys.

The county health department had been involved with the school previously in various activities such as programs designed to help students understand the nature and cure of venereal diseases. When staff members of this group were approached, they readily agreed.

Enlisting the support of the adoption agency was somewhat more difficult. Officials were skeptical about (1) providing a program for all boys and girls and (2) parental reaction to such a program. The officials did agree that girls needed more information about what they should do if they become pregnant and about the nature of adoption procedures. After three sessions, the agency officials agreed to assist the program on a trial basis. The final program, which was installed as a component of the health program, was as follows:

1. Health Care during Pregnancy
2. The Unwed Mother
3. The Unwed Father
4. Adoption: Pros and Cons
5. Returning to School after Pregnancy

Two components were left out of this program because of school board policy. These were components on birth control and abortion.

Dealing with Alcoholic Parents

A junior high school counselor found that he was spending great amounts of time with students who had either one or two alcoholic parents. The counseling that he had been providing was primarily supportive, but it seemed to result in more requests. As a result he contacted the director of a local alcoholic rehabilitation center. He relayed to the director that at least six of his students had problems with alcoholic parents and were at a loss to deal with them effectively. He indicated that a program was needed to assist these students in coping more effectively with their parents.

It was decided that the most efficient means of assisting the students was to have a series of group sessions directed at developing an understanding of alcoholism and helping students learn skills that would enable them to deal with a drinking parent. One problem that surfaced was that none of the counselors on the staff of the center had experience with younger students. It was therefore decided that the junior high school counselor would colead the first few group sessions as a model for the rehabilitation counselors. The program was then initiated and at this writing is in its third year.

Helping Retarded Students Enter the World of Work

A high school resource teacher worked diligently with the vocational education staff to develop programs for mentally retarded students. As a result, several programs were developed. However, she found that local contractors, service stations, and businesses were reluctant to hire students from these programs because they had heard that some of the students were retarded. This led to an immediate effort to delabel all students.

However, it was decided that a more aggressive approach to dealing with the various businesses was needed. As a consequence, the personnel officers of two businesses and the manager of one large filling station were contacted and asked to take *one mentally retarded student each* on a trial basis. Finally each agreed to do so on a ninety-day basis.

Each employer was contacted weekly to determine the progress of the employee, which was entirely satisfactory. However, at the end of the first month one personnel officer reported that some of his employees had started making fun of the student, and he was considering terminating the agreement because of the disruption. The resource teacher suggested that perhaps the employer could recruit from the work crew one or two "sponsors" to help the student on the job. She also volunteered her services to provide information to the "sponsors" about the mentally retarded. This suggestion was accepted, and the problems on the work crew diminished. It should be noted that *all* new workers were assigned sponsors after this incident.

After this pilot program was completed, letters were sent to other employers in the area telling them of the success of the program and urging them to hire graduates of the vocational programs. Placement problems were greatly eased at this point.

SUMMARY

The purposes of community-based consultation are to bring to bear forces that can provide both remedial and preventive services to students. It is, in a real sense, an attempt to develop a community oriented toward providing mental health services and promoting mental health.

Needs assessment was identified as the first step in community consultation, for the view here is that community groups respond best whenever hard data are available regarding specific problems in the community. Subsequent steps in community consultation were listed as entry, goal setting, strategy selection, and evaluation. Finally, some examples of successful community consultation were presented.

REFERENCES

APGA *Guidepost.* Washington, D.C.: American Personnel and Guidance Association, February, 1973.

Brown, D., and D. J. Srebalus. *Contemporary Guidance Concepts and Practices.* Dubuque: Wm. C. Brown, 1972.

Drum, D. J., and H. E. Figler. *Outreach in Counseling.* New York: Intext Educational Publishers, 1973.

Glidewell, J. C. "The Entry Problem in Consultation," *Journal of Social Issues,* 15 (1959): 51–58.

Goode, W. "Family Disorganization." In *Contemporary Social Problems,* ed. R. K. Merton and R. Nisbets. New York: Harcourt Brace Jovanovich, 1971, pp. 481–501.

Hager, D. L., A. M. Venes, and C. S. Stewart. "Patterns of Drug Abuse in Middle America," *Journal of Counseling Psychology,* 18 (1971): 71–76.

Hoppock, R. *Occupational Information,* 3rd ed. New York: McGraw-Hill, 1967.

Jarvis, P. E., and S. E. Nelson. "Familiarization: A Vital Step in Mental Health Consultation," *Community Mental Health Journal,* 3 (1967): 343–348.

Lewis, J. A., and M. D. Lewis. *Community Counseling.* New York: John Wiley & Sons, 1977.

Menacker, J. *Vitalizing Guidance in Urban Schools.* New York: Dodd, Mead & Co., 1974.

Norris, W., F. R. Zeran, R. N. Hatch, and J. R. Engelkes. *The Information Service in Guidance,* 3rd ed. Chicago: Rand McNally & Co., 1972.

Purdue Opinion Panel, *Counseling and Educational Needs of Adolescents Poll No. 93.* Lafayette: Measurement and Research Center, January, 1973.

Seymour, W. N. *The Young Die Quietly.* New York: Morrow, 1972.

Shertzer, B., and S. C. Stone. *Fundamentals of Counseling,* 2nd ed. Boston: Houghton Mifflin Co., 1974.

The Report of the Commission on Population Growth and the American Future. New York: Signet, 1972.

United States Bureau of the Census. *Current Population Reports.* Series P-23, No. 36, "Fertility Indicators: 1970," 1971.

United States Bureau of Narcotics and Dangerous Drugs. *Drug Abuse and Law Enforcement Statistics.* Washington, D.C.: U.S. Government Printing Office, 1970.

United States Department of Justice. *Uniform Crime Reports.* Washington, D.C.: U.S. Government Printing Office, 1972.

United States Department of Labor. *The President's Manpower Report.* Washington, D.C.: U.S. Government Printing Office, 1975.

CHAPTER ELEVEN The Evaluation of Consultation

It has become increasingly important that consultants be able to document that their efforts do have an impact upon students. In fact, some state legislatures have mandated that all school employees demonstrate that their efforts have a discernible influence on the various aspects of student development (Hawthorne, 1973). The consultant's dilemma is not only how to produce the data necessary to support his or her contention that interventions are successful, but to generate this information in a manner that is not so time-consuming that it detracts from other activities. The purpose of this chapter is to provide methods and techniques for evaluating consultation that will allow the development of data documenting the value of consultation efforts.

Because of the nature of consultation, this chapter will be broken into two sections, one dealing with evaluating the outcome of consultation aimed at individuals and small groups, and one that will address the issues involved in assessing the impact of organizational change.

EVALUATING CONSULTATION WHERE INDIVIDUAL BEHAVIOR CHANGE IS THE GOAL

Much of this volume has been directed toward consultation with parents, teachers, and students. In each of these cases the consultation relationship is initiated for the benefit of an individual or a small group of students. Since the primary purpose of the consultation session is to bring about meaningful behavior change in target students, these students must be the focus of the evaluation. However, a secondary purpose of consultation is the development of a knowledge base and skills to enable the consultee to cope with similar situations in the future. Thus, this objective also deserves attention in the evaluation process. Let us turn first to examining means by which evaluation of change in the target population can be conducted.

Burck and Peterson (1975) point out seven methods that are commonly utilized in evaluation efforts. These methods they label as sample-of-one, Brand A vs. Brand X, sunshine, goodness-of-fit, committee, shot-in-the-dark, and evaluation by the anointing of authority. Briefly, Burck and Peterson define a sample-of-one method as a situation in which the individual simply gives his or her opinion that a technique or program is of value. Brand A vs. Brand X evaluation occurs whenever an individual or group compares a new program or procedure (Brand A) to a traditional approach (Brand X). Usually this approach is not appropriate because the groups are not equivalent and valid comparisons cannot be made. The sunshine method of evaluation is simply to provide a great deal of exposure for a given program or procedure, thus developing widespread support for the idea. Unfortunately this procedure has little to do with the value of the operation. Neither does the goodness-of-fit method, which is simply a device that tends to determine the extent to which a program fits into the existing program. Burck and Peterson facetiously point out that a foolproof method of evaluation is by committee. All that is required in this method is to convene a group of congenial people. The shot-in-the-dark method entails examining a program after it has been developed, usually without consideration of goals or objectives. Without considering objectives, there are no guidelines for evaluation and thus the "shot-in-the-dark" label. Finally, a consultant might bring in an external evaluator who is an authority in the field to pass judgment on his or her efforts. This procedure, like the others listed here, has little to offer in the way of producing meaningful information.

More seriously, a major issue in the evaluation of the efforts of consultants is whether or not the traditional experimental methods of science must be used. These methods, which most people have encountered at some point in their educational careers, require that groups of individuals be compared to other groups of individuals. This approach requires at least four or five members in each group and random assignment of the group members. Once the groups are established, both are typically pretested, one given an experimental treatment, and then both groups are posttested. The data derived from the testing procedures are then analyzed, using inferential statistics, and conclusions are drawn about the value of the experimental treatment. If, in this extensive design, subjects are selected randomly and are thus representatives of a larger population, it is presumed that the results can be generalized to this population. For example, one might take two groups of students who were chronically out of their seats and inattentive. If after their teachers had introduced a contracting procedure, one group showed significant reduction in these behaviors when compared to students whose teachers had not used contracting, we could conclude, tentatively at least, that the contracting intervention was responsible for this change.

One problem with the experimental method described in the foregoing paragraph is that we know that individuals respond differentially to treatments and that the reason for lack of significance in much of our experimental research is because the gains of some subjects are canceled out by the losses of others. This occurs, according to Browning and Stover (1971), because of the idiosyncratic learning histories of the individuals. It may also be, as Chenault (1965) suggests, that our models that are based upon assumptions of "uniformity, order, permanence and constancy of nature" (p. 7) may be faulty. Indeed, physical scientists have for the most part abandoned these assumptions (Chenault, 1965; Thoreson, 1972) and, increasingly, social scientists are doing so. What has arisen as a substitute for the experimental, extensive design is the intensive, or case-study, approach.

N=1 and Small N Evaluational Designs

Defining Behavior The first step in the evaluation of consulting research needs to be the development of precise definitions of the behavior that is to be changed (Miller and Warner, 1975; Thoreson, 1972). There will be times when this task will be relatively easy. For example, if a junior high school teacher wishes to deal with the behavior of completing homework assignments, he or she can define what he or she means in this case. Other easily defined behaviors involve staying in seats, participating appropriately in class, completing a percentage of mathematics problems correctly, and identifying letter sounds. However, let us consider the problems involved if we are interested in increasing interpersonal skills. In this case, we may be able to define in terms of verbal contacts with peers or participation in cooperative activities such as games or work activities. However, we must consider a wider variety of activities and situations, thus increasing the complexity of a chore. The task would become even more difficult if we should decide to attempt to focus on negative responses to an authority figure such as a teacher. Such a definition is particularly difficult, because a negative response can be done with a nonverbal expression, an intonation of a word, or a variety of other subtle ways. As a result of this difficulty, some consultants have attempted to steer clear of those behaviors that are more difficult to define. Doing this is a mistake, since much of the behavior that consultants attempt to alter falls into this category.

Finally, Skinner (1953) has indicated that in defining behavior we need to take into consideration such factors as color, space, time, and velocity. We have already discussed time to a certain extent, and we are accustomed to talking about behavior in the context of a time dimension. John Smith will complete a paper by the end of the grading period, and so many algebra problems must be completed during a specific time interval. However, we may be unaccustomed to conceptualizing behavior in terms of color, even though we are aware that some individuals blush (turn red) when embarrassed and others blanch (turn white) when they become anxious. We are also aware that behavior takes place within a certain space (a classroom, a play area, et cetera), but we do not use this concept as often as we do time. Finally, certain types of behavior, such as running and crawling, take place at a certain velocity (feet per second), and this idea may help us to describe the target behavior more adequately.

Once a behavior has been carefully defined, an objective or target for the intervention should be stated. Sanborn and Schuster (1969) point out that goals should be established in such a manner that there is a reasonable chance that they can be met. Burns (1972) indicates that the objective should be established in a fashion that includes the behavior as it has been defined, provides some indication of level and rate of responding, and specifies a time period in which the expected behavior change is to occur. The following are some examples of this type of objective:

1. Tom will be completing his homework with 80 percent accuracy, by March 1.
2. Tina will participate in class at least once a day in a voice loud enough to be heard by all of the children in the class, by January 15.
3. Terry will exhibit more interest in school, as indicated by participation in at least two school activities, during this semester.

Observation Once a target behavior has been identified and objectives established, baseline data must be collected. Browning and Stover (1971) refer to this process as establishing an uncontrolled baseline: that is, a measure of the behavior while it is not under some type of treatment. A consultant might ask a parent to ascertain the number and duration of temper tantrums prior to the development of an intervention. The measurement of an uncontrolled baseline is an A design in single-subject and Small N research.

Hall (1971) points out that collection of baseline data may occur in at least three ways, with the method to be used dependent upon the goal of the consultation. First and perhaps most commonly, data may be collected regarding the rate of a response within a given time period. For example, we might find that a high school student disrupts the classroom by punching, hitting, or speaking to another student at least twenty-five times per fifty-five minute period. Another, younger student might be out of his seat three times every five minutes. However, in some instance the frequency of response within a time period might not give us the information that we want. If, for example, we were attempting to help teachers in increasing reading skills, one important variable in learning to read would be time on task. Therefore, the amount of time spent within the reading period *attending* to reading would be more valuable information than the number of times the child *looked* at a reading book. Although frequency of response and duration or amount of time of response are often used in establishing a baseline, perhaps a more typical approach to collecting data is through a time sampling procedure. Instead of observing our high school student for an entire class period, we might decide to observe segments of the period. If a time sampling procedure is to be utilized, it is important that sampling be done in a manner that insures the collection of representative behaviors. Our first grade reading student might spend more time on reading during the middle part of the period than he or she would during the early or late portion of the period. Obviously a time sampling procedure that looked at just the beginning of the reading period or the beginning or the end would result in erroneous information about the amount of time spent on reading.

Hall (1971) notes that time sampling approaches to collecting baseline data are particularly useful with teachers since they make observations while they are teaching.

Recording Observations Bijou et al. (1964) point out that there are two major approaches to coding responses: making a specific response code for each situation and using an electromechanical device. The development of a specific response code will be considered first, although, as we shall see later in this section, mechanical devices have certain advantages in an applied setting.

Let us suppose that we are interested in the disruptive, acting-out behavior of a ninth grade boy. This behavior has been defined as talking without permission, dropping a book or another object, throwing any object, and hitting or pushing another student. We have decided that our observations would occur during the first ten seconds of each ten-minute class period, which with sixty-minute classes would mean that we would have six observations per class period. Our recording chart would be set up as shown in Figure 11.1. We could then ascertain whether or not the student was manifesting any type of disruptive behavior and simply mark the appropriate observation box with a 1 or a 0, depending upon whether or not the student was exhibiting the behavior. This approach has another advantage in that the incidence of the target behavior can be reported in times per minute, a frequently used unit of reporting.

As was mentioned earlier, some behaviors are more complex and may have to be broken down into a variety of subunits. Let us return to our example of the development of interpersonal skills. Because interpersonal skills actually involve a series of behaviors, we might be interested in observing eye contact, being engaged in a conversation, physical contact, and smiling. In this situation our observation recording device would necessarily be more complex, as is shown in Figure 11.2. Bijou et al. (1969) point out that we may be interested in observing the incidence of positive as well as negative behavior, and thus response codes must be modified to accommodate the recording of this type of datum. This would, of course, be quite easy to accomplish.

Finally, we may be interested in observing the nature of the interactions in a given situation in order to determine the relationship of two or more sets of behavior (Bijou et al., 1969). We might, for example, be interested in the extent to which a student was out of his or her seat. We might also be interested in the teacher's reaction to that particular behavior. In this situation

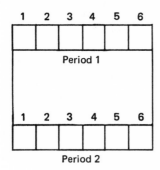 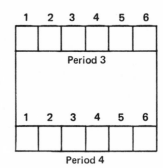

Legend: time sample = 10 seconds.
   1 = student is exhibiting disruptive behavior.
   0 = student is not exhibiting disruptive behavior.

FIGURE 11.1.   Observer recording sheet

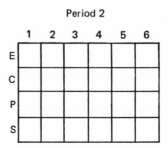

	1	2	3	4	5	6
E	1	0	0	0	0	1
C	0	0	0	0	0	0
P	0	0	0	0	0	0
S	0	0	1	0	0	0

Legend: Observation period = 10 seconds.

   1 = student is exhibiting behavior.
   0 = student is not exhibiting behavior.

FIGURE 11.2.   Observer recording sheet

we might set up our response code with boxes divided in half, as shown in Figure 11.3. In these boxes the upper part would be used to indicate the incidence of the student's behavior and the bottom half to rate a teacher's reaction, such as reprimanding the student. It is also possible to use multiple rows in much the manner that was shown in Figure 11.2 and simply use one row to note the student's behavior and a second row to indicate the teacher response. This approach has the obvious advantage of allowing the recording of multiple behaviors.

Bijou et al. (1969) point out that mechanical recording devices have definite advantages over the procedures that we have just described. Perhaps the major advantage of a device like a wrist counter in an applied setting is that it requires that the observer attend less to the task of recording and may as a result enhance the accuracy of the observations. Further, if the observer is also a classroom teacher, a parent, or a consultant who is directly involved with the student, mechanical recording can allow continuation of an activity (teaching, parenting, group leadership) with a minimum of disruption. The major disadvantage of mechanical means of recording is that only a limited number of behaviors (usually four) can be monitored in a given observation setting. Although devices exist that are more complex than the wrist counter, they are usually expensive and thus not practical in a school setting.

Bijou et al. (1969) raise one last issue that needs to be addressed here: the length of the observation interval. They make the point, which is an obvious one, that the frequency of a response is limited by a time interval: that is, if your observation periods are ten seconds long, the behavior cannot occur more than six times per minute. Bijou et al. go on to suggest that small intervals be used whenever the incidence of a behavior is high and longer intervals whenever the incidence is low.

Rater Reliability Sidman (1960), Bijou et al. (1969), and Browning and Stover (1969) all point out the importance of establishing interobserver reliability before proceeding to the intervention stage. In the simplest terms, interobserver reliability is the degree of agreement between two or more raters who presumably have been trained to observe the target behaviors. Typically a rho-correlational coefficient is computed and reported. However, a simpler method of computing is to (1) determine the number of intervals that observers rated the same; (2) divide that number by the number of intervals agreed plus the number of intervals where observers disagreed; (3) multiply by 100 (Bijou et al., 1969). This computation will result in the percentage of rater agreement.

FIGURE 11.3. Observer recording sheet

The question that must be raised here is whether or not procedures such as the determination of observer interreliability are necessary for the evaluation of consultation. Many consultants are averse to any type of systematic research, and the involvement of two observers to introduce rigor into the evaluational work certainly complicates the process. The answer to the question of the need to determine interobserver reliability is a qualified yes, however. The qualification is inserted only because there are times when it will not be possible to involve two observers and because the evaluation process may be tentative and thus not for dissemination to the consultant's various publics. If the data that are to be collected are going to be used to support the consultant's functioning to administrators, teachers, parents, school board members, and so on, two or more observers should be utilized and interobserver reliability determined. Unless this step is taken, the consultant can never be certain that the outcomes obtained are the result of the treatment or some observer error or bias.

If observers need to be involved, the obvious questions are who can be involved and what training needs to occur prior to the observation periods. First, high school students could easily serve as observers. The only prerequisite for their involvement would be the rather obvious ones of having the time to follow the evaluational procedure through to its completion and the ability to attend to a task. It is conceivable that students younger than high school age could also be used under some circumstances.

Observers must be trained in first identifying the target behavior(s) and then in recording the observations accurately. Bijou et al. (1969) suggest that the first step is to familiarize the individual with the apparatus. The observers should also be asked to memorize the behaviors that are to be recorded, so that they will not need to refer to notes or written work. Then the observer should be trained to record behaviors. This should be done either in the setting or with the assistance of a videotape or movie and should continue until a reasonable level of interobserver reliability is attained (80 to 85 percent).

One last note about the use of observers should be made. The presence of observers in a classroom or other school situation can distort the situation. No observations should occur until the raters are accepted in the situation. Additionally, observers should be stationed so that they will be as unobtrusive as possible.

Graphing Data in Small N research are not presented as means and standard deviations. They are presented more typically in line graphs or in histograms (bar graphs). In both instances, the vertical side of the graph is used as an indicator of the frequency of response and the horizontal portion of the graph to portray the time dimension. Examples of a line graph and a bar graph are shown in Figures 11.4 and 11.5 respectively. Because histograms are somewhat harder to construct and have no definite advantage over the line graph, it is recommended here that data collected be shown on line graphs.

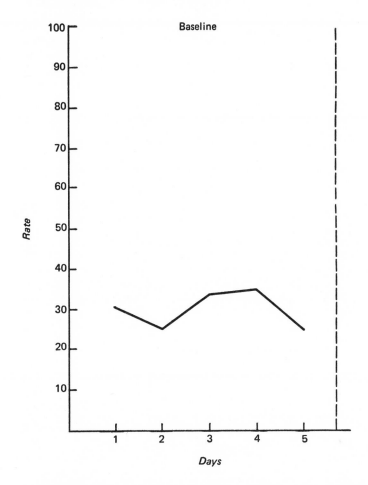

FIGURE 11.4. Line graph, depicting baseline data collected on disruptive fifth grader

With the graphing of the baseline data the counselor is ready to proceed to the intervention. Observation should be continued to ascertain the effectiveness of the intervention.

The A B Design

The A Design was defined earlier as simply the collection of uncontrolled baseline data. Up to this point, much of this chapter has been devoted to describing the techniques and procedures for collecting the data. These same procedures are utilized to collect data once the first intervention (B) is introduced. This ap-

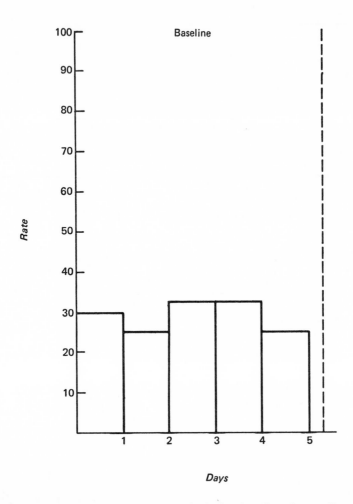

FIGURE 11.5. Histogram, depicting baseline data collected on disruptive fifth grader

proach to evaluation is known as the A B Design. Browning and Stover (1971) point out that we could have simply introduced the intervention (B Design), but they hasten to point out that this is the crudest of all possible designs, since there is no experimental control and no meaningful comparisons can be made. Data are collected continuously in order to ascertain the effectiveness of the intervention and are reported in a graph similar to that shown in Figure 11.6. As can be seen in the graph, the intervention that was introduced was generally ineffective. If the intervention had been effective, the data line would have dipped toward the horizontal axis of the graph. Obviously what is called for is the redevelopment of the intervention.

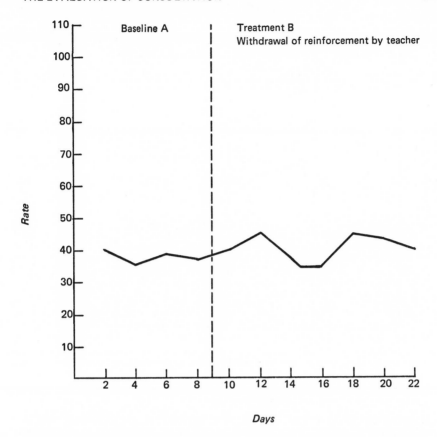

FIGURE 11.6. Line graph, depicting baseline and intervention data for disruptive fifth grader

A B C Design

From a research point of view the A B C Design is weak because it is difficult to parcel out the effects of B, the first intervention, when the second intervention (C) is introduced. However, practically speaking the A B C Design allows the consultant to redesign his or her strategy without starting over (Browning and Stover, 1971). To be sure, any data that arise from this situation must be interpreted carefully. However, let us continue to consider the case of our disruptive fifth grade student who did not respond to our first intervention (B). After careful consideration, we discover that we have overlooked a critical factor and thus institute a third intervention, which may or may not encompass the first. The results of our strategy are reported in Figure 11.7. The data in the graph show that our second intervention appears to be working and that the

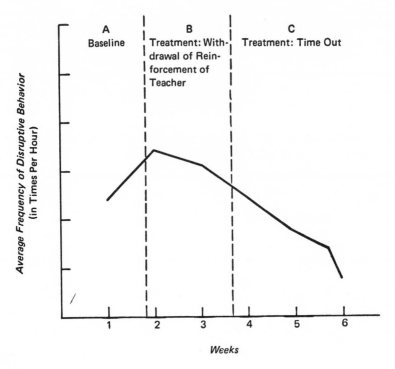

FIGURE 11.7. A B C strategy

incidence of disruptive behavior is decreased markedly at the end of six weeks. Of course, the intervention will have to be continued in order to ascertain its true value.

Reversal Designs

There will be times when the consultant may want to establish that the intervention designed as a result of the consultation process is indeed the variable that has caused the behavior change. Reversal designs can be used for this purpose.

As the letters A B A suggest, this design is the establishment of an uncontrolled baseline, then introducing an intervention, and finally returning to an uncontrolled baseline condition. One problem with this particular design is that frequently there is never really a return to the baseline, and thus a total reversal is not possible (Browning and Stover, 1971).

A second difficulty lies in the rather obvious fact that it may be unwise or unethical to withdraw merely for the sake of evaluating that strategy an intervention once it is initiated. Third, and finally, if an intervention has been designed carefully, there should not be a return to the baseline: that is, the level of responding during the intervention period should maintain itself. This would in effect make the attainment of the A condition theoretically impossible.

The A B A B carries the A B A design one step further, in that the intervention is reinstituted after the second baseline period. From a purely theoretical basis, what has occurred is that the original baseline and intervention strategies have been replicated. In reality this does not occur, for reasons already mentioned in the preceding paragraph.

There are a number of other reversal designs, including A B A C, in which a second intervention is introduced, typically as a result of a discovery that our first intervention (B) has a weak or negligible effect. A B A C D designs include the establishment of an uncontrolled baseline, intervention, replication of the baseline condition, the implementation of a third intervention, followed by still another intervention, much in the same manner as was presented in the discussion of the A B C Design. Needless to say, the more complicated the design, the more difficult it is to implement. However, complexity is not the major barrier to the use of these reversal designs, in the author's view. Taking away an intervention that appears to be working may add to the confidence of the consultant that the strategy employed was worthwhile. However, one cannot help but wonder about the impact upon the student.

Multiple Baseline Designs

Fortunately there are designs which permit us to evaluate precisely the effectiveness of our intervention strategies without some of the problems noted with the reversal designs. These designs are called multiple baseline designs (Risley and Baer, 1970; Schmidt, 1974). Multiple baseline designs are of three types: across behaviors, across individuals, and across situations. Let us consider each of these separately.

Across Behaviors   In this design, uncontrolled baseline data are collected on two or more behaviors manifested by the same individual in the same situation. To return to an earlier example, a student might have low incidence of eye contact, maintain a serious countenance, and not initiate conversations. The first step in this design is to establish baselines for each of these behaviors. This step should be followed by the successive introduction of the intervention. If the intervention produces desirable results on each of the behaviors, we can state with some degree of certainty that the behavior change is the result of the intervention and not due to some extraneous variable. Figure 11.8 depicts the results of an intervention where an across-behaviors, multiple baseline design was utilized. As can be seen in Figure 11.8, the incidence of the three behaviors was very low in each case, but in each case the number of responses rose markedly at the point where the intervention was introduced.

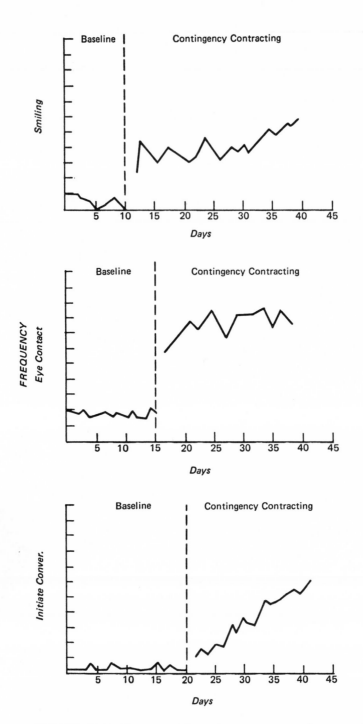

FIGURE 11.8. Outcome of contingency contracting procedure upon the initiation of conversation, smiling, and eye contact of fifth grade boy

Across Individuals Another way of evaluating the impact of a certain intervention is to collect baseline data on two or more individuals in the same situation. After the baselines are established, the interventions are applied successively and data are collected. Figure 11.9 shows two records of the outcomes of utilizing time-out procedures to reduce the incidence of hitting in sixth grade boys. The design can be strengthened by including two or more boys in each treatment

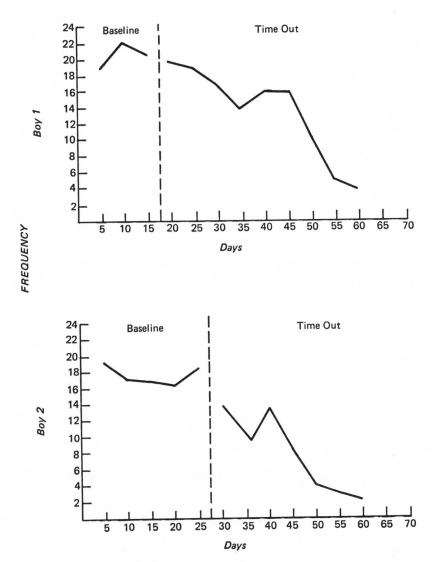

FIGURE 11.9. Outcomes of utilizing time-out procedure to reduce the incidence of hitting in two sixth grade boys

period. Schmidt (1974) stresses that the time period between the initiation of interventions is essential to maximize the possibility that the observed outcome can be attributed to the intervention.

Across Situations Still another type of multiple baseline design that can be employed is one in which an intervention is applied to the *same* behavior but in different situations. An eleventh grade student may "talk back" to both his science teacher and his English teacher. In Figure 11.10 there is an example of how the across-situations design can be employed to determine the value of an intervention, in this case ignoring the behavior. As can be seen in Figure 11.10 the curves obtained were somewhat similar in both English and science class. On the basis of this similarity we can conclude that the decrease in the incidence of "talking back" is attributable to the intervention, ignoring, and not to some extraneous variable.

Mixed Designs It is possible to combine multiple baseline and reversal designs in order to increase the rigor of our design procedures and, as a result, increase the certainty with which we can make statements about our work. These designs increase problems such as record keeping, are vulnerable to deficiencies already discussed under reversal designs, and, perhaps more important, require the consultant to focus great amounts of time and energy on relatively few students. For these reasons the mixed designs will not be discussed further here.

ANALYSIS

The data resulting from reversal and multiple baseline designs can be analyzed using sophisticated statistical procedures such as repeated measures analysis of variance. However, most consultants have little need for this type of sophisticated evidence and therefore the charts that depict the behavior change process will suffice as an analysis procedure. For the practitioner wishing information about more sophisticated analytical procedures Sidman's (1960) book *The Tactics of Scientific Research: Evaluating Experimental Data in Psychology* should be examined.

CRITERION-REFERENCED TESTS

The intensive research design described in the foregoing section will be useful in the evaluation of interventions involving a few students. However, consultation should often result in changes that affect the entire class. In this situation, different types of evaluational procedure must be used. Whenever these innovations involve academic areas, it is suggested that criterion-referenced tests be used.

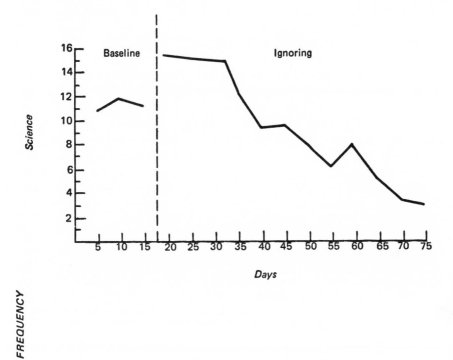

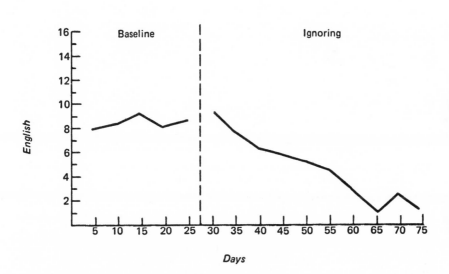

FIGURE 11.10. Outcome of utilizing "ignoring" as a means of eliminating talking-back behavior in an eleventh grade boy

In order for a test to be truly criterion-referenced, it must meet six criteria (Gronlund, 1973):

1. The area to be measured must be clearly defined.
2. Objectives must be established in observable, measurable terms.
3. Within the objective, the standard for proficiency must be established.
4. Tests must be constructed so that they adequately sample the area to be measured.
5. Test items must be selected in a manner that reflects instructional objectives.
6. Test scores should reflect the student's performance in the area being measured.

Defining the Area

In the elementary school, particularly in the early grades, it is easy to analyze subject matter that defines somewhat specifically the area to be taught. As subject matter becomes more complex, the difficulty of this task increases. However, if a social studies teacher is teaching a unit on World War I, he or she should be able to specify what it is he or she hopes to teach about World War I and how he or she expects to know that students have learned what they have been taught. An understanding of what is to be taught and how knowledge acquisition is to be measured is crucial to the development of criterion-referenced tests. In this case, the social studies teacher wished the students to know (1) crucial dates, (2) historical antecedents of the war, (3) roles of significant persons during the war, and (4) the implications of the outcome of the war for the next quarter-century.

Writing Behavioral Objectives

Behavioral objectives are written in a manner that establishes expected outcomes in observable, measurable terms and establishes expected standards of proficiency. First graders are expected to print the alphabet in a legible fashion with 100 percent accuracy, add two-digit numbers with 90 percent accuracy, identify letter sounds with 95 percent accuracy, and so on. These types of objective tend to focus instruction on the tasks that have been identified and to identify the level of performance expected on the measurable criterion that has been set.

Constructing Test Items

The social studies teacher mentioned earlier must develop measurement devices that will determine whether or not the material deemed appropriate has been mastered by students at a level deemed appropriate by the teacher. Thus, the difficult task of test construction begins. The important concern is that the test items be drawn from the area defined at the outset as important and that they are in line with the instructional objectives. Multiple-choice items that require the students to utilize concepts learned, recall pertinent information, and recognize associations take time to construct but are worth the effort.

In some instances teachers may use a theme to measure what Good et al. (1975) call a "behavioral expression" of the knowledge believed to be important. "Statements that specify learning outcomes but which do not provide tight guidelines for 'how' to demonstrate the skill can be viewed as behavioral expressions" (Good et al., 1975, p. 151).

Test items must obviously sample the domain of expected knowledge and skills. This is why measurement devices other than multiple-choice and other traditional objective testing devices will need to be used.

Scores should reflect criteria. If a teacher expects 100 percent accuracy in adding two-digit numbers that require carrying, the test score should reflect this expectation. Similarly, if our social studies teachers expect students to identify three economic, political, and historical factors that led to World War I, the students' feedback should reflect the extent to which this criterion has been met. It is also desirable that when scores are reported, the next step in the learning process be specified. For example, the feedback might direct the student to advance to the next unit or recycle by involvement in a teacher-directed experience, engage in a self-study procedure, or complete an autoinstructional unit designed by the teacher.

THE CASE STUDY

A form of single-subject research that has been utilized by consultants for decades and that has recently been advocated as an evaluational procedure is the case study (Miller and Warner, 1975). Case studies typically begin with the collection and assimilation of large amounts of data, data that are, one hopes, related to the problem manifested by the student. As Traxler and North (1966) pointed out, the primary purpose of conducting a case study is to bring about better adjustment on the part of the student. Traxler and North went on to list three outlines for making case studies. These have been synthesized and are presented here.

1. Statement of problem. This should be a succinct statement regarding the difficulty being manifested by the student.
2. Health information. (This section should include only that information which pertains to the problem.)
3. School history.

4. Family history. Discussion should be restricted to data pertinent to problem (4, 5, 6).
5. Social history.
6. Other developmental data.
7. Diagnosis or working hypotheses regarding nature of problem.
8. Intervention. (This should contain a complete description of the design and implementation of the intervention.)
9. Follow-up and evaluation. (What was the outcome of the intervention?)

Readers who are familiar with traditional approaches to case studies will instantly recognize that the outline just presented is a greatly abbreviated version of the case study method. The authors believe that the case study approach lost its appeal, at least in part, because recommendations were made that all possible data be included as a part of the study. This seems neither wise, when one considers the time variable, nor useful to the practitioner, whose primary concern is the evaluation of his or her work.

The case study approach has some definite advantages as an evaluative device. First, most consultants already have the skills required to utilize the case study approach. Second, the consultant will not need to become involved in identifying and training raters, since case studies are typically reported in more general terms. Third and finally, the case study method can help consultants to increase their understanding of human functioning and its change. The disadvantages of the case study, like the advantages, seem to be threefold. The case study approach is time-consuming. Even the abbreviated version recommended here requires the consultant to spend a great deal of time perusing records, discussing the student with the family and gathering data from the student's teacher(s). The case study also has the disadvantage of producing a type of datum that is general in nature and thus may have less utility than data pertaining to specific areas of behavior. Finally, the data resulting from a case study are more open to criticism because of the subjective manner in which they are collected.

In sum, the case study is an evaluative procedure that can be used by consultants. However, as Miller and Warner (1975) pointed out, we often need more explicit data than that typically produced by the case study approach.

EVALUATING THE SECONDARY OUTCOMES OF CONSULTATION WITH INDIVIDUALS AND SMALL GROUPS

The reader should recall that consultation has two primary purposes. First, consultation should result in an observable change in the client group: in our case, students. Second, consultation should have a beneficial effect upon the consultee. Norman and Forti (1972) indicate that these secondary benefits should be in the areas of increased objectivity, problem solving, and general role competency. To this list should be added an increased ability to understand human functioning and the competencies needed to facilitate individual and group development. As Norman and Forti did in their study of the outcomes of mental health consultation, it is suggested that these secondary outcomes be assessed by the use of consultant-designed questionnaires.

It is outside the scope of this book to go deeply into the design of evaluation questionnaires. Perhaps it will suffice to say that it is recommended that the questionnaire be rather simple in nature and that the items should grow directly out of the expected secondary outcomes that were enumerated in the previous paragraph. To this should be added that the format used in the development of the questionnaire should also be rather simple. The following are some sample questions that might be used to construct a questionnaire of the type under discussion. Each would be prefaced by "As a result of consultation."

SECONDARY OUTCOME: OBJECTIVITY
1. I am better able to understand my students. Yes____No____Unclear ____
2. I have gained a new perspective regarding student behavior. Yes____ No____Unclear____
3. My biases no longer are the determining factor in the way I deal with students. Yes____No____Unclear____

SECONDARY OUTCOME: PROBLEM SOLVING
1. I am better able to establish priorities. Yes____No____Unclear____
2. I now use a more systematic approach to problem solving. Yes____ No____Unclear____
3. I can say with some certainty that I am a better decision maker. Yes____No____Unclear____

SECONDARY OUTCOME: ROLE COMPETENCY
1. I am a better teacher (parent, administrator, etc.). Yes____No____ Unclear____
2. I feel more confident about my ability as a teacher (parent, administrator, etc.). Yes____No____Unclear____
3. I can deal more effectively with my classroom (home, school) situation. Yes____No____Unclear____

SECONDARY OUTCOME: UNDERSTANDING HUMAN BEHAVIOR
1. I have gained greater understanding of the principles of human functioning. Yes____No____Unclear____
2. I feel confident that independently of the consultant I can utilize the principles which I have learned. Yes____No____Unclear____

3. I have a sufficient understanding of human development principles so that I feel that I could explain them to others. Yes____No____Un-clear____

SECONDARY OUTCOME: FACILITATING HUMAN DEVELOPMENT
1. I am better able to design approaches that will be helpful to my students. Yes____No____Unclear____
2. I have developed new approaches to students that will facilitate their overall development. Yes____No____Unclear____
3. I feel confident that I can develop interventions (may specify) for students in the future. Yes____No____Unclear____

While each consultant will want to design a questionnaire that fits his or her own situation, it seems that questions should be included that are aimed at evaluating each of the secondary outcomes.

Finally, although the foregoing questions were designed for the consultee, it may also be wise for the consultant to complete the same questionnaire and then, with the consultee, compare perceptions of the gains made by the consultee. This feedback session may lead to closure or may in fact serve to perpetuate the consultation process.

EVALUATING ORGANIZATIONAL CHANGE

In theory, the process of evaluating the impact of organizational change is much the same as that of evaluating individuals' outcomes. In practice, evaluation of organizational outcomes is much more complex.

The process of evaluating organizational change starts with the establishment of objectives. These objectives should be stated in observable, measurable terms, should be comprehensive in that they include the affective, cognitive, and psychomotor domains, should specify the temporal dimension — that is, the time in which the change is to occur — and should establish a performance level. It should be noted that each of these objectives should be stated in terms of student behaviors.

The focus of objectives upon student behavior causes a particular problem for the organizational consultant in that not only must he or she have some intermediate objectives — that is, objectives which focus on teacher behavior, administrator behavior, and/or certain organizational processes such as decision making or communication — but the ultimate impact of these behaviors or processes on students should be considered. To be sure, an innovation designed to increase staff morale by using a different communications system is worthwhile if it is effective, whether or not it has a discernible influence on students. However, just as industry concerns itself with net earnings, so must educational organizations concern themselves with student outcomes.

Some school districts have established thousands of objectives, each designed to reflect some expected outcome of a particular program. Perhaps the first step in the evaluation of an organizational change is to determine which among the myriad objectives the innovation is expected to influence. These then become the focus of the evaluation.

Another important problem in evaluating the effectiveness of an educational organization is making direct inferences that observed changes are the result of innovations. For example, some school districts have been openly criticized by their publics because of a decline in students' scores on standardized achievement tests. However, as Featherstone (1974) points out, we have known for some time that scores on achievement batteries are influenced more by family background and socioeconomic level than they are by a particular approach to schooling. Therefore a decline in test scores or other measures of academic achievement may not be attributable to the educational program. Conversely, an increase in these measures may not be indicative of the success of a particular program.

Pinkham and Hardie (1971) describe a procedure where the results of standardized tests can be utilized as meaningful evaluative instruments. However, the focus of the evaluation must be upon the total profile rather than an individual area. To be more specific, let us assume that we have given the Iowa Test of Basic Skills (ITBS) at the end of each grade, starting with grade three and ending with grade eight. Let us further assume that for our school districts the test scores on all subtests have remained near the mean on national norms except in the area of mathematics. In mathematics the scores have fallen to the twenty-fifth percentile, a decline that cannot be accounted for by chance variation. This datum clearly indicates that we have reason to believe that our mathematics program has some deficiencies *if* the ITBS measures those skills and concepts that we hope to teach.

The problem involved in inferring that scores on standardized tests are the results of academic programs offered in the school is not an isolated area. Although the school attempts to influence other student behaviors in the affective and psychomotor domains, it is likely that the family and the community at large have a greater influence in these areas. Thus we are always in the uncomfortable position of not really knowing why perceived outcomes occurred as they did. Nevertheless, as was stated at the outset of this chapter, educators are increasingly forced to evaluate their efforts and report their conclusions to a public demanding accountability.

SUMMARY

This chapter has focused upon evaluation of the consultation process. Because of the nature of consultation it has been divided into two sections: one dealing with evaluating consultation that focuses upon individuals and small groups and one on consultation focused upon organizational change. Much of the chapter addressed itself to the former and specific designs for evaluating one-to-one consultation efforts. Specifically, designs that have arisen primarily from the work of behavioral psychologists, such as A B Designs, reversal designs, and multiple baseline designs, were presented.

REFERENCES

Bijou, S. W., R. F. Peterson, F. R. Harris, K. E. Allen, and M. S. Johnston. "Methodology for Experimental Studies of Young Children in Natural Settings," *The Psychological Record*, 19 (1969): 177–210.

Browning, R. M., and D. O. Stover. *Behavior Modification in Child Treatment*. Chicago: Aldine-Atherton, 1971.

Burk, H. D., and G. W. Peterson. "Needed: More Evaluation, Not Research," *Personnel and Guidance Journal*, 53 (1975): 563–569.

Burns, R. W. *New Approaches to Behavioral Objectives*. Dubuque: Wm. C. Brown, 1972.

Chenault, J. "Research and the Monolithic Tradition," *Personnel and Guidance Journal*, 44 (1965): 6–10.

Featherstone, J. "Measuring What Schools Achieve," *Phi Delta Kappan*, 55 (1974): 448–450.

Good, T. L., B. J. Biddle, and J. E. Brophy. *Teachers Make a Difference*. New York: Holt, Rinehart & Winston, 1975.

Hall, R. V. *Managing Behavior: The Measurement of Behavior*. Lawrence: H and H Enterprises, 1971.

Hawthorne, P., ed. *Legislation by the States: Accountability and Assessment in Education*. Denver: Cooperative Accountability Project, 1973.

Miller, E., and R. W. Warner, Jr. "Single Subject Research and Evaluation," *Personnel and Guidance Journal*, 54 (1975): 130–133.

Norman, E. C., and T. A. Forth. "Study of the Process and Outcomes of Mental Health Consultation," *Community Mental Health Journal*, 8 (1972): 261–270.

Pinkham, F., and J. Hardie. "The Yardstick Project." In *Planned Change in Education*, ed. D. S. Bushnell and D. Rappaport. New York: Harcourt Brace Jovanovich, 1971, pp. 78–90.

Risley, T. R., and D. M. Baer. "Operant Conditioning: 'Develop' Is a Transitive-Active Verb." In *Review of Child Development Research*, Vol. 3: *Social Influence and Social Action*, ed. B. Caldwell and H. Ricciuti. Chicago: University of Chicago Press, 1970, pp. 124–153.

Sanborn, B., and W. Schuster. "Establishing Reinforcement Techniques in the Classroom." In *Behavioral Counseling*, ed. J. D. Krumboltz and R. E. Thoreson. New York: Holt, Rinehart & Winston, 1969, pp. 131–152.

Schmidt, J. A. "Research Techniques for Counselors: The Multiple Baseline," *Personnel and Guidance Journal*, 53 (1974): 200–206.

Sidman, M. *The Tactics of Scientific Research: Evaluating Experimental Data in Psychology*. New York: Basic Books, 1960.

Skinner, B. F. *Science and Human Behavior.* New York: Macmillan, 1953.

Thoreson, C. E. "The Intensive Design: An Intimate Approach to Counseling Research." Unpublished paper presented at American Educational Research Association meeting, Chicago, 1972.

Traxler, A. E., and R. D. North. *Techniques of Guidance,* 3rd ed. New York: Harper & Row, 1966.

Author Index

Subject Index